Banking on Ethic

Today's perception is tomorrow's norm

Banking on Ethics

Today's perception is tomorrow's norm

George Möller

Published by
Euromoney Institutional Investor PLC
Nestor House, Playhouse Yard
London EC4V 5EX
UK

Tel: +44 (0)20 7779 8999 or USA 11 800 437 9997
Fax: +44 (0)20 7779 8300
www.euromoneybooks.com
E-mail: hotline@euromoneyplc.com

The author's photo on the back cover of the book is provided by corbino.

Typeset by Phoenix Photosetting, Chatham, Kent

Printed and bound by CPI Group (UK) Ltd, Croydon, CR0 4YY

For Oscar Nickson

Contents

Foreword

Following the collapse of Lehman Brothers in September 2008, great changes have taken place that have not only affected the financial landscape but have also had an impact on how we view research and education, in particular within the financial sector. The narrow focus on rational agents that are purely profit-oriented has come in for much heavier criticism, and belief in the relevance of social interaction for macroeconomic outcomes is greater today than it has ever been. The Harvard MBA has been accused by critics of concentrating solely on maximising profits, and this has not gone unnoticed in the Netherlands. While it is indeed true that ethics came to be neglected over time in most business and economics curriculums, there has been a reversal in recent years. Economists have started, for instance, to study once more the work of Friedrich Hayek, in which the discovery of norms in complex societies plays a significant part. More than ever before, there is an awareness that human behaviour is of relevance for both market processes and organisational change. The importance of ethics in the financial sector and in financial degree programmes is therefore obvious.

Banks and ethics are closely connected. If even economic theory demonstrates that the banking sector is inherently unstable, because the risk of a bank run always exists, it is clear that, in order to understand how financial systems need to work, more is required than rational behaviour alone. For a long time, George Möller, himself a graduate of the University of Groningen, has been at the forefront of thinking in this area, and the results of his reflections are presented in this book. Under the auspices of the University of Groningen, this work has been further developed within the Faculty of Economics and Business and the Comenius course on leadership in the financial sector. The University of Groningen is very proud of the fact that George Möller has given a new impetus to thinking on ethics in the financial sector, and the fruit of his labour is a book I wholeheartedly recommend.

Elmer Sterken
Rector of the University of Groningen
Professor of Monetary Economics

Acknowledgements

At a lunch in London in the spring of 2011, Naveed Siddiqui, who worked for Euromoney at that time, introduced me to his colleague, Sanjeevi Perera. This introduction marked the start of this book, and the beginning of a serious effort by many, including Annemarie van der Tuijn, who was responsible for editing the Dutch text, and Joanne Victoria Trees and Kristine Kohlstrand, who produced the English translation. Many of my thoughts were further crystallised as I dealt with issues as part of my day to day duties, but it was a particular pleasure to be able to share them in an academic environment at Comenius, an institution through which the University of Groningen provides postgraduate executive programmes. I would like to thank Boudewijn de Bruin, Professor of Financial Ethics at the University of Groningen, for going over the transcript with me and providing me with insights that proved invaluable. We also disagreed at times, which led to some very interesting debates.

I obtained a great deal of inspiration from my patient family: my daughters Maaike and Tessa, and my wife Saskia. And I was of course tremendously inspired by the little man born on that beautiful, memorable day, 8 November 2011, in the St John of God Hospital Subiaco, Perth, Western Australia. He surveys the world with his beady eyes, and clearly he expects a great deal from us.

About the author

George Möller has been involved with the international financial industry for over 40 years. He worked for MeesPierson in London for 10 years, from 1987 to 1997, during which time he served as a member of the Board of Liffe. In London he was one of the founding members of the Futures and Options Association, and he was granted the honour of the Freedom of the City of London. He was one of the founders of Euronext and worked for the exchange operator in Amsterdam, Paris, London and Brussels. He also served as Chairman of the Federation of European Securities Exchanges (FESE) between 2000 and 2004. In 2004 he became the CEO of Robeco Group, the largest international asset manager in the Netherlands. He was also a member of the committee that formulated the Dutch Corporate Governance Code, better known as the Tabaksblat Committee.

George Möller is currently the Chairman of the Supervisory Board of the Netherlands Authority for the Financial Markets (AFM), and is also a member of the Board of NASDAQ Dubai. He is the Chairman of the Supervisory Board of Leiden University Medical Centre (LUMC) and is a member of the Board of Winton Futures Fund. He is also a member of the Advisory Board of the Securities and Commodities Authority (SCA) in the United Arab Emirates.

George Möller is the initiator of a Dutch postgraduate course on financial ethics provided by Comenius, an institution that forms part of the University of Groningen.

George Möller is a Dutch national.

Will ethics pay my bills?

No, but without them you could lose your job.
Dominique Strauss-Kahn, the former Chairman of the IMF.

No, but without them you could lose your newspaper.
Rupert Murdoch, the owner of the News of the World, a UK tabloid that ceased publication on 10 July 2011 after 168 years in print.

No, but without them you could be impeached.
Bill Clinton, the former President of the US, who faced charges following the Monica Lewinsky scandal.

No, but without them you could lose your triple A status.
Barack Obama, the President of the US.

No, but without them you could discredit your country and cause a crisis of trust.
Silvio Berlusconi, the former President of the Council of Ministers of the Republic of Italy.

No, but without them you could lose your company.
Dick Fuld, the former Chairman and CEO of Lehman Brothers.

No, but without them you could lose your reputation and much more.
Rajat Gupta, the former CEO of McKinsey, former member of the board of Procter & Gamble and former director of Goldman Sachs Group Inc, who called Raj Rajaratnam of the Galleon Group just 16 seconds after learning of some price-sensitive information. Mr Rajaratnam conducted trades the next day, before the market in the relevant security moved.

No, but without them you could lose your job as CEO of BP, although you would get your life back.
Tony Hayward, the former CEO of BP, who demonstrated a total lack of compassion during his handling of the Gulf of Mexico oil spill.

No, but without them you could face charges brought by the SEC for misconduct in office.
Brian Stoker, a former Citigroup employee.

No, but without them you could risk losing your case in the European Courts of Human Rights.
George Soros, the well-known, successful and highly professional investor, who was convicted in France of insider trading. His defence was that at the end of the 1980s, when the offence was committed, the French rules on insider trading were too vague for him to realise he had broken them.

No, but without them you could be convicted of market abuse.
David Einhorn, a hedge fund manager who claimed he was unaware of the UK's rules on insider trading.

No, but without them you could be seen to lose your integrity as a monarch and the honourable chairman of the WWF.
King Carlos of Spain, caught hunting and killing elephants in Botswana during a trip made at the invitation of Mohammed Eyad Kayali, a Saudi businessman.

No, but without them you could ruin the IPO of the bank you head and partly own.
André Esteves, fined by Italy's Consob for insider trading, a fact that had to be incorporated into the IPO documentation as the Brazilian bank BTG Pactual went public.

No, but without them the credibility of your institution will be destroyed and thousands of believers will turn their back on what they once believed was their personal faith.
Successive Popes who knowingly allowed child abuse to take place under their authority.

No, but without them your words lose all meaning.
Christine Lagarde, the head of the IMF, who accused the Greeks of failing to pay taxes while being exempt from paying taxes herself owing to her position.

Chapter 1

A wink

A cautionary tale with a wink.

On Monday 29 August 2011, a security van lost part of its load on the A2 motorway near Beek in the Dutch province of Limburg. At around 10 o'clock that morning a case full of banknotes fell out of the back of the van. Its doors, which had not been locked properly, burst open, scattering hundreds of notes all over the motorway. Scores of passing drivers pulled over to pick up the money, sometimes risking their own lives in the process. The motorway and the verges were soon picked clean by the greedy crowd. By the time the police arrived half an hour later, all of the scattered banknotes were gone, and all the drivers had left the scene.

The chaos on the motorway was caused by an experiment conducted by the financial ethics department at the University of Groningen. The driver of the security van had deliberately dumped the case of banknotes at a designated location, and a number of researchers attached to the university were there to observe what happened. They filmed the behaviour of the other drivers so that they could study it in more detail later on. Their hope was that they could use the data obtained in this way to gain a better understanding of existing theories of behaviour.

However, the behaviour they observed still came as a great surprise to most of the researchers. They had taken many factors into consideration, but they had not expected that greed would play such a dominant role in human behaviour. On seeing all that scattered money, the drivers who pulled over were concerned with one thing only: picking up notes, and preferably as many as possible. All of a sudden the drivers no longer cared about the risks that this entailed. Only a few of them returned the money to the unlucky driver of the security van. Most of the drivers that stopped to pick up notes continued their journey with their loot instead. Another surprising finding was that hardly any of those involved felt any remorse, even after they had come to their senses. Twenty-four hours later, only a tiny fraction of the banknotes had been returned to the police. As most of the money had to be considered lost, the experiment cost the University of Groningen a great deal more than it had budgeted. Despite this, the prevailing feeling was one of satisfaction as the data obtained in this way turned out to be of inestimable value from a research perspective.

The experiment generated so much data that the researchers believe they can use it to gain new insights into theories on human irrationality. The finding that people lose their ability to think rationally as soon as they see money is particularly intriguing, as is the suggestion that people can temporarily switch off their conscience in certain situations. It has been discovered that this tends to happen when people are able to get hold of money that is not theirs and can act quickly. At such times any sense of values quickly disappears.

The researchers repeated their experiment in a scaled-down form in the US to investigate whether American drivers would behave differently in identical circumstances. If they did, this could indicate that cultural differences exist. However, the American drivers reacted in the same way as the drivers on the A2 near Beek in the province of Limburg. Based on this, the experts in Groningen concluded that greed is universal and is not culturally bound. People are predators without a specific conscience or demonstrable ethics, particularly when it comes to money.

The events described above are true, in that the unfortunate affair with the security van actually happened and passing drivers really did grab the cash. However, rather than being an experiment by the University of Groningen, it was a tragicomic incident. Nevertheless, the conclusions drawn from this 'spontaneous experiment' are still valid. When it comes to money, we lose all reason. Given this, the time seems ripe for a book on the morality of financial markets.

Chapter 2

A walk in the dunes

How important are financial ethics? How does the financial world deal with ethical issues? Are they given enough attention? And is there really such a thing as a specific ethic for the financial world?

Winter was a long time coming in the last few weeks of 2003. It had not got very cold and even Christmas had been exceptionally mild. And wet. The weather slowly began to change on 27 December as temperatures gradually fell and the rain finally stopped. My daughter Maaike and I decided it was good weather to go hiking. As in previous years, we chose the area of the dunes between Bergen and Schoorl/Groet in North Holland. It is on the doorstep of where we live and in my opinion it is one of the most beautiful natural environments in the Netherlands. The dunes are broad and unusually high because the wind had free rein there for centuries. Heavy storms from the sea blew sand higher and higher until entire villages were buried by the relentless force of the wind. To hold back the sand, part of the area was planted with trees two centuries ago. Although this slowed the inland migration of sand, the wind has never entirely given up its capricious game. In the summer the huge sand dunes are an irresistible draw to nature lovers, and especially to children, but in the winter the area is enchantingly quiet. Maaike and I enjoy being in that environment immensely.

We set off early on that fine December day. We walked from Bergen in the direction of Schoorl and then continued north until we reached the village of Groet. We decided to stop there to catch our breath and have a bite to eat at a restaurant before heading back. As the kilometres passed almost imperceptibly, we chatted a great deal. I asked Maaike about the special medical ethics course she had just completed. As a medical student at the University of Bristol she had had the opportunity to spend a year studying a related subject. She chose ethics, and contributed to a book, *The Practical Guide to Medical Ethics & Law* (2002). We talked at length about her findings and my profession. By that time I had held various positions in the financial industry, while she was doing her best to become an outstanding doctor. We discovered that these two very different professions had one important thing in common: people. But we also came to the conclusion that there was also a major difference: the role that ethics play.

The medical world attaches great value to ethics, and the subject is on every trainee doctor's curriculum. This stands to reason, since doctors continually have to make choices and deal with moral issues in the course of their work. Technical medical training alone is not enough. But surely this should also be true of people working in the financial industry.

Are all the managers, politicians, policy-makers, economists and lawyers who work in this industry sufficiently well-schooled in ethics? I considered this question as we made our way through the dunes. And the longer we walked, the more convinced I became that the financial world was just muddling through where ethics were concerned. In 2003 the financial industry had just come through troubling times. The recent crisis in the technology industry and the collapse of the US energy giant Enron had been followed by the demise of the telecom company WorldCom, the Ahold scandal in the Netherlands and the Parmalat disaster in Italy. Fraud was widespread and it seemed as if the financial industry did not take ethics seriously. Of course, the medical world deals with matters of life and death, unlike the financial industry, where all that matters is money and numbers. But is that really true? Is that really all there is to it?

Not in my opinion. If there is one place where we need to talk about how people should conduct themselves, it is in the financial industry. Employees' actions in this industry can have mammoth consequences. Pensioners who have saved for retirement throughout their lives and are ready to start enjoying their old age can be ruined by the wrong financial advice and decisions. Savings can evaporate at a time when starting over is no longer an option. In addition to personal tragedies of this kind, the widespread sale of unsound financial products can also lead to collective suffering. Examples include extortionate insurance – ridiculously expensive policies that cover nothing but the seller's bonus – and the Madoff affair, in which funds intended for future generations went up in smoke as a result of deliberate mismanagement and fraud. Sometimes, squandering one's financial heritage can be as bad as destroying one's cultural heritage. In the end, neither can be reproduced. Moreover, financial crises can cripple society for years, and their impact can spread beyond a country's borders. The mortgage crisis in the US caused worldwide damage. Owing to securitisation, a financing technique based on bundling and selling debt papers, the malaise spread around the world like an aggressive, unstoppable virus that took a long time to present symptoms. And when the symptoms appeared, it took a very long time to cure the disease. In short, the consequences of irresponsible actions in the financial world can be tragic and cause serious social disruption. Financial ethics are therefore concerned with extremely serious matters, and sometimes quite literally with matters of life and death: there is no shortage of examples of investors who have taken their lives after a financial catastrophe.

However, there is something else at work here. The financial world can sometimes seem to be detached from the real world, but in fact the financial world is the inverse of the real world. If, for example, I want to buy a house, I will need a mortgage. That is how an action in the real world (buying a house) becomes an event in the financial world (applying for a mortgage). The source of the lack of morality can often be found in the real world, not the financial world. The confusion stems from the fact that the consequences of an action that is wrong are only visible in the financial world. The financial industry is the real economy's relief valve. It is not where the problem originates, but where the steam can escape. For the sake of convenience we call it a financial crisis when, in fact, that is not entirely true.

Sometimes the only way to combat amoral behaviour within society is with measures imposed by the financial world. Having failed in this respect, bankers now find themselves in a new position. They may no longer be the source of evil, but they have become accessories. Money-laundering practices are a good example. The financial world is not the source of criminality, but criminals use the financial sector to bring illicit funds back into circulation legally. If bankers help them by looking the other way, that is an ethical failing. Providing active assistance in such practices is, of course, even worse. The same can sometimes be said of inflation. Monetary measures are used to achieve price stability, even though the source of inflation is due to tensions in the real economy. These may include a struggle for scarce resources, in which people are not prepared to accept the consequences of the scarcity, or a refusal to keep wages in check with productivity. Expanding the money supply, which is currently happening on a wide scale under the guise of quantitative easing, is tantamount to acting as an accessory to the inflationary process – a process involving an unintended and undue transfer of wealth. Some would call it theft.

The interference between the real world and the financial world means that it is very important to make a clear distinction between cause and effect, for example in relation to the crisis affecting countries in the eurozone. Ireland's problems arose because the banks had particularly lax credit policies and took on way too much risk when financing property. They did not restrict their actions to Ireland or to their duties as a utility: the bankers also financed extravagant projects across the Irish Sea in Great Britain. It was their own strategy; no one had asked them to come up with it. When their problems became too big, the Irish government – and in effect Irish taxpayers – had to come to the rescue. The opposite is true of Greece. The Greek banks were not affected by the crisis of 2007–2008, in fact they came out of it in a healthy state. However, the banks were overexposed to the bonds issued by their own government. Once it emerged that the Greek government could not balance its books, as its citizens were very reluctant taxpayers, the banks were in trouble. The Greek banking system was not saved but destroyed by the taxpayer. Italy is in a similar situation. Every year a significant portion of the annual budget deficit ends up in Swiss bank accounts. The end result for these countries is the same: a major crisis in government financing. However, the causes, and therefore the moral issues, are different. According to German chancellor Angela Merkel, we cannot solve the problems of Greece and Italy by getting the European Central Bank to print more money. And she is correct. It is not a monetary issue, but a problem with a significant social and political dimension.

It is often much more difficult to judge behaviour in the financial world than it is in the real world. The financial world is abstract, which makes it difficult to distinguish right from wrong. This is easier in the real world. If I found a wallet full of money on the street, I would take it to the nearest police station. Fortunately, there are many others who would do the same. Once, on weekend trip to Berlin, I left a full wallet behind at a restaurant next to the autobahn. It was very careless, to be sure, but, perhaps surprisingly, three days later I was able to collect my wallet at the restaurant on my return trip. A cleaner had found it and handed it in to the manager. I got it back, neatly sealed, and with all of its contents. It is not always like that in the financial world. Investors too are sometimes careless with their wallets. They can get into trouble, for instance by placing a securities order in the market with the wrong price. It is easy to make a mistake by accidentally hitting the wrong key, putting in one zero too many or a decimal point in the wrong place. Or by dividing by the exchange rate rather than multiplying by it. When the traded equity options market first opened in Europe in the 1970s, exercising the wrong option – a call option instead of a put option or the wrong strike price – was not uncommon. The result was that the other party to the option transaction had unexpected amounts credited to their accounts. They knew all too well that a mistake had been made, but the money was quickly withdrawn and it disappeared into the pockets of the lucky finder. By the time the mistake had been discovered, and the lucky recipient had been traced, the money was gone. If you forget your wallet in the world of finance, you will never see it again. All the textbooks argue that this behaviour makes the market efficient, and so it is permitted. Efficient markets are a positive thing. And arbitrage is a word with a positive meaning, but sometimes it stands for theft.

Back to my hike in the dunes with my daughter Maaike. The more we talked, the more I wondered why the financial world pays so little attention to ethics. This question stayed with me as the first snowflakes fell from the sky at the end of the day. In fact, on that day, as the dunes slowly disappeared under a beautiful blanket of snow, I decided to write about ethics in the financial world. It would not be a book full of high-minded theories and reflections, but a clear narrative that would create some awareness of values and a sense of what one can and cannot do. The need for such a book was also prompted by what I saw as a contradiction when it came to financial regulations. We tackle every crisis by imposing more rules, but we are often unable to make those rules universally binding. We resolve the problem by identifying the exceptions. The result is an accumulation of rules of conduct and exceptions to those rules. However, this mechanism only creates more confusion. Certainty is possible only if one follows the letter of the rule, and this encourages, even forces, people to disconnect their moral compass. Moral judgments are made on automatic pilot. In other words, too many rules discourage, rather than promote, good behaviour.

In the winters that followed 2003 I often took the same walk through the dunes. Something gnawed away at my conscience every time. Why had I still not started on my book? Was it still necessary? Or had people learned enough from their mistakes and were crises now a thing of the past? Nothing was further from the truth. The financial markets and their players continued to provide food for thought. And that was not all. There was a crisis in 2008, and another in 2011, which had major social consequences. There was widespread public opposition to the behaviour seen in the financial markets. The US-based protest movement, Occupy, quickly spread to many European cities, including London and Amsterdam. People were simply fed up with the behaviour of the financial sector. European voters are starting to punish not only their bankers but their political leaders. Even more telling, the protest singers long gone, reappeared. Bruce Springsteen led the way with songs such as 'We take care of our own' and with statements such as 'the banker man grows fat, working man grows thin' in his song 'Jack of all trades'. The social system is under threat. That is how far we have gone off track. Now that you know why I decided to write this book, we can get down to basics, starting with a critical evaluation of the assumptions made by scholars when studying the market. Does this branch of learning do enough to encourage the development of a moral compass? Or does it take the easy way out?

Chapter 3

The economy plays a shell game

Positivism and other approaches have led economics to abandon its normative responsibilities. According to leading economists, value judgments have made way for value-free thinking. However, is this entirely true? Surely low levels of inflation and low unemployment are normative goals?

People have wondered about their existence for centuries. The world around us has been a constant source of study, as has humanity itself. This study, philosophy, is literally the love of wisdom. The original philosophers were scholars, teachers and advisers who concentrated on the fundamental areas of philosophy: science, logic and ethics. Classical scientists were mainly interested in identifying unchanging order in natural phenomena, and hence in principles establishing uniformity. Their focus was on matter. In the case of logic, matter was subordinate to ideas. Whereas the observable world, that is matter, was subject to constant change, some concepts were eternal. One such eternal concept is honesty. It has existed for as long as humanity itself, but in this constantly changing world its meaning may be subject to interpretation. The third branch of philosophy was ethics. Socrates, one of Ancient Greece's first and best known ethicists, focused entirely on what people do and what they try to achieve through their actions. More modern ethicists, by contrast, study morality to determine which behaviour leads to the greatest possible happiness for the largest number of people. They try to work out which actions are good and which are bad. In order to do this they need a norm. This, however, raises the question of what the norm is, how one arrives at it and who defines it. In the context of norms we would talk about principles and rules today, but the Greek philosophers considered good behaviour to be embodied in virtues. Plato, the famous sage, applied the theory of virtues, and this theory was further developed by his pupil, Aristotle, in the fourth century BC. The theory describes aspects of character that result in virtuous actions. Virtues are a human predisposition. They can be acquired, but they are also genetically determined to a certain extent. The theory of virtues gradually fell into decline in the centuries after Aristotle. During the Reformation virtue became a duty, and during the Enlightenment it became a right. We have moved away from the theory of virtues and continued down the road of principles until we now find ourselves terrorised by rules. A certain amount of historical reflection is therefore called for.

The founder of economics was also a philosopher. Adam Smith (1723–1790), a student of Francis Hutcheson and one of the most important figures of the Scottish Enlightenment, was primarily preoccupied with politics and ethical issues related to government. Smith was known mainly for his books, *The Theory of Moral Sentiments* and *The Wealth of Nations* (see also Chapter 5). In *The Wealth of Nations* (1776), Smith sets out a framework for enhancing prosperity which earned him his reputation as one of the most important economists of all time. You would not, for example, find any of Smith's books in the philosophy section of Kinokuniya, the large Japanese bookstore chain, as they are all located in the economics section. And Kinokuniya is not the only bookstore that does this. Smith would probably have been surprised by this, and it might even have worried him. This, however, says less about Smith than it does about economics, which at the time was a relatively new field of study with its origins in moral philosophy. Smith was a leading advocate of an economy within which people were free to promote their interests and to act without government intervention. What ensures that this freedom does not lead to excesses? To answer this question, Smith revisited some of the ideas of the classical philosophers. The arguments set out in *The Theory of Moral Sentiments* (1759) are based on a system of virtues, such as thrift, justice and generosity. According to Smith, this system forms the basis for how the free market keeps itself in check. The formulation of free market theory therefore took place in a clearly defined value framework, while economics was comfortably embedded in moral philosophy. After Smith's death, his work was overshadowed by newer, often more modern insights, but the concept of the invisible hand made a comeback with the return of the belief in free markets in the 1960s. There was, however, one significant difference this time. The safeguards in the form of virtues and ethics, which Smith described as essential for keeping an unregulated market in check, had been left out. The vehicle for economic progress was back, but it had been stripped of a sound moral braking system. Was this perhaps a cardinal error?

Why did Adam Smith slowly disappear into obscurity after his death? He was followed by Thomas Malthus, John Stuart Mill and Alfred Marshall, all of whom were influential professors and can be considered moral economists. They took as their starting point the fact that the economy cannot remain indifferent to the behaviour and roles of people in society. In other words, human behaviour formed part of the study of economics, and the views of economists regarding desirable behaviour were not value-free. Mill was the first to describe the concept of the *economic man*, that is, man as a wealth maximiser. However, as a devotee of political economy, Mill did pay attention to social aspects, and the judgments he made in this area were not value-free either. He wondered, for instance, how to deal with wages that are so low that people cannot reasonably be expected to survive on them. During the time Marshall was writing (between 1880 and 1920), a fierce battle was waged that was aimed at separating economics from the moral sciences completely. There was great pressure to see economics more as a natural science with a purely scientific bias and to curb discussion of normative issues in the exact sciences. Human behaviour was considered 'normal' by definition, and any behaviour that could not be termed normal had to be dealt with by another branch of science. The tide could no longer be turned, and after Marshall the idea of economics as a moral science fell into serious decline. It was now just about mathematics, about collecting and interpreting data without adding a value judgment. Positivism, a philosophy that attaches value only to knowledge that is based on empirical evidence, was a major force in the shift towards value-free economics.

During the first half of the 20th century, the pressure to see economics as a natural science only grew. Some of the leading names in this school of thought were Lionel Robbins,

Milton Friedman, Harry Markowitz and Paul Samuelson. Samuelson believed that mathematics was a very important tool in economics, and he argued that economics could learn a great deal from physics and the laws of mechanics and thermodynamics. Samuelson's most influential theories were the efficient market hypothesis and the option pricing theory. As its name suggests, the former states that markets are efficient. This means that the price of a financial asset already takes account of all available information concerning future events. The price can therefore only be affected by new information. In support of this hypothesis, Samuelson referred to an underappreciated theory developed by Louis Bachelier. This French scholar made a significant intellectual advance in 1900 that many people consider to be the start of financial mathematics. Bachelier had studied the publications of the Scottish botanist Robert Brown, who was fascinated by the motion of particles in gasses and liquids. These particles seemed to be able to move randomly, even though they consisted of non-living matter. Bachelier asserted that share prices were essentially the same as particles, stating that they moved randomly too, only on the financial markets. This model was described in his thesis on the theoretical basis of speculation.

Samuelson repackaged this thesis. He asserted that in markets where information is available and which are competitive and speculative, price movements are random. Following the publication of his concept, there was no stopping it. The development of theory and the subsequent construction of models in the field of economics was improved and further refined between 1960 and 2008. Big securities companies, realising that this was a new way of making money, hired academics and paid them excessively. No one doubted the appropriateness of this trend. Academic ambitions and honour had to make way for greed, and this greed became the driving force behind more research and development. Money makes people blind, and so the models became the new reality.

That this was not entirely true became painfully obvious on Black Monday, the day of the 1987 stock market crash. Why had the models failed to predict the losses resulting from the dramatic fall in share prices? This was the first sign that the models have a habit of letting us down just when we need them most. Models are based on prices being set on a continuous basis and assume that financial markets are always liquid. They are therefore unable to cope with a price formation process that is discontinuous, and they do not work at all when markets lose their liquidity. Yet that is precisely what happens in every crisis, including the one that occurred in 1987. The name Black Monday also refers to something vitally important. The word that should be stressed in this case is not Black, but Monday. The UK had been hit the previous Friday by one of the worst storms in centuries. There were power failures in London, and the road and rail networks were seriously affected by fallen trees. Since most investors had been unable to reach the financial heart of London, the Bank of England had been forced to declare that Friday a bank holiday. There was, therefore, a three-day weekend. When trading closed in continental Europe that stormy Friday, share prices in the US began to fall. It was soon rumoured that insurers had sold their shareholdings en masse in order to release funds to cover the huge number of claims. The models had simply failed to predict a scenario in which the entire catastrophe would take place while the markets were closed. The markets opened substantially down on Black Monday. The losses were severe, and they were much larger than the models had calculated the previous week. It came as a big shock to us all. The reason this had happened was that the models assumed investors in derivatives (assets based on formulae) would be able to limit their losses by selling their shares in the intervening period. The formulae did not take account of markets that were closed and markets that had no liquidity. The panic that followed was also difficult to capture in models. The fat tails of a normal distribution were referred to in mocking tones, in recognition of the fact that models based on a normal distribution underestimate the likelihood of extreme circumstances (as a result of which the 'tails' at each end of the bell curve are thicker). The economists' assumption that human behaviour can be compared with the motion of particles was completely disproved by the behaviour of real people. Human beings are imperfect and irrational, and they have no intention of being banished from economics as an independent explanatory factor.

Black Monday was a clear warning, yet it was not heeded. People carried on as before, and this could not turn out well. The next warning came just over a decade later, in 1998, in the form of the spectacular collapse of Long-Term Capital Management (LTCM) (see also Chapter 5). Excessive speculation and Russia's rouble crisis had paved the way for the fall of this unregulated investment company, which led, on the threshold of the new millennium, to one of the greatest emergency situations seen on Wall Street in the last century. LTCM was run by Robert Merton and Myron Scholes, the same scholars and Nobel Prize winners who had broken new ground in financial thinking three decades earlier. No one had a better understanding of the assumptions used in the models. According to books about the LTCM crisis published later, academic purists were having pangs of conscience, since one cannot act outside the bounds of one's own assumptions without impunity. However, the temptation was great and that behaviour compromised the fruits of pure academic thinking.

Despite the devastation caused by this disaster, the LTCM crisis did not lead to reform either. Although it had come as another great shock to all, once again no one learned from this crisis. It was only when the 2008 credit crunch hit that people started to realise the models only work properly during uneventful periods, and not during crises, when they are actually needed. At times of panic their results are way off. The models therefore turned out to be about as useful as the bankers who lend their umbrellas when the sun is shining and want them back the minute it begins to rain. Why is this? There are countless explanations, but they all come down to the same thing: markets are not efficient because people are not efficient. People are irrational and are subject to animal behaviour that cannot be captured by sterile models. In his book *Deceit and Self-deception* (2011), the American biologist Robert Trivers delivered a damning verdict on economics. His somewhat cynical conclusion was that despite an impressive mathematical apparatus and an annual Nobel Prize, economics is not a science. Economists are really playing a shell game. Economics focuses on maximising utility, but it fails to work out what this utility is and how it is created. Trivers asserted, unsurprisingly given his background, that this utility can largely be explained in biological terms. As far as he was concerned, economics fails to pay anywhere near enough attention to this fact, as a result of which crucial links are missing. And surely the whole point of the natural sciences was to discover the unchangeable order? If economists believe that they are able to gain insight into the future in this way, they will soon find they are thwarted by irrational, biological human behaviour that is the result of evolution.

The 2008 crisis is often referred to as a perfect storm. This, however, is incorrect, since the crisis was not a natural phenomenon but something that was caused by people. The

2011 government debt crisis was also created by people, particularly in the cases of Greece, Ireland, Italy and Spain. The main cause in this instance was overconfidence in the property sector and a lack of morality, specifically when it comes to paying taxes. Often the problem is not abnormal behaviour on the part of a single individual, but collective abnormal behaviour. Human collective behaviour is so influential, and can be so destructive, that it needs to be given a place, and perhaps even claim a leading role, in the development of economic theory. This will inevitably raise questions about which kinds of behaviour lead to the greatest possible prosperity for all, which kinds of behaviour cause catastrophes, and what type of behaviour is morally just. The markets are not efficient, that much is clear.

Why has economics shifted so far towards mathematics and models and drifted away from highly unpredictable human behaviour? Abstracting this unpredictability creates tools that in many situations produce visible results, which lead to excellent scientific articles, results based on figures, and public attention, and to Nobel Prizes for some. Economists who did not use many models in their work appeared to be much less effective, and were less able to recycle their thinking in numerous articles or permutations of thoughts. They consequently received less praise. The 2008 credit crunch proved that Hyman Minsky (1919–1996, see also Chapter 19) was completely right, but Minsky was never held in the same esteem as his more mathematically oriented colleagues. This brings us back to the practices used in scholarly methods. Is the world to be described first, after which models are distilled from the description of unchanging order? Or should things be done the other way round? Fisher Black and Myron Scholes worked jointly and individually on developing a formula for determining the value of conditional contracts, in other words options, or equity options to be even more precise. Their efforts met with failure until they came up with the concept of replica portfolios. An option contract could be represented by a replica contract whose size kept changing. This major find allowed them to develop an option pricing formula. It was, however, dependent on a market and liquidity always being available for pricing the instruments in the replica portfolios and adjusting the size of the portfolios. This assumption was made quickly and solved a knotty problem. That clinched the matter. However, something vitally important had happened. The guiding principle was no longer reality, but a modelled reality, a reality that could be shaped by the models. This reality is often true, but sometimes it is not. And the development of all the theories based on the concept of the economic man, or *homo economicus*, is in keeping with such thinking and behaviour.

In the autumn of 2010, I was invited to give a lecture at an event marking the anniversary of Rotterdam University. Naturally I decided to argue in favour of elevating economics to a normative science once again. Arnold Heertje, the well-known Dutch emeritus professor and fervent Keynesian, was present on that October day as a speaker at the event. He approached me after my lecture. 'Economics is a science that is free of values,' he said. 'Telling people how they should behave has no place in our discipline.' I could tell that he was angry, furious in fact. We debated the matter briefly. I told Heertje that unethical behaviour had had a major impact on the economy, and obviously this fact could not be ignored as that would mean leaving other branches of science to sort out the problem. 'If human behaviour, including its unethical aspects, has had such a great impact on economic events that almost all of your economic predictions have been wrong-footed, then that behaviour is our problem,' I said. 'You will then have to declare, as an economist, what kind of behaviour is desirable in order to bring about economic stability. These are issues of a normative nature.' Heertje took a different view and I do not believe that either of us shifted our position. But Heertje is not alone in his views. He is in fact in good company.

Alan Greenspan believed in value-free economics all his life. He served as chairman of the Federal Reserve of the US (the American central banking system) from 1987 to 2005, and his policies always relied heavily on models and statistics as the source of all wisdom. Holding the same beliefs as Friedman and Samuelson, Greenspan developed and justified his views always on the basis of objective facts, making him a true proponent of positivism. Following his retirement he wrote *The Age of Turbulence* (2007), an interesting, readable vision on economic thinking and behaviour during the crucial period between 1987 and 2005. It describes the development of the capitalist system once it was no longer in competition with the communist model. Even more interesting is the epilogue Greenspan included in later editions of his book, in which he sets out his views on the credit crunch. Writing the epilogue was a somewhat defensive move, since the former chairman of the Federal Reserve has come in for a great deal of criticism. Excessively low interest rates, lavish amounts of cheap liquidity and the failure of models and risk systems caused the world's greatest financial crisis.

Greenspan reached the conclusion that the macroeconomic models and risk models used by financial institutions are unable to incorporate irrational human behaviour (the animal spirit), which he termed a large missing explanatory variable. He is less concerned with whether human behaviour is rational or not; what matters to him is that it is observable and systematic. According to Greenspan, we can solve the problem by incorporating this form of human behaviour in models through 'add factors'. In his view, those who build models need to tweak their comparisons to include irrational behaviour. In an article published in the *Financial Times* in 2009, he stated that 'we have never successfully modelled the transition from euphoria to fear'. Why is this? And why will we never be able to do this, even if we tweak the system? There are many reasons why this is the case, but there is one reason in particular. Models, once globally endorsed, are used by literally everybody, and that affects the model's outcome. This is an externality. A model cannot predict what will happen if everyone who uses that model starts to panic. It is like a dog biting its own tail. The model is its own worst enemy. Greenspan is evidently unable to admit that he was let down by his beliefs. Economics has simply become too mathematical. But the issue goes even deeper than that. Human behaviour has been banished from the development of theory, yet the root cause of both the credit crunch and the crisis affecting eurozone countries was human behaviour. For this reason, forming judgments about good conduct needs to return to the centre of economics and the development of theory. The truth is out: economics is a moral science.

This amounts to bringing back judgments of actions performed by people as economic individuals and restoring normative thinking to economics. It goes beyond merely paying attention to human behaviour and its impact on financial markets. We need to develop a vision on what constitutes good conduct and bad, at both an individual and a collective level. If human behaviour plays such a decisive role and forms such a threat to our society, maybe we can do something to repair the broken structure. If such a remedy can be introduced, the next crisis may not be a systemic crisis but rather a 'regular' crisis that is easier to bring under control and causes less damage. This would, so to speak, reduce the hurricane to a storm. If we manage to do just that, we will have achieved a great deal. That said, the current trend towards more normative behaviour goes further than merely looking at behavioural risks. Society is demanding that the financial world becomes socially engaged. Social engagement should be the rule, not the exception. When investing in companies that manufacture cluster bombs or use child labour, for example, investors can no longer hide behind intellectual neutrality. Companies, too, are increasingly taking humane working conditions and dignity into account. For example, Nestlé, the major Swiss food and nutrition company, has incorporated sustainable business practices in its purchasing policy. The group selects cocoa producers on the basis of the way in which they treat people rather than on the basis of price. Value has made a comeback. It is not just a response to catastrophes or bad decisions; it is also backed by public opinion, based on a positive way of life.

This is a good thing, but there is still much more to be gained. The financial world has tried time and time again to deal with all kinds of business collapses and disasters by developing new rules and codes, as if the world can be saved by an instruction manual containing detailed rules of conduct. But are we still able to see the bigger picture despite all the rules? And are these rules still in keeping with our sense of justice? Even if this is not the case, there is an unstoppable proliferation of rules and regulations in the financial sector. I would like to offer an alternative to this. Returning to the principles of human behaviour, what motivates people to behave in accordance with generally accepted principles that we consider the norm? How is this norm defined, and could a single issue involve more than one norm? How can we operate in such a complex, abstract financial world without a rulebook and still avoid violating norms? What should our guiding principles be? How can we recognise patterns in the abstract world that are in keeping with our principles? I worked in the financial industry for many years and I have always hated rules. The rules did not make for a good read and they provided little real guidance. I preferred to let my conscience guide me through complex situations. Although this meant I sometimes broke rules, I frequently abstained from actions that were not actually prohibited. I believe that those of us working in the financial industry need to make a serious effort to reduce the number of rules and bring back principles, and this book can be considered as a step in that direction.

What do we need to accomplish this aim? First, we obviously need to have a sense of which forms of behaviour are permitted according to the general norm and which are not. This matter is looked at in more detail, often using real-life examples and my own experiences as a basis, in later chapters. Before this, in the next chapter I would like to say something about the view of humanity I have drawn on in this book. I have had to make an assumption about the kind of people we have to deal with in the financial industry, because without such a presupposition any attempt at analysis is doomed to failure. Given the example I provided of the outlandish behaviour of the drivers on the A2 near Beek in the Netherlands, you may well already have an idea of the course this view will take.

Chapter 4

The ethics of a beggar

What motivates people's actions? Do people take others into consideration or only themselves? Which is stronger, the positive or negative view of humanity? What are the implications of this when it comes to the supervision of conduct in the financial world? Where should the emphasis be: on education and encouragement, on rules and enforcement, or on punishment?

I was so annoyed. It was just gone seven and time for dinner. I had just come out of a long meeting with the members of the Federation of European Securities Exchanges. Back then, in 2001, I was the chairman of the federation. It was a position I had held for two years and which enabled me to explore the European exchange landscape and learn all about lobbying in Brussels. We had got through a lot of material that day, including plans to place trading screens in the US. The European exchanges had not been able to secure the required approval of the US authorities for these plans. The official line was that the subject was still under consideration, but in reality the US authorities were adamantly opposed as our screens would have given US investors unrestricted access to markets that were not subject to US regulation. If anything went wrong, those investors would naturally turn to their own regulators, who were said to be less than enthusiastic about the idea. We had a strong suspicion that competitive arguments also played a role. At the New York Stock Exchange, specialists still traded on the floor. They held on to orders for minutes at a time, searching for the best prices. Screens controlled from Planet Europe, displaying share prices that at times were in direct competition with those of the specialists, were not welcome. The many reservations and the legal jargon of the regulator masked a further misgiving: the suspicion that companies would use these screens as a backdoor route to acquiring a listing in the US while remaining beyond the reach of the long arm of the SEC. That was entirely at odds with the interests of its own regulated capital market. Investors in the US had to be protected by US regulations and by the US regulator. The Americans did put forward a pragmatic alternative: apply for exchange status in the US. Well, quite. We concluded in our meeting that this would be a lengthy process, full of bureaucratic obstacles and complex issues. The federation regarded the standpoint of the Americans as a refusal and unconstructive. My own, somewhat ironic, conclusion was that it would perhaps be a good thing if the problem was never solved. The European exchange organisations were competitors as well as colleagues. There were not usually many subjects we agreed on, and the American question was the one point of the agenda on which we could close ranks. Of course, I kept my opinion to myself, but I am pretty certain that many members shared my views.

Back to the evening of the meeting, and the beginning of an informal dinner at the exchange. Why was I annoyed? Jean Schmidt, the chairman of the Luxembourg Stock Exchange, was supposed to join us for dinner but he had not yet arrived. Because it had been a long day and everyone was tired and hungry, I decided to ask the guests to take their places at the table. Most of them would be flying back to their home countries that same evening, and airplanes wait for no one. There would just have to be an empty place next to mine, and if it got too late I would ask the waiter to remove the place setting. It is not unusual for someone to fail to show up at a business dinner without prior notice, but it is not a habit I like, which is why Schmidt's absence annoyed me. Michael Machiel, the CEO of the Luxembourg exchange, was also concerned. Where was his chairman? Apparently Jean Schmidt had failed to tell him too. Michael decided to call his chairman's mobile phone. It rang for a long time, and when it was finally answered Michael became even more confused. He could not recognise the voice at the other end of the line at all. It was not Jean Schmidt, it was someone else. Had he dialled the wrong number? It was someone speaking in Dutch, but fairly incoherently. It later emerged that Michael had been talking to one of Amsterdam's homeless people. He said that he had found an almost motion-less man on a bench. The bench in question turned out to be just across the street from the stock exchange. Michael and my colleague André Went rushed out into the street. At first I was unaware of what had happened and I even gave a brief welcome speech. When Michael and André failed to return, people began to suspect that something was seriously wrong. I heard someone say that Jean Schmidt had collapsed in front of the stock exchange, possibly from a heart attack. The police and an ambulance had already arrived. I could not believe it, and I rushed to the nearest window. On the other side of Damrak I could see a large group of bystanders, flashing lights and some paramedics who were apparently trying to resuscitate someone. That was all I could see from my distant vantage point, but it was enough. The vague images confirmed the rumours. Jean Schmidt was rushed to hospital but never regained consciousness. He died that same evening, before the hastily curtailed dinner finished. It was an unreal, macabre evening that I shall never forget. But the reason I am telling the story now is not because of Jean, but because of the beggar. On a bleak February evening, the chairman of a stock exchange died on the street, and the only person who came to his aid was homeless. The beggar took care of the stranger, and set the emergency services in motion by answering the phone when Michael called. And when Michael arrived he handed him the mobile phone, symbolically handing over responsibility to him. The story has an almost biblical quality, the beggar tending the dying stock exchange chairman. What would have happened if the tables had been turned? What motivates a homeless person to behave scrupulously and not take advantage of the situation? He could have easily lifted Schmidt's wallet out of his jacket and walked away with it, but he did the opposite. What instincts drive someone to behave the way this man did? What prompts this kind of action, which we undoubtedly consider to be 'good'? Is it our conscience, our instincts, or is the decision to act in such a manner somehow pre-programmed and stored on our own hard disk? Was Charles Darwin right to argue that we are hardwired by evolution? I will come back to this later.

First, let me give another example. A car plunges into the water and a fireman dives in without hesitation to the save the lives of the people inside. Stories like this often inadvertently take a tragic turn. The dog on the back seat is unharmed while the fireman's courageous efforts cost him his life. And yet there are always more firemen prepared to do the same thing. Apparently there is something that makes human beings want to save others, even when it means putting their life at risk. The need or urge to help transcends every form of self-interest, even one's own life, the most precious thing we have, and the riskiest thing to wager as a gesture of love for one's fellow man. And yet it does happen, quite frequently. However, this does not detract from the extraordinary story of the beggar in Amsterdam, particularly as the opposite is so often true in the financial world.

In the financial world people behave selfishly; they are entirely focused on their own self-interest. Take the example of the management of a company that announces a reorganisation. The market responds positively to the news, even though the reorganisation will cost many people their jobs. The market valuation of the company goes up, as do the prices of its shares and stock options, and the personal wealth of the company's management increases as a result. This is a deliberate construct aimed at making a profit by aligning the management's interests with the interest of shareholders. Egoism and self-interest have been given an official role in our industry. The employee loses, the shareholder wins, although sometimes the reverse is true. In some cases the construct is beneficial from an economic perspective, in others the process is a battle motivated by self-interest, and often it is an assault on human dignity. Bernard Madoff, once a respected member of the financial community in the US, did exactly the opposite of the homeless man in Amsterdam. Madoff embezzled tens of billions of dollars, going so far as to cheat and impoverish his best friends. He ruined his favourite charitable organisations. Figuratively speaking, Madoff stole the exchange chairman's mobile phone, his wallet and his smart watch, and then left him to die in the street.

The gap between the real world and financial world became painfully obvious after the 9/11 attacks in New York. The firemen who responded to the call to duty on that tragic day in September 2001, courageously stormed up the staircases of the fatally damaged towers of the World Trade Center, perhaps against their better judgment. They ran through thick curtains of smoke, into the crowds of fleeing people, carried people out and went back again. Time after time. Many firemen died that day, many others are now sitting at home with lung and respiratory diseases, trying to make ends meet on limited benefits. Some of them get nothing at all. These true heroes are scarred for life. How different things are for the 'heroes' of the financial world. Charles Gasparino's book *King of the Club* confirms what I heard from different sources at the time. During the attack on the World Trade Center, Richard Grasso, the CEO of the New York Stock Exchange, was locked up with his staff on Wall Street. He was later praised for his extremely cool-headed behaviour. While the Twin Towers imploded, and the situation on the ground became more and more life-threatening, Grasso remained calm and convinced everyone on the exchange floor to do the same. He prevented panic from breaking out, and for that he deserves to be praised. But Grasso is celebrated primarily because of his headstrong will, his persistence and his efforts to open the exchange again as soon as possible after 9/11. He moved heaven and earth and spurred everyone on to work day and night in pursuit of that goal. It was an enormous effort, as many exchange members had lost not only their offices and their infrastructure as a result of the cowardly attacks, but also many of their co-workers. The human loss for the brokerage companies in the Twin Towers was huge, but other companies were also affected. In spite of the terrible losses, it was important that Wall Street, the symbol of American capitalism, was not closed for too long. The exchange reopened within days of the attacks. Trading resumed and indices were calculated again. The symbolic value was inestimable: it was a confirmation of American resilience and invincibility. And it was all down to Richard Grasso. It was his moment of glory. The board rewarded him with a special US$5 million bonus at the end of the year, bringing his annual salary to US$30 million, US$4 million more than in 2000, the last year of the bull market. When I heard this I could not believe my ears. In times of war, soldiers and generals are in it together. They all have to eat from the same tin plate. You may be awarded a medal but you do not get paid extra for doing your patriotic duty. That was the situation for the firemen. Some time later, one of Grasso's colleagues was in Amsterdam. I told him how surprised I was at Grasso's bonus, and I clearly showed my disapproval. He was shocked by my reaction. He hesitated and then, to my great surprise, stammered that he had received a bonus too.

This set me thinking about how ordinary people, whose lives are sometimes without dignity, can still behave impeccably, while people such as Madoff and Grasso and his colleagues at the exchange behave in what I would call an unethical manner. It is not just down to these individuals but evidently the entire system. It was the members of the board of the New York Stock Exchange who decided to award a special bonus to Grasso; all he did was accept it. Ethics involves critical reflection on the right course of action, but the examples given are not consistent with my idea of what is right. How can people choose such widely divergent courses of action, and how do they square it with their conscience? How can a leading institution such as the board of a US stock exchange approve such special bonuses, and how is it possible that the decision drew no comment? (Bonuses were not criticised until years later, by which time the amounts involved were much higher.) In other words, what motivates people to act in a way that is considered good behaviour while others behave unethically?

There is no universal agreement on the subject. There is no book defining what is right and what is wrong, certainly none that can take into account ever-changing circumstances. The material is far too complex, which is precisely what makes it so fascinating. What is the process by which people weigh good behaviour against bad? How is good behaviour then achieved? An individual may well have a strong sense of values but still be unable to identify the relevant norms or have problems respecting them. He may have a value system in place, but lack the necessary internal discipline. The opposite may also be true. Some people who appear to lack a value system behave impeccably. The beggar in Amsterdam is a good example. Great philosophers and ethicists have studied the question of good and evil for centuries. They have tried to formulate answers that can help us understand this complex material. Natural laws were promoted to theory but many of these theories are highly coloured by the historical context in which they were conceived. One philosopher may have been traumatised by religious wars while another spent his formative years in peace and security. What these theories have done is give us greater insight into the how and why of human actions and whether they are right or wrong. They have also given us tools for detecting good and evil. Does this mean that we are now closer to a universal truth? Have we finally found absolute wisdom? Unfortunately not. Our human tragedy is that we are better at analysing than at drawing conclusions. We are masters of hindsight, but having foresight has proved extremely difficult. In other words, our rear view mirror is in better shape than our crystal ball. Maybe this is because just when we think we have grasped the truth about ethical behaviour, it eludes us as people create new circumstances and present new dilemmas. The same is also true – perhaps especially so – of the financial world.

There is no absolute truth, but the theories of Jan Verplaetse, a professor at the University of Ghent, provide insight into what determines certain forms of human behaviour. Verplaetse has done a great deal of research into the natural origins of our morality. He wondered whether people had a sixth moral sense in addition to the other five senses. There is no evidence of this in the brain, but the concept of a moral sense works very well as a metaphor. The metaphor feeds into the idea that morality is not just a layer of civilisation, but something rooted deep in our biological nature. Morality is to a large extent the result of biological, automatic and emotional processes. What is common to all human morality is that it limits our individual freedom. This serves a higher purpose: survival and the preservation of the community we belong to. We could not survive without these communities. It also introduces a degree of evolutionary thinking into our vision of morality. Morality is based on the preservation of the human race and the survival of our species. In his book *Het morele instinct (The Moral Instinct)* (2008), Verplaetse defines moral and immoral behaviour as the expression of five moral systems. Four of these systems are based on instincts and emotions (the attachment ethic, the violence ethic, the cleanliness ethic and the co-operation ethic), and only one (the ethic of principles) is rational. All of these moral systems create obligations to act, or not act, but on different grounds and in different ways.

The attachment ethic regulates our actions on the basis of empathy and respect for people to whom we feel attached. People form attachments to others through all kinds of processes, and are willing to step into the breach for one another. Such bonds exist not only between a mother and her child, or members of the same family, but also in long-term friendships. As attachment is also related to a strong sense of interdependence, it creates feelings of solidarity. It helps to stem aggression because we are reluctant to hurt people we feel connected to. The attachment process can even take on extreme, irrational forms, such as when hostages form an attachment to their captors. This psychological phenomenon, first identified in Sweden, came to be known as Stockholm syndrome. A famous example of this is the American hostage Patty Hearst, the granddaughter of the wealthy publisher William Randolph Hearst. After being taken from her apartment in 1974, she eventually sided with her kidnappers. She even went so far as to reject her family and participate in a bank robbery with her captors. And in 1977, a group of people who had been held hostage for weeks in a hijacked train in the north of the Netherlands were full of praise for their Moluccan captors but critical of their liberators. From a rational point of view, this is very difficult to understand, but if it is seen as a manifestation of the will to survive under any circumstances, it can be understood. People attach themselves to those they depend on. If an act of liberation suddenly destroys that dependence, the attachment instinct may continue to work. The attachment ethic is one of the factors that drive human behaviour in the financial industry. People in the financial industry work with one another in relative isolation, and often depend on a few individuals who bring in business and determine the success of the operation. People are often more attached to individuals within a company than to the company itself. Innocent people can easily become attached to unprincipled individuals, which can lead to all kinds of undesirable processes and outcomes.

The attachment ethic is not suitable for situations in which we are threatened. At such times the violence ethic comes into play. Although people are social beings, they can also be violent. Violence is an important survival tool, and this is why the instinct is so much a part of human behaviour. Violence is a means of influencing others, as in religious wars when the sword is used to spread brotherly love. Violence has another function: it helps people conquer their fears, and enables them to make calculated decisions. In the financial world violence (and the negative manifestations of power and influence) is a common occurrence. People use every means available in the struggle for survival or in order to land a big order or a bonus. Even though no actual sabres are rattled, the means employed are comparable to violence. No strategy is overlooked in this battle. Those in power do not hesitate to damage the interests of parties who are in an inferior position or to take advantage of an information gap. The abuse of power is commonplace in the financial world, and this has everything to do with the violence ethic, as happened in the case of former IMF chairman Dominique Strauss-Kahn's inappropriate relationship with a New York hotel employee. The ethic of violence also plays a role when the most animal of human instincts – the sex drive – takes over. Our ethical instincts are therefore not always moral. This can be seen in the financial world. In a world that is so far removed from the real world, the ethic of violence is given free rein.

Verplaetse's third kind of morality is the cleanliness ethic. Good and evil are often associated with feelings of cleanliness and dirtiness. We say we 'wash our hands in innocence' because cleanliness is associated with innocence. Despicable acts are often described as 'dirty' practices. No one wants to shake hands with a murderer, and if we accidentally do, we feel the need to wash our hands. In short, moral repugnance creates the need for cleanliness. There is now an awareness of how much needs to be cleaned up in the financial world, and action is being taken. After a crisis, a truth and reconciliation committee is set up and bankers have to repent on camera. The current discussion about whether bankers should apologise to a US congressional committee or to a Dutch parliamentary committee is all part of the cleanliness ethic. The recriminations will not end until hands have been washed, preferably in the form of a detailed report that identifies the guilty parties; only then can confidence be restored. The forced resignation of a senior manager, guilty or not, is part of the cleanliness ethic.

The last of the emotion-based ethics is the co-operation ethic, which teaches us that no one can survive without co-operation. It is an ethic that is deeply rooted in human nature. We co-operate because it benefits us individually or as a group. Co-operation is based on trust: we assume that others will do their part. This makes us very vulnerable to abuse and ignorance. The financial world, like the real world, depends on co-operation. One person cannot achieve much alone and may find it difficult to survive. This encourages co-operation. Your own objectives count, but if you cannot achieve them through co-operation you may be willing to help colleagues achieve their objectives, provided certain conditions can be met. There has to be something in it for you too; this is the essence of coalition building. And if you cannot reach agreement, opposition is always an option. Unfortunately, people in the financial world frequently favour the latter. Luckily, not everyone chooses co-operation out of self-interest. Other motives include a sense of responsibility and generosity.

The four ethics described above are driven by emotions and instinct. They are deeply rooted in our innermost being, and can come to the surface unbidden and unexpectedly – remember the beggar in Amsterdam – but they are not enough to constitute a moral life. That requires a morality driven by rationality: the ethic of principles. This is not about what we do, but what we are supposed to do. We refer to this as a normative world, but moral philosophers prefer to call it ethics, a rational ethic. Because moral principles play a fundamental role in every ethical debate, Verplaetse calls this the ethic of principles, which are based on the rights and obligations of individual citizens and minorities. The question then arises as to what we want to achieve with the norms we have developed. What are the objectives of our norms? The answer has to do with the continued survival of humanity, not from a biological perspective, ingrained in us by evolution, but rather as rules we have to observe in order to secure our continued existence together.

I incorporated the ideas of Verplaetse into a lecture I gave in February 2009 at the annual alumni day of my alma mater, the University of Groningen. It took place at Allersmaborg, a monumental 15th-century structure in the north of the province of Groningen. The university had leased the building the year before as a retreat for students, academic staff and professors, and as a meeting place for alumni. The *borg* – a farmhouse expanded to create a country estate – is near Aduarderzijl, on the banks of the Rijtdiep, in one of the most remote places in the Netherlands. At night it is completely silent and dark. The village is connected to the outside world by a single winding road, and it seems to be largely unaffected by that world. There, in the middle of an empty landscape, lies Allersmaborg. Once inside, the memory of the desolate location quickly receded. It was crowded and I met old acquaintances, deep in discussion with one another. I was nearly overwhelmed by the cacophonous din. What a contrast! My presentation focused on human behaviour as the primary cause of the financial crisis. That evening I spoke about the concept of man as a coalition-forming animal, and man in the financial world as a capricious, calculating egoist. I described a *homo economicus* who, while he may be looking for co-operation, acts primarily out of self-interest. Moral agents working in the financial world know that they cannot survive alone. They need the help and support of others in order to satisfy their own needs, but these do not always have to be the same people. People are continually forming new coalitions, and I cynically noted that *homo economicus* hopes to get more out of the coalition than he invests in it. In one sense this is a variation on the relationship between the individual and the tribe, a modern form of contract theory. In all possible forms of society, and at all times, people have lived in tribes: small, manageable social units. Tribes were more important in the past, before the advent of the nation state, but they have lost little of their significance today. People feel comfortable with this easily manageable type of social structure. They form attachments and rely on the support of the tribe, from which they derive human dignity, and more importantly, economic and social security. Tribes function on the basis of unwritten codes and clearly delineated rights and obligations, duties and responsibilities. In our complex world, moral agents can be members of more than one tribe, at work and elsewhere. Such other tribes could include the local golf club, the Hells Angels or the family. The tribal principle is the same. Loyalty to the group is much greater than to the organisation in which the group operates. This leads to the formation of networks and subcultures within organisations, the power of which is largely informal.

It is important to realise that the objectives of the network of coalitions within an organisation are not necessarily those of the organisation itself. In fact, they often conflict. The company where the group works is simply a platform for achieving ambitions. The mission statement in the annual report is a dead letter, and the company is not an objective in the life of the group member, simply a means of achieving his own group objective. Coalition man optimises his own self-interest by becoming a member of different groups.

When I introduced the concept of coalition man, Martin van Hees and Lodi Nauta, both professors of philosophy, took exception to it. In preparation for my lecture I had written an essay on which they had commented. In their opinion, my view of humanity was too one-sided, and outdated as well. According to Nauta, my narrative was reminiscent of Thomas Hobbes. Although at the time I was not quite sure who Hobbes was, I took this as a compliment. I decided to find out more about my supposed soulmate. It turned out that I do indeed share some of the notions of this English philosopher. Thomas Hobbes (1588–1679) thought that people strove for self-preservation. Their will to survive means that they take no account of the effect of their behaviour on others. Hobbes refers to the social contract but argues that it is a covenant that the individual enters into with an absolute ruler who has absolute power. The ruler is necessary to determine the limits to which man can pursue his own self-interest. The limits of self-interest are defined by the threat of the absolute ruler's sword. I do not think that this notion is outdated at all. On 25 February 2009 the head of the British financial regulatory body, the FSA, appeared before a committee of inquiry investigating the collapse of the British banking system. The FSA had come under heavy fire as a result of the 2008 credit crisis and was accused of having been too lenient with the banks and the financial markets. That day the committee was questioning Lord Adair Turner, the FSA's chairman, and Hector Sants, executive director at the time of the crisis. Lord Turner promised to restrain the baser instincts of bankers, and admitted that the weak regulatory regime had been a major mistake. It is the regulator's responsibility to take the bottle off the table when the party starts getting out of hand.

Van Hees and Nauta are of course right to say that my vision of humanity was too one-sided. The reality is more nuanced. That became clear the day after the FSA enquiry, when a Turkish passenger jet crashed next to a motorway near Amsterdam. On attempting to land at Schiphol airport, it fell out of the air and dropped into a muddy field like a tired child collapsing onto a mattress after a sports contest. The mud turned out to be a stroke of luck; the plane broke in half but did not go up in flames. 'Only' nine people died, but there were many traumatised and wounded passengers. People who witnessed the accident parked their cars in the emergency lane, jumped over the guardrails and made their way to the plane. Some of them even climbed into the plane to help the wounded escape. Later, a journalist asked them if they had realised at the time that the plane could still have caught fire and exploded. Some of them said they had, but that they had weighed up the risks. Others said it had not even occurred to them. One of the helpful bystanders could have been someone from the financial or business world. It could even have been a hedge fund manager whose work consists of profiting from the setbacks of others, someone I just disparagingly described as coalition man. He may be egotistical, but on that unfortunate day he put his own life at risk to help others. That brings us back to the beginning of my argument. People are not all good or all bad. The instincts that determine human behaviour are also influenced by circumstances. This is a generic truth about the world we all live in, but one aspect of that world – the financial industry – has revealed a distinctly Hobbesian nature. The players in this world need to realise that their behaviour is too mired in the theories of a 16th-century philosopher, and make a concerted effort to change it. They can do so with the help of their own insights and self-discipline, but the metaphorical sword is still necessary.

In the next chapter I will take a closer look at the ideas of Thomas Hobbes and their impact on others, including Adam Smith, and on modern society.

Chapter 5

The visible hand

Markets closely resemble people. They are very good at regulating, but not necessarily at regulating themselves. Should governments monitor the markets, or should the markets keep governments in check? Who regulates whom?

Thomas Hobbes was born rather prematurely on 5 April 1588, during the Anglo-Spanish war of 1585–1604. That spring the Spanish Armada set sail for England, causing a great deal of fear among the English. On the matter of his birth, he would later go on to say, 'My mother gave birth to twins: myself and fear.' The Armada would be defeated that year, but Hobbes was not born under a lucky star. His father, who had little interest in him, got into trouble due to his own bad behaviour and eventually left the family. The young Hobbes had a rich uncle who was concerned about his fate. He raised his nephew and arranged the means for him to study at the University of Oxford, where he focused primarily on the study of classical philosophy texts. Hobbes was a scholar and fascinated by the issues of his time. He belonged to a group who took a sceptical view of the effectiveness of moral values, partly because of people's drive to protect their own self-interests. Early in his career, Hobbes asserted that moral values were totally ineffective if they were not enforced. At first he was mainly interested in the natural sciences. He believed the laws of nature needed to be studied, and that by applying these laws it would be possible to obtain answers to questions, including those about humanity. Moreover, our understanding of social and political problems ought to be based on the application of such laws to matters of a more social nature.

Hobbes's views were influenced by events during his lifetime, such as the religious wars in Europe and the political revolt in his own country. England had been ruled with a stern hand by King Charles I since 1625. However, the monarch struggled constantly with Parliament, and these struggles became so fraught that he dissolved Parliament and reigned without it for eleven years. In order to raise funds for his war against the Scots, however, Charles I had to call Parliament to session. In this way the power of Parliament grew as the position of the monarch became steadily weaker. The religious conflicts and the struggle for power triggered the outbreak of the English Civil War in 1642. This led to the beheading of Charles I in 1649 and the replacement of the monarchy by a Protectorate governed by Oliver Cromwell. Cromwell died in 1658, and the monarchy was restored, with Charles II as King. According to Hobbes, the conflicts were due to a struggle for power between groups, and these groups could put forward arguments that were both right and wrong. But that did not matter, because Hobbes believed that human behaviour was driven by self-interest. Some critics of his work have interpreted this as a pure form of psychological egoism and have therefore argued that Hobbes's theories have little to do with ethics. According to Hobbes, humanity was mainly motivated by the desire to avoid war and create the basis for a common wealth in which people could benefit from a 'contented life'. Unusually for the time, his moral philosophy was based on reason and rationality, rather than theology and the Bible. Reason focused on self-preservation, while rationality drove people to prevent avoidable deaths. Hobbes thought that religion formed a constant threat to the stability of the common wealth. Are all these theories outdated now? Has humanity evolved from a social perspective since the defeat of the Armada? Do we now live in a social paradise compared to the early modern Hobbes? The world has not changed as much as we might like to think, and for this reason we still need to take his views very seriously. For example, in 2011 a woman living in the Libyan capital Tripoli was asked how she thought the battle between Colonel Gaddafi and the rebels would go. 'To be honest,' she replied, 'the truth is that I want to live.' This single sentence speaks volumes.

Returning to Hobbes, he believed that the goal of morality was peace, and this could only be achieved if there was a proper common wealth. To achieve this, each individual needs to transfer rights to a sovereign who rules with a stern hand and enforces moral conduct. These early notions of a social contract derived from a starting point that Hobbes called the state of nature. In this state of nature, people live without any social, political or legal structures, and are only concerned with survival. This means constantly struggling and having no time or opportunity to provide for, let alone enjoy, a comfortable life. According to Hobbes, people eventually realise that there is a better world, in which they cede some of their rights in the state of nature to a sovereign. In exchange for this, they receive security and peace. In peaceful times, people can work on the common wealth, in other words on the economy. A number of objections can be raised against Hobbes's ideas, for example as regards the extent to which people are completely egocentric. Moreover, is the state of nature as bad as he describes? Nevertheless, such criticisms do not detract from Hobbes's greatest achievement: he was one of the first to describe a model of government that was not related to any organised religion. His most important conclusion was that only a central power was in a position to combat some forms of human behaviour seen in society. Without this absolute monarch there would be chaos. Or, in other words:

> Subjects cannot manage on their own; the government is the solution.

Adam Smith was basically interested in the same issue as Hobbes: the social process aimed at increasing wealth. Smith lived in a different era, and naturally this coloured his view of society. In the mid 18th century, the church and state had a stranglehold on society. This led to stagnation and misery in Scotland too, or perhaps in particular, where Smith lived. Trade and colonialism had generated more liberal ideas as well as a new view of society and how it should be governed. The Low Countries were a model of free thinking and liberalism in Europe, but Smith was also greatly inspired by America, where the colonies were rebelling against British rule. There was a realisation that the middle and lower classes were entitled to a piece of the wealth and that the pursuit of an increase in overall wealth was good. Smith's insights can be summarised as three concepts:

- division of labour, allowing production to be increased;
- trade as the driving force behind resource allocation (if labour is divided, there needs to be more trade to ensure that everyone gets their share of the goods produced); and
- self-interest as the driving force behind economic prosperity.

As self-interest increases productivity, the pursuit of self-interest is a positive thing that brings growth and progress. The size of the cake increases, benefiting everyone, including those who only get a small slice. Among other things, Smith introduced the concept of 'national product'. He believed that growth benefited everyone. His view on humanity was different from that held by Hobbes, but Hobbes was considering people at a lower point on their hierarchy of needs. Hobbes was concerned with safety and security, while Smith's focus was increasing wealth.

In *The Theory of Moral Sentiments*, Smith provided grounds for his proposition that the pursuit of self-interest is good. He believed that people who are driven by self-interest were also familiar with the very important principle of benevolence and sympathy. He argued that this was one of the qualities that separate people from animals. Sympathy forms part of the system we use for imagination. It goes further than emotions and is more than just a product of physical experiences. Our imagination makes sympathy meaningful and powerful. Our imagination fuels judgments about our feelings and those of others as well as the ensuing actions. This concept of judgments guided by the imagination was termed 'the impartial spectator' by Smith. He asserted that when we develop morality, our natural sympathies are shaped into thoughts and actions as if these were the thoughts and actions of an impartial spectator. In my view, the moral spectator described by Smith basically corresponds to the conscience and to the ability people have to transcend themselves and reduce their own self-interests to socially-acceptable proportions. This requires empathy.

In *The Wealth of Nations*, Smith grappled with the causes of stagnation, such as government interference, high taxes, fixed rewards, cartels and monopolies. According to Smith, the government had a role to play when it came to infrastructure, but economic actors needed to find their own way within this infrastructure. In Smith's view, this resulted in the best allocation of capital goods and wealth creation. The 'invisible hand' is associated with this way of thinking, although the concept has been subject to many different interpretations since Smith first committed it to paper. The most common interpretation of the concept is that the invisible hand is the mechanism through which economic freedom creates economic progress. What this comes down to in practical terms is a small government that gives economic actors free rein. Smith therefore puts forward a different proposition from Hobbes, which is:

> The government is the problem, and subjects are the solution.

So who is the problem, and who has the solution? These questions continue to occupy us and divide politicians and economists. Major theories on financial markets have been developed by economists on the basis of assumptions of free markets versus regulated markets, and responsible behaviour versus irrational behaviour. The rationality of a person can be described on the basis of the individual's preferences and choices, but for rational markets these criteria need to apply at an aggregated level. Guido Erreygers, a professor at the University of Antwerp, is the author of an essay on efficiency and rationality in financial markets that made a major contribution to the book *Explorations in Financial Ethics* (2000). Erreygers gives two criteria that markets need to satisfy in order to be considered rational. Markets are rational if: (i) they give participants accurate price signals; and (ii) trends in the markets are related to trends in the real economy. This assumes that individuals act on the basis of rational expectations. Markets are closely connected with the concept of efficiency. Efficient markets are markets in which prices accurately reflect the available information. During the 1960s, two key concepts – the capital asset pricing model (CAPM) and the efficient markets hypothesis (EMH) – were developed on the basis of rational, efficient markets and fleshed out in models that have been widely applied and enjoyed broad acceptance. These models were used to our great satisfaction for half a century, but the crises have shown us that they let us down at crucial moments.

Amid all the violent tones of a discipline that had come to be based increasingly on natural sciences, John Maynard Keynes (1883–1946) managed to make his presence felt. This important British economist had a less mechanical perspective and saw social and economic trends in a broader perspective. He described the psychological mood that had led to the Great Depression in the 1930s as well as the sentiment that accompanied the recovery. Keynes studied the causes of business cycles (including psychological causes) and coined the term 'animal spirits'. He was not at all convinced that the market consisted solely of nice, decent, rational players, declaring 'Markets can stay irrational longer than you can remain solvent'. In Keynes's wake, the US economist Hyman Minsky (1919–1996) tried to come to a better understanding of the causes of financial crises. He warned against debt accumulation and developed the financial instability hypothesis, which claimed that the economy swings between the two extremes of robustness and fragility. 'Mature' economies were more vulnerable, and according to Minsky the only way to deal with this was through government intervention. Thomas Hobbes would go along with this.

Animal Spirits: how human psychology drives the economy, and why it matters for global capitalism, by George Akerlof and Robert Shiller, was published in 2009. This book breathed new life into Keynes's concept of animal spirits. Banking and the stability of the system are a matter of confidence, and this brings us right to the heart of the psychology of markets and participants. Akerlof and Shiller describe five key animal spirits and how they influence economic decisions. These concepts are confidence (and the lack of it), fairness, corruption, the money illusion and stories.

One of the main causes of crises and periods of rapid market price increases relates to confidence in the future. Judgments about the future are not always reached rationally, and many are irrational. People take decisions based on whether it feels right or due to emotional factors. Confidence (or a lack of it) is often based on past experience that does not necessarily bear any relation to the future. For instance, an asset manager who has been disappointed by a company's management once too often will refuse to touch the company's shares ever again. This is understandable from an emotional perspective, but as management changes over time it makes no sense rationally speaking. Confidence breeds confidence. If someone has already obtained good results by taking a particular decision, this gives us confidence. Copying another person's success can provide a significant amount of confidence, and it is much harder to win others over for new initiatives than it is for proven strategies.

In connection with this, Akerlof and Shiller, pointing to theories developed by Keynes and another economist, John Hicks, refer to the multiplier effect. According to Keynes and Hicks, each dollar that is injected into the economy by the government can do its work many times over. Akerlof and Shiller argue that the same can be said of confidence. When customers develop confidence in a particular product, the number of people who want to have that product grows. The banking industry plays a key role in this. Every increase in a bank's assets, which are often created by retaining profits, has a multiplier effect on the possibility of granting new loans. Every loss, however, results in a proportional reduction. When things are going well in the banking industry and the capital base is growing, there is a tendency to be generous when it comes to lending, which boosts confidence in the market. The reverse is also true. Excessive lending is the source of recklessness – something we now know all about.

Confidence can soon turn into overconfidence (irrational exuberance). Many entrepreneurs start off by making plenty of money and then make even more, only to lose it all. Entrepreneurs whose initiatives turn out to be successful tend to think that achieving this success was easy. It gives them a boost, which frequently means they not only repeat their success once, but on multiple occasions. They then borrow money from the bank and market their idea on an even larger scale. Their success can get out of control, and this puts the continued existence of the business in great danger. From a management perspective, there is no stopping success. Shareholders want success to continue, analysts are jubilant, employees get drunk on it, and all the while the competition lies in wait with initiatives that pose a threat. Executives often argue that they have no choice other than to continue investing, but this can be disastrous. Sometimes the opposite happens. In times of great crisis, people may rush to throw everything overboard, including the business's best assets. This is irrational shrinkage.

Akerlof and Shiller's second key animal spirit, fairness, takes us from psychological into more ethical territory. The authors illustrate this concept with the story of Albert Rees, a professor in labour economics at the University of Chicago. In his later years, Rees came to the conclusion that economics had failed to give any consideration to the concept of fairness. Economists, led by Adam Smith, studied the exchange of goods and services for money or other goods and services. The exchange of goods and services and the associated price are described as technical phenomena. However, no attention is paid to the experience of those who take part in this process. If they sense that a process is unfair, this leads to irrational behaviour. They start to oppose the process. Irrational acts occur that are no longer aimed at achieving the best possible economic outcome. Reason makes way for feelings of vengeance and ill-will. For example, if employees think that the appointment of new management was not handled correctly or if the outcome of their appointment is not in line with expectations, this can lead to an exodus from the business. The employees may benefit more from staying, but that is irrelevant. What matters is how they feel, their emotions. People often say that they are at their wits' end, but this has nothing to do with reason. Neither do strikes. The process for arriving at the best possible economic outcome is abandoned and the head butting begins. During strikes, gaining the support of the public is much more important than striving for the best possible outcome. The outcome of recent elections in the eurozone countries can be partly attributed to this effect as well. Revenge is victorious over reason.

Corruption and bad faith, Akerlof and Shiller's third key animal spirit, are major reasons why outcomes are different from what one should expect based on rationality and efficiency. Or more accurately, this is the purpose of corruption. Corruption is everywhere in our society. It interferes with the efficient allocation of all kinds of resources, ranging from human talent to capital goods. The impact of corruption goes beyond a specific incident and the advantages obtained by a particular individual. It has consequences for the entire system. The best examples of this are Greece and Italy once again. These countries have to contend with a corrupt, inadequate process for collecting public funds. This created national financial crises that became social crises and later a global crisis. The economic process of allocating resources and goods has become totally disrupted. Adversely affected individuals and institutions claim that the process is very unfair and have also started to act irrationally. Reason tells us that other European countries need to come to the aid of Greece, but the people of those countries feel differently. They have questioned why they should have to pay more taxes while the Greeks do not pay theirs.

Besides being based on corruption, which primarily relates to the payment of taxes, wrong decisions can also be the result of bad intentions. Personal preferences, such as excessive sympathy for one party or a dislike of another, can also play a role. Favouritism and nepotism are commonplace and certainly cannot be underestimated as disruptive factors in the economy. Corruption and bad intentions were instrumental in causing the 2008 banking crisis. The products sold to unsuspecting investors in the run-up to that crisis were not developed with the best of motives. Bad intentions, and the greed that accompanies them, are a matter that touches on ethical behaviour, financial structure and relationships. General ideas concerning remuneration are of crucial importance when it comes to guiding and controlling the course bad intentions take.

The fourth key animal spirit, the money illusion, is what I term nominalism. This phenomenon arises mainly when decisions are taken on the basis of the naked equation, without considering the dimensions of the variables. The following example illustrates this. When the euro was introduced, there was a money illusion, particularly in the restaurant and pub sectors in countries where the value of the local currency had been close to the value of the euro. In Germany, for instance, a cup of coffee that used to cost two marks soon cost two euros. Customers were caught out because the price did not appear to have changed. In nominal terms they were right, but in real terms they had been cheated. Figures have an exaggerated impact on our decisions. Anyone from continental Europe who drives a vehicle in the UK will be aware of this fact. Once one is used to driving on the left and has practised shifting gears with one's left hand, there is another challenge: not speeding. Those who normally drive at around 120 kilometres an hour have to get used to speeds of no more than 70 miles an hour. Another good example is what being a millionaire means for a very rich person. Can he or she still be considered very rich after decades of inflation? Quite ordinary people can be found walking around annual Millionaires Fairs these days. We remain fixated on the number, while the reality of what the number means changed long ago. This is what is known as the money illusion. I will take a closer look at one form of this phenomenon, specifically the inability of people to reconcile a figure that indicates a difference in return with the difference in the risk that they run, in Chapter 9. This inability leads to the level of risk being underestimated or overestimated, and that, together with bad intentions, was one of the main causes of the euro crisis.

The fifth and final key animal spirit mentioned by Akerlof and Shiller was the fact that the human brain thinks in terms of stories. According to the social psychologists Roger Schank and Robert Abelson, storytelling plays a vital role when it comes to gaining and passing on knowledge. Stories either fuel or damage confidence and they draw attention to key behavioural concepts and virtues, such as honesty and justice. Stories can also be used to explain truths or make connections more easily, and they contain knowledge that is transferred from one generation to the next. The Bible is a good example of this, and each culture and religion has its own traditions. Stories are also important for the economic process. When people come to know about an entrepreneur's success, for example, it encourages others to start their own business ventures. Stories are often one-sided, only exposing part of the truth, but this is their strength. Stories romanticise matters and make them abstract. The tale of a successful entrepreneur with a nice yacht, a house in France, and probably a young second wife too, appeals to many. However, we very rarely hear about the many others who have failed and are condemned to live a life without glory. The fact that the young second wife spent so much money the successful entrepreneur died penniless is not mentioned either. But none of this matters. A half truth is often a palatable truth, and that is what we like to hear. The opposite usually applies in newspapers, where bad news prevails. We read that another crisis is happening, there has been a disaster somewhere or that someone has been murdered. The misery is magnified, and this appeals to our imagination. This is how stories start to influence our own behaviour.

In *Animal Spirits,* Akerlof and Shiller tackle behavioural economics, a discipline that focuses on the cognitive processes involved in the decision-making process. Individuals rarely take financial decisions that are entirely rational, as their actions are also determined by their emotions and opinions, which are based on a subsection of reality. According to relativism, an explanation of variant behaviour derived from nominalism, we are particularly focused on the difference between two numbers. We want to earn more than our neighbour, and our business should be bigger than our competitor. What we want to achieve in absolute terms is rarely mentioned. This variant behaviour was one of the main factors behind the disappearance of ABN Amro as an international financial institution and a listed company. Countless other forms of variant behaviour can have a major impact on decision making. Most investors are more driven by fear of losses than by the allure of profits. Personal motives are another important aspect of the decision-making process. The motive may be money, status, power, or a boost to the ego. It could also be fear. Many mergers, for example, were concluded because the businesses were afraid to go it alone in tough economic times. The decision to merge has little to do with economic reason. Bankers and consultants have a ready-made business case, based on economies of scale. Moreover, we live under the assumption that someone who is closer to the source and has more information than we do must know best. But is this true? If you zoom in on an object too much with a strong telescope, the contours of the object disappear. Reducing the level of magnification produces a clearer picture. In other words, we unwittingly become blinded when we are too close to something.

That said, the main source of irrationality is herd behaviour. It is practically impossible for the human mind to weigh matters up objectively when a choice has to be made between an individual's own insights and those of the herd. Behaving differently from the group takes a great deal of courage. This fact, in combination with the hubris seen in times of prosperity, leads to people becoming detached from social reality. This is partly because every decision to invest or consume has a delayed effect, and the impact of this delay is difficult to assess. But once economic reality becomes apparent, it is too late to reverse the decision. It is a fate that affects many businesses. As soon as a new head office is built, the economy collapses and cuts have to be made. When Fortis and the Royal Bank of Scotland were given final approval to proceed with the consortium bidding for ABN Amro, the economy was already in trouble, and this is just one of countless examples. As far as Fortis is concerned, technically the deal could have been called off, but psychologically speaking there was no way out. This is often the problem. Once we find ourselves in a tunnel, we run the danger of becoming detached from reality. We usually fail in our efforts to break out of that state as we are, essentially, herd animals.

In this context, it is also important to consider the relationships between an individual's rationality and the rationality of the market. Many relationships were identified by Charles Kindleberger, who made a key contribution to behavioural economics. Two of these relationships are explained below. First, when an investor acts irrationally it is unlikely that the market is rational. In fact, the market is very probably irrational as well. Kindleberger asserted that the reverse is also possible. If every participant in the economic process acts rationally, the system may still produce irrational outcomes and even collapse. This is because everyone will be doing the same thing. Kindleberger termed this a 'fallacy of composition', the incorrect attribution of one or more parts of a whole to that whole. For example, a passenger ship has many more people on board than permitted by law. During its voyage along the Norwegian coast, the sea mist that has obscured the view for hours unexpectedly clears up. Suddenly the beautiful coastline is visible, and no one wants to miss it. All of the passengers rush to the port side of the ship, and you can guess the rest. The vessel lists, so the captain asks the passengers to move to the starboard side. This means quite a climb because the ship is listing so badly. At the same time, everyone is watching what the others are doing, just as a herd would. If no one makes a move, the inevitable happens: the ship capsizes and disappears into the sea. Events can take a similar turn on the financial markets. If all investors do the same thing, even if it is the right thing, the system will go under. Nevertheless, this is what we do, driven by our herd instinct. The herd is large, and moves in the same direction en masse. Modern communication technology means that geographical and time differences no longer have a mitigating effect. People all over the world were able to see a plane hit the Twin Towers at the same time. We all have front row seats in the theatre that is the world. Regulators have good reason for warning that one-sided, synchronised behaviour can, when taken to excess, create systemic risks.

Nevertheless, for a long time a large number of economists refused to believe that behavioural aspects have an impact. They admitted that the markets were not rational on occasion, but in their view this did not have any consequences for the most important theoretical assumptions. In 1988, for instance, the US economist Eugene Fama noted that the evidence was not strong enough to form a serious threat to the efficient markets hypothesis.

However, that was three crises ago. These economists will, I hope, think differently today. Any defence of efficient markets today means fighting a rearguard action against reality. As noted above, the markets are not efficient in times of crisis, and that is the nub of the problem. That is precisely when efficiency matters most and we need to be able to rely on the underlying assumptions. The collapse of Long-Term Capital Management (LTCM) in 2000 and the 2008 banking crisis have provided us with interesting new insights. The assumptions we made in our hypotheses and on which we base our models vanish during a crisis. David Harding, the founder, chairman and head of research at London-based Winton Capital Management, is one of the most successful hedge fund managers in the world. His investment approach is based on the inefficiency of markets. Techniques recognising market trends early can often help by being in the vanguard and thus create an extra yield. In an interview with the *Financial Times* in November 2011, he questioned the traditional theories of efficient markets, and stated:

> The financial crisis is a direct result of their hubris and blind faith in their models. The efficient markets hypothesis is a religion... Facts are not relevant to these people.

How could we have been so mistaken? It is because the efficient markets hypothesis assumes that markets are a match for the universe in terms of space and size. However, this assumption is incorrect. Fear and a lack of confidence mean that liquidity disappears from the markets in times of crisis. The seemingly infinitely large market shrinks, and may sometimes disappear completely. Banks stop lending and regulators impose all kinds of impediments, such as bans on securities lending, as a result of which arbitrageurs can no longer work to make the market efficient. The presumption of eternal liquidity is disproved by the spectre of fear. Fear reigns, just as it did when Thomas Hobbes's mother heard that the Spanish Armada had set sail for England, but the models have no place for fear.

The models also contain another aspect that can seriously disrupt the markets. Economic theory has developed on the basis of the assumption that the market prices of different asset classes are not only related to one other, but that this relationship is a stable one. Some asset classes are positively correlated, others negatively. If there is a low correlation, or a negative correlation (low or otherwise) between two asset classes, the theory is that investing in both classes can be considered a safe strategy, since they will never both drop in value at the same time. The extent of the relationship between the values is referred to as covariance and is calculated on the basis of long time series. Covariance is an important element in risk models and can be found in extensive covariance matrices. These models allow us to run a greater risk (absolute or otherwise) than would be considered wise if we were to add together the risks attached to each investment position. This is because we can adjust the risks with a factor corresponding to the covariance. In this way, we accumulate risk. Moreover, people claim that one risk covers another (hedging), allowing them to take even more risk. And so it goes on.

There is a great risk that a stable negative correlation may suddenly and unexpectedly become a positive correlation. That became apparent in 1998 when LTCM collapsed. This hedge fund concentrated on profiting from small differences in the prices of related bonds. As the price differences were so small, the fund held large positions in numerous markets, including the markets for government bonds issued by Britain (gilt market) and Germany (bund market). At first this strategy produced excellent returns, but the trouble began when the Russian rouble crisis broke out, causing widespread panic. The fund management at LTCM realised that banks would soon reduce the amount of credit they provided, and so the fund had to dispose of positions in order to generate liquidity. Since liquidity in Russian government bonds had dried up, LTCM decided to reduce its positions in gilts and bunds. As a consequence, the Russian crisis had an impact on the prices of British and German government bonds, caused by a speculator that had found itself in a corner. The covariance matrix broke down. This story does not have a happy ending. The fund was unable to liquidate its positions and got into great difficulties. What is more, most of the money that had been invested was borrowed. A bailout fund, financed by a number of major US investment banks, was required in order to prevent all of Wall Street from being dragged down. Bear Stearns refused to participate in the bailout, and there are suspicions that this score was settled on 5 March 2008. LTCM was wound up and liquidated in 2000. Animal spirits had spoiled the party and dispelled our notion that certain financial assets have a low price correlation. Yet we failed to learn any lessons from this event, which is why it happened again in 2008. This means that portfolios that are properly diversified can suddenly become very dangerous, as JP Morgan found out in March 2012 when their London operations reported a loss of more than US$2 billion. Even the king of risk management was fooled by the unexpected behaviour of markets.

Let us now return to Hobbes and Smith. During the 1960s, the theories of Smith were hijacked by economists and politicians who favoured small government and believed markets could take care of themselves. But these policy-makers were guilty of being selective. They took only certain parts of the theories, and omitted other parts that appealed to them less. They ignored the parts of Smith's theory that were vital for keeping the free markets in check, the virtues that could counterbalance greed and egoism, in other words the conscience that ensures our actions respect the interests of others. Since the virtues were taken out of the dogmatic approach developed in the 1960s, the system we admired at that time became unbalanced. Consequently, self-regulation failed. However, something else has changed since Adam Smith put his ideas of the 'invisible hand' down on paper. The belief that markets are able to self-regulate is based on a multiform market where there is a pluriformity in demand and supply. In a pluriform market, if a supplier goes bankrupt many others will step into the fold and take over the supply shortfall. These will be the better run suppliers. In this way, Darwin's law can also be applied to the financial markets. However, this is no longer the reality of the situation. Globalisation and standardisation has led to the emergence of dominant suppliers that are vital for keeping our global economy going. As well as banks, these suppliers include businesses such as Microsoft and, possibly, Google. We cannot allow these businesses to go, so the healing power of bankruptcy no longer works in their case. These businesses represent systemic risks and we need to change how we think about them.

In this context, it is interesting to look at the interview given by Sheila Bair on retiring as the chairperson of the Federal Deposit Insurance Corporation (FDIC) in the US. According to Ms Bair, the monetary authorities should have let the bank Bear Stearns fail. She believes it is wrong that big banks can never be allowed to fail, and does not think that the regulators can adequately regulate these banks. In her opinion, we need market discipline. Ms

Bair is in favour of legal measures that would allow big banks to be wound down. Former chairman of the Federal Reserve, Alan Greenspan also continues to believe in the power of the market. Regulators cannot take over the disciplinary power of the market. He asserts that regulators are poorly equipped as they are unable to catch more than a glimpse of even the simplest financial system. According to Greenspan, the global invisible hand has, with the single exception of the events of 2008, ensured relatively stable exchange rates, interest rates, prices and wages. Evidently not all dinosaurs are extinct.

The 2008 banking crisis proved Thomas Hobbes right. In those tense times, everyone felt the need for an absolute ruler. That was Hank Paulson, then US Secretary of the Treasury, who was accompanied by a number of intrepid key political figures, such as Gordon Brown in the UK and Wouter Bos, the Dutch minister of finance. Even Alan Greenspan had to admit he had been mistaken in the extent to which he believed executives at financial institutions would be able to ensure the continued existence of the financial system. Although Greenspan had thought that individual boards could fail, he was shocked by the failure of collectivity. He was not alone in this. I hope this fact will serve to convince the reader that we cannot run financial markets without the wisdom of courageous governmental leaders. However, just when we had started to believe that governments were the solution, they got into trouble themselves. Some heads of government behaved no less unethically than CEOs at some big businesses. In other words, governments have their own problems and are far from infallible.

Agreements were reached on ceilings on budget deficits at the time the euro was introduced, but not a single one of Europe's national governments adhered to the agreements, and no one forced them to. Former high-interest-rate countries got drunk on these low borrowing rates and went on a spending and investment spree. When the market decided the situation could not continue, the governments talked of speculators trying to bring down the euro. In literature, speculators are frequently depicted as vultures without a conscience that attack the public interest, but in reality they are the market forces that enforce good behaviour when politicians fail to do so. Without such intervention, Greece and Italy would have continued down the road they were following and their problems would have only grown. Spain would have continued to build houses for nobody. In fact, the speculators should have struck sooner. But instead of learning lessons from this political incompetence, the European Commissioner for the Internal Market and Services, Michel Barnier, wants to deprive rating agencies of their influence. American senators hurled abuse at Standard & Poor's after it downgraded the US, a move that in my eyes was both brave and necessary. Politicians have shot the messengers. Can things get any worse?

The above brings me back to the question I raised earlier on in this chapter. Whose theory is correct: Hobbes's theory, or Smith's? As I have explained in this chapter, the answer can be found in two recent crises. In 2008 the 'subjects' (that is, banks and consumers of financial services) were guilty of creating one of the worst financial disasters in history. The governments managed to keep the system going, and this brought an abrupt end to free-market thinking. Were we mistaken in this? Should we have regarded government as the solution? The answer came in 2010 when governments, led by Greece and Italy, with many others following in their wake, caused serious international economic chaos. Financial institutions and citizens were presented with the bill for this. Banks had to make contributions, the people had to pay more tax and public services were cut. Even the US has now learned that it cannot defy the law of financial gravity. And that is not all. In the Middle East, the power of absolute monarchs crumbled before the eyes of an astonished global audience. Absolute rulers are also fallible, and they are certainly not the first people to whom we should delegate power unconditionally. Clearly, Smith's proposition (letting subjects arrange matters for themselves) failed, but so did Hobbes's theory (giving government the task of meting out discipline). What is interesting about the current situation is that there is a state of mutual dependence. The market has to be kept in check by government intervention and regulation, but it also has a message to give to politicians. Markets and government need to regulate each other. Unfortunately, by no means everyone has realised this yet.

As I looked out of the windows of Dubai's Emirates Towers hotel in 2006, I believed I had come across a perfect example of irrational exuberance. The emirate had more construction cranes than anywhere else in the world except for China. Nearby, the rising silhouette of what was to become the tallest building in the world, Burj Dubai, crept upwards at a rate of two floors a week. As I wondered what had made this possible, I came to understand at least one thing. My insight was related to the reason why this tower's name was changed from Burj Dubai to Burj Khalifa just minutes before the opening ceremony. It was an insight that deserved to be included in the conclusions of this book.

Chapter 6

Eudaimonia

The Greek word 'eudaimonia' relates to the central concept of Aristotelian ethics. It is the feeling of happiness that can be achieved by making the right choices about our actions. How do we choose the right course of action? What are the underlying ethical theories? Do these theories give us anything to go by, and can they help us solve modern-day problems?

Despite all of the unpleasant subjects I touched on in previous chapters, we should not forget that most people want to lead a good life and try to do this by giving their life meaning. It is important for us to act in a way that promotes our welfare and happiness. This relates not so much to what we actually do (*is*), but more to how we should act (*ought to*). The Scottish philosopher David Hume (1711–1776) was convinced that moral conclusions could not be drawn from factual circumstances. Normative statements based on factual evidence are not permissible because, according to Hume, normative statements require a process of moral judgment. For moral philosophers, the gap between *is* and *ought to* is the basis of their discipline. Having said that, it is unrealistic to assume that there is no relationship at all between *is* and *ought to*. Let us just say there can be a healthy tension between the two, a degree of covariance as it were, but I will consider this later. First I want to discuss the concepts of *is* and *ought to* in greater detail because not everything related to how things ought to be has a moral dimension.

Imagine that today I ought to have taken the rubbish out, but I simply forgot. Of course, this has nothing to do with moral ethics and everything to do with household organisation. Morality is about social interactions, about how we deal with others and with society as a whole. Normative ethics are not about what we think we need or ought to do for ourselves, but about standards of good behaviour and the moral evaluation of those standards, about our actions towards other people and the rest of society. In general, we can look at our actions at two different levels: as individual actions, and as a person's general behaviour. We can form an opinion about a person's character on the basis of the latter. Is the person virtuous or not? Some people are virtuous, others less so. Some may have specific virtues but lack others or, even worse, may also have vices. Judging the virtuousness of a person and his or her character allows us to draw some conclusions about the correctness of his or her actions, now and in the future. For example, a person may be very courageous. Generally speaking, actions resulting from courage are virtuous. But courage can become reckless-ness, which is a vice. The actions resulting from that vice are subject to criticism. This is termed virtue ethics. There is, however, a third approach to normative thinking: pragmatic ethics. According to this philosophy, norms are derived from the social context in which we operate. Summarising, we can say that the three factors that from an analytical point of view determine good behaviour are those that are integral to the action itself, to the character of the person who performs the action and to the society and the social context in which the action takes place. These three determinants can lead to the same conclusion, albeit via different routes. But they can lead to different outcomes as well.

When we talk about good and moral actions, there is one principle that almost all cultures recognise in one form or another. This principle is the Golden Rule, which says we should treat others as we would like them to treat us. The Golden Rule is formulated in slightly different ways in different cultures – 'as you sow, so shall you reap', 'he who hurts another hurts himself', 'do unto others as you would have them do unto you' – but they all have the same basic meaning. They express a neat, simple rule that uses one's own feelings to judge actions directed at another person. It implies that the person acting must consciously take those feelings into consideration when making moral decisions. The Golden Rule is based on an aspect of human nature that is present in both private and professional life: the feeling that reciprocity is a fundamental component of integrity.

Returning to moral principles, what is the frame of reference we should use for our normative behaviour? What is the magnetic north by which we should calibrate our moral compass? How do we arrive at answers to our questions about how we ought to act? These are questions that reflect a longing for a value judgment. One of the oldest precepts of Western philosophy is that *we are moral because we are rational.* For the ancient Greeks and Romans, reasoning and moral judgment was founded on rationality. However, with the advent of Christianity, religion replaced rationality. Believing meant there was no need to seek rational explanations. Moreover, religion provided answers to questions for which there appeared to be no rational explanation. The Word of God determined human behaviour, and the Word was moral by definition. Reason fell out of favour, but was it difficult to ignore it altogether. In the Middle Ages the concept of a morality based on religion began to lose ground. There was more independent thought and people dared to openly doubt the Word of God. This was due not only to the different ways in which it was interpreted, but also to the different ways in which people lived in accordance with the Word. Real problems arose when people began to defend their interpretation with the sword instead of with reason. Atrocities were committed in the name of God, and chaos and misery were the result. It was time to look for new sources of moral wisdom.

Natural law theory is a normative theory linked to the image of God. It explains the good in terms of the logic of natural laws, which form our frame of reference. The basic assumption of natural law theory is that the world cannot be shaped to meet the needs of humans, and we must therefore live according to the laws of nature. However, these laws are so rigid and restrictive that they rob humans of the opportunity to shape the world themselves. That is an unpalatable fact because it is human nature to want to shape and change the world; it is part of our genetic make-up, and it is very difficult for us to suppress that urge. What should then be the guiding principle of good behaviour? To determine that, we need to look at the essence of human desire. Every human being's most fundamental desire is security. We want to survive, and preferably lead a pleasant, healthy, prosperous life. Human beings are social animals and cannot survive alone. A lack of protection makes human beings vulnerable, and without social interaction they die of sadness, hunger and cold. That is why a caring, protective and stimulating social infrastructure is crucial. The right to existence also needs to be sustainable, and this gives human beings a long-term perspective. They want to share their achievements with children and grandchildren, and ensure they have an inheritance to pass on to their descendants. The concept of inheritance goes beyond money and material goods, and people have always had rituals for passing on knowledge, skills, culture and cultivated nature. The desire to preserve family reputation is also a bond between the generations. Even though survival as a hunter or farmer depends on a daily food supply, and therefore encourages favouring the short term over the long term, the desire for long-term security is also instinctive and structural. This desire encourages people to create order, since order is a means of achieving their objectives and a lack of order constitutes a threat.

The struggle for security raises an important question: do people only want to secure their own future, and that of their immediate family and friends, or do they also act in the interests of a broader social unit, for example, their village or a country? To answer that question we must again make a distinction between *is* and *ought*. Moral agents often have a highly egotistical nature (Thomas Hobbes's psychological egoism). However, that factual statement says little about how desirable, or undesirable, egotistical behaviour is. The key to that can be found in the concept of ethical egoism. This theory states that it is right to pursue egotistical goals because they also serve the broader interests of society. Modern theories of the market economy share this vision, maintaining that the pursuit of self-interest is the motor that drives economic growth and hence improves general welfare. Here egoism is a rational force, a concept that has a much wider impact than previously thought. For example, an entrepreneur's egoism may lead to results that benefit society as a whole, such as job creation, opportunities for talented employees and tax revenue for the government. To secure their social status, entrepreneurs are also likely to donate money to the causes they support. Senior business executives like to see their names on libraries and museums. This may seem philanthropic, but it often merely serves to emphasise the donor's success. Millionaires sponsor football clubs to boost their own ego. Great leaders like to play the role of the hero, and this can have major benefits for society. It goes without saying that not everyone shares this vision of egoism as a beneficial driving force. Some egoistic behaviour is detrimental to other people's interests. For this reason many believe that the long-term interests of humanity are better served by more socially responsible attitudes and behaviour that help one's fellow man directly instead of indirectly. Clearly, there are different ways in which to secure one's right to existence.

Looking at individual choices regarding actions and behaviour, we can use two of the main theorems of normative ethics to determine whether or not a particular action or behaviour is ethical: deontology and consequentialism. Deontology determines whether an action is ethical or not on the basis of certain moral suppositions, independent of the outcome of that action. This approach is quite consistent with Christian ethics, which state that good behaviour is the product of adherence to commandments and rules. 'Thou shalt not kill' and 'thou shalt not steal' are laws that cannot be broken under any circumstances. By contrast, consequentialism looks at the outcome of an action or behaviour. Deontology is also referred to as Kantianism, after the German philosopher Immanuel Kant (1724–1804). Kant was the fourth of nine children born to a poor harness maker. Thanks to the benevolence of a local clergyman, he was able to attend Latin school from the age of eight. At 16 he went to university, where he first studied theology and then philosophy, mathematics and physics. He graduated at the age of 22 and became a tutor. Kant was appointed to the position of private lecturer at the University of Koningsberg in 1755, the same year in which he published his doctoral thesis, and in 1770 he became the professor of logic and metaphysics at the university's faculty of philosophy.

According to Kant, it is moral law that determines whether an action is good or bad, not the outcome of that action. Kant based his argument on the concepts of the maxim and the categorical imperative. In the philosophy of Kant, the maxim is the intention that prompts or is the foundation of a person's actions. The maxim is a subjective principle based on an individual's intention, and it is therefore the principle underlying that individual's actions. The individual formulates the maxim, thereby defining the action. Whether the action is good and morally justifiable can be determined by comparing the maxim to the categorical imperative. This means that one should act according to the maxim only if one wants it to become a universal law. Every action is subject to the test of universal reality or the desire for universal applicability. According to this line of reasoning, stealing is wrong because a universal law allowing theft would result in a world in which no one would want to live. Kant believed that we could determine right from wrong by means of rational thought. Kant's philosophy makes a practical distinction between the categorical imperative and the hypothetical imperative. To illustrate the hypothetical imperative, let us consider some examples. If I am ill and I want to get better, I have to go to the doctor. Or if I want a higher return on my investments, I will have to accept more risk. The action (going to the doctor, taking more risk) is not compulsory, but if I want to achieve the objective (getting better, getting a better return on my investment) I have no choice. By contrast, the categorical imperative is an unconditional instruction that must be obeyed.

When formulating the categorical imperative, universalising the maxim can lead to a contradiction in logic or a contradiction in will. For example, if we do not speak the truth, the truth cannot be discovered, and that leads to a contradiction in logic. In other words, the system can no longer function. To clarify this, Kant used an example from the financial world. Lying to secure a loan that you know you are not going to repay is an immoral action. If everyone did this, the financial system would be unable to function. Two centuries later, that insight could have saved us from the mortgage crisis. Another example relates to tax avoidance. If no one pays their taxes, the government cannot balance its budget and will cease to function. If we had known that, we could have avoided the government debt crisis. Unfortunately, it was not meant to be. A contradiction in will is less far-reaching than a contradiction in logic. The system continues to function after the maxim is universalised but the resulting situation is undesirable. For example, if everyone drives an SUV, the world will undoubtedly continue to function. The question is whether we would want to live in that world.

In addition to avoiding any action that does not meet the test of universal applicability, Kant had a second ethical rule. He said we have a duty to treat humanity as an end in it itself, and not as a means to some other end. We should see our fellow humans as autonomous beings, not as an instrument in the hands of others. According to Kant it is unacceptable to manipulate people for one's own ends. Autonomy, the fact that individuals can decide their own fate, is an unshakable reality.

Although Kant is regarded as one of history's most influential thinkers, he has his critics too. His categorical imperatives are seen as binding, stringent and too rigid as they take no account of the outcome of actions and make no allowances for the evaluation of actions on the basis of past outcomes. Nor does Kant take any account of exceptional situations or circumstances that could affect the outcome. It is of course wrong to kill another person, but it is possible to think of circumstances in which it could be justified, and there are many other examples. In spite of the criticism, the idea of testing the universality of every action and deciding whether it would be socially impossible or undesirable is an attractive one. It is a way of thinking that we seem to have lost, and we feel its absence.

Consequentialism starts from a different point altogether. It is not the principle that determines the moral admissibility of one's conduct, it is the consequences. If the consequences of an action help to achieve the objective of a good and healthy life, that action is morally justified. The consequences are the determining factor. Utilitarianism is the most important form of consequentialism. Utilitarianism measures the moral value of an action according to its contribution to the general good, and to society as a whole. Jeremy Bentham (1748–1832) developed the theory of utilitarianism, which was revised and expanded by John Stuart Mill (1806–1873). Bentham, who originally wanted to be a lawyer, developed his theory as a reaction to the barbaric way in which people who broke the rules were treated at the time. He opposed torture and corporal punishment, and wondered why such people were punished even if their actions did not harm society in any way. Bentham believed that it was pointless and unjust to punish people simply for a violation of principles. He approved of actions that promote the happiness of the individual, and believed that it is *the greatest happiness of the greatest number* that is the measure of right and wrong. Because utilitarianism is based on the maximisation of overall good, it is sometimes referred to as hedonism. Utilitarianism occupies an important position in moral and ethical philosophy, primarily as a method rather than as a result of its practical applicability. This is because people find it hard to measure the quality of a decision, and to immediately evaluate the resulting action, because they cannot foresee what its benefits will be, or who will benefit. Moreover, not all benefits are equal; some are more desirable than others. According to the law of diminishing marginal utility, if I have already consumed a great deal of a particular item, the utility of a subsequent unit will diminish. There are other reasons why this method of judging morality is not always applicable. A person may decide on a particular course of action because of the expected result of that action. The outcome is uncertain and is not only determined by the quality of the decision, but also by the way in which the action is performed. The quality of the performance is not part of the decision-making process, but it does help determine the outcome. Two identical decisions can lead to two entirely different outcomes. The painful part of a decision is usually is not the decision itself, but its implementation. Going ahead with an action can be seen as something separate, but in fact it is not. It is an action that is linked to the decision. Chance can produce two different outcomes from two identical decisions, but since we do not know that when we make a decision this factor cannot be taken into consideration. That is why when chance causes a decision to go awry, it is important to know that the decision was made with good intentions.

The following examples serve to illustrate this. We are all aware of the rules governing how we should behave in traffic. If we wish to avoid fines, these rules are categorical imperatives. However, almost all of us exceed the speed limit at one time or another, whereas hardly anyone would run a red light. And yet these two norms are more or less the same: both are rules governing traffic. Even though we are not allowed to break these rules, we are calculating. We know that running a red light is much more dangerous than driving too fast and can have more serious consequences. The risk of causing an accident and harming others is much greater. It also involves much more personal risk for ourselves, in the form of damage and injury. Apparently, while we do take the norm into consideration, we pay more attention to the consequences of violating the norm. We adjust our actions based on the consequences of deviating from the norm. If we consider this in the light of the philosophical theories discussed above, we see that we behave both deontologically and consequentially in traffic, and we do this more or less simultaneously.

One current debate has more relevance in terms of consequentialism, although it also touches on deontology. It concerns the failure to act when action is clearly called for and the moral agent has decided against taking action. This issue may arise in the context of situations involving abuses as well as disasters. Is it morally reprehensible not to save a toddler from drowning? Was it wrong for drivers who saw the Turkish passenger jet crash near the motorway (see Chapter 4) not to stop? Was such action unethical? Perhaps not, but we can narrow the focus of the question by looking at a person's social responsibility. A leadership position, for instance, has implications for morality, and a manager has a moral responsibility not to look the other way. A good example of a person who failed to accept this responsibility is James Murdoch, the son of the media magnate Rupert Murdoch.

On 10 November 2011, James Murdoch was required to appear for a second time before a special parliamentary committee in the UK. He was questioned about phone tapping practices used to gather information for the *News of the World*. Doubts had arisen as to the truth of his testimony during the first hearing in July. At the time he said that even though he had approved enormous payments to the victims of phone tapping, he had not been aware of the e-mails confirming that the practice was systematic and had not been a one-off. Colin Myler, a former editor of the *News of the World* who was not appointed until after the phone tapping scandal, and Tom Crone, the newspaper's highly skilled and experienced legal adviser, contradicted James Murdoch's version of events. Documents that surfaced later confirmed that he must have known that the illegal practices were systematic. Yet throughout the second hearing he continued to deny all knowledge and to maintain that he had therefore not been in a position to take steps and put a stop to phone tapping.

> Myler and Crone went to James Murdoch's office to obtain authorisation for a payment to Gordon Taylor. The amount in question was a six-figure sum. Murdoch received no documentation, and he did not ask any questions about why the payment was necessary or why Taylor's phone had been tapped. His only question concerned the amount of the payment. The meeting lasted 15 minutes.
>
> *Financial Times*

The members of the parliamentary committee concluded that if Murdoch's testimony was true, he took a very unusual view of his managerial responsibilities.

> What kind of manager shows absolutely no curiosity about a large payment made in controversial circumstances? A fraudulent manager, or an incompetent one?

Can you hold a manager responsible for abusive practices even if he has no knowledge of them? The answer is yes, provided the incident is serious enough and it can be demonstrated that he ought to have known about it. Looking the other way, failing to ask the questions that would have uncovered the truth, or creating a corporate culture that impedes the flow of information, all of these are the equivalent of not acting. And that is incriminating behaviour if someone is in a position to stop unauthorised actions. Many executives struggle with this dilemma while in fact they have no choice.

In addition to consequentialism and deontology, there are two other theories of normative ethics: pragmatic ethics (also known as contract ethics), and virtue ethics. Pragmatic ethics concerns situations in which people derive moral values from agreements. The agreements – written or verbal – take the form of a contract. In the previous chapter, I referred to Thomas Hobbes and his view that people are prepared to give up a degree of freedom and enter into a contract in order to escape from the dangers of the natural state. That state is so undesirable that we are willing to exchange freedom for security. We judge whether or not conduct is moral on the basis of the contract. There are many examples of this concept, including, at the national level, constitutions, the legal codes based on them and general rules governing civilised behaviour, and, at the supranational level, the human rights that most governments recognise. The principle of contract theory can also be translated to the financial world, and to the principles governing the money and capital markets. These are formulated in directives issued by national and international regulators and included in rule books. I will discuss this in greater detail later in this book.

As noted in this chapter, virtue ethics refer less to individual actions than to generic actions and the general character traits of the actor. Plato described four cardinal virtues (wisdom, justice, courage and moderation), and four corresponding vices. Christianity added three divine virtues: faith, hope and love (particularly in the form of charity). Virtue ethics were all but forgotten during the Renaissance, and they were not rediscovered until the 20th century. In his book *Geografie van Goed en Kwaad (The Geography of Good and Evil)* (2010), Andreas Kinneging of the University of Leiden complains that many virtues have fallen off the radar, the only exception being tolerance. I would like to add one more: transparency.

Deontologists find virtue ethics too non-binding. They would prefer to see hard and fast rules that everyone must obey, and this is difficult to reconcile with a human being whom society regards as virtuous and who therefore has a licence to act more or less as he sees fit. Virtue ethics offer more scope for discretion, freedom of action, and trust in an individual's actions, provided that individual has made good choices in the past. This is in sharp contrast with the current, widely accepted notion that 'past results are no guarantee of future performance'. It was only natural that virtue ethics were among the first ethical concepts developed by Western culture. The ancient world had fewer laws and rules. Good behaviour was primarily down to the individual, not a specific action dictated by a categorical imperative.

Which aspect of human nature is instrumental in deciding whether an action is good or bad? If we are looking for something to replace the divine orientation of early Christianity, we need to examine the innate qualities of human beings: rationality, intuition and emotion. This topic has also been the subject of heated debate, sometimes verging on religious warfare. David Hume's theories regarding human emotions were influential. In the tradition of Thomas Hobbes, Hume had a worldly view of ethics and used science as the starting point for his theories. Hume also rejected religion as a moral guideline, but his perception of human nature was much less gloomy than that of Hobbes. Hume attributed feelings of sympathy to people, and believed that this sympathy could create social unity. He consequently saw no need for coercion as a means of creating social cohesion. Our feelings are the source of ethical actions. Hume does not preclude reason as a major determining factor, but he thought that reason alone could not distinguish good from evil. Reason is only used to collect the information needed to guide the process. In the end, we act on the basis of emotions such as sympathy and desire.

Although David Hume was 12 years older than Adam Smith, they were good friends, and Hume was a great source of inspiration and a role model for Smith. Smith expanded the concept of emotions as an important factor in determining human behaviour. Immanuel Kant took a different view. Although he admired Hume, he vigorously rejected the notion of emotions as a source of ethical behaviour. According to Kant a sense of morality is what distinguishes human beings from animals, which are guided purely by instinct. In addition, people are capable of reflection and logical reasoning. Kant regarded desire and emotion as unreliable indicators of good behaviour and thought they also led to different outcomes for each individual. They provide no basis at all for a universal theory of morality. It is interesting to consider just what reason is exactly. What are the grounds for concluding that an action is reasonable? That question can only be answered on the basis of the end result of a reasonable action. Apparently we cannot separate the result from the reasonable action. That is a somewhat consequentialist statement, and perhaps we are better off not turning to Kant for an answer.

Returning to the discussion of deontology and consequentialism, we need to ask ourselves whether these two schools of thought are in opposition, or if they are complementary. Perhaps a compromise is possible. If a decision that is not based on clear moral principles goes awry, the decision was the wrong one. The same can be said of a decision that goes awry even though it is based on clear moral principles, but because the intention was good the decision is easier to defend. The opposite is also true. A decision that turns out well but is not based on moral principles may still be the wrong decision. The first thing we can conclude from these statements is that the intentions on which a decision is based should be ethically sound. The second is that there should be the greatest possible chance of a good outcome. Based on what I have described in this chapter, my conclusion is that it is possible to combine deontological and consequential theory, and that doing so can increase the quality and the moral calibre of a given action.

Chapter 7

Cultural relativism

Can culture be used to explain differences in behaviour? Are cultural differences always an acceptable excuse for behaviour or do we need to look beyond that concept?

Following the historical and philosophical considerations raised in the preceding chapters, I would like to touch on a lighter subject, which nevertheless shares some common ground with the normative theories discussed earlier. This is the subject of cultural relativism. All over the world people have learned to live together and work together, often in order to increase their own personal happiness or prosperity. There is wide cultural variation in the way in which people choose to live, think, behave and, most importantly, interact socially. These cultural differences may be coincidental or the result of external factors such as climate, geography, and historical and socio-economic circumstances. But even if cultures differ, the outcome of different social interactions may be very similar. Americans and Germans, for example, speak different languages and behave differently. They happen to celebrate Christmas in a very similar way. Both countries produce cars; the cars are different but they all still take people from A to B. And while they produce cars they run their companies very differently as well. There are many well-run companies in both the US and Germany, but each country has its own interpretation of what that means. The difference is culturally determined. American culture has a command-based structure, which means that the boss is in the driver's seat. The traditional Anglo-Saxon approach is to replace bosses who are no longer effective. Businesses operating under Germany's Rhineland model, by contrast, have two-tier management structures: a managing board and a supervisory board. This model is based on a separation of powers and is geared towards consultation, consensus and shared responsibility. Americans dislike the idea of shared responsibility. The chairman of the managing board of a German company is not its CEO, but its *Sprecher*, the board's spokesperson, and unions are represented on the supervisory board. Germans find it difficult to accept the American model in which the top manager is both chair and CEO. This combination of powers made the US great, contributing to the enormous success of companies such as Apple (which was managed by Steve Jobs for many years until his recent death). However, it also led to disastrous results at WorldCom, Lehman Brothers, AIG and Enron. The Anglo-Saxon model extols the concentration of power that is forbidden by law under the Rhineland model. Yet the outcomes of the economic endeavours of the two cultures are surprisingly similar. The US is a great industrial power, as is Germany, and both have had their fair share of business disasters.

The more or less comparable results of the two different cultural blocks make it difficult to gain comprehensive insight into how a specific culture produces those results. For the outsider, actions within a given culture resemble a kind of black box. It is difficult to pass judgment, and to isolate and ethically dissect individual actions, in someone else's cultural domain. Germans raise their voice as a means of reinforcing their argument, while the Dutch would regard this as a sign of having already lost the argument. In the Middle East, shouting would be regarded as an insult. If the desired result can be achieved within a culture, shouldn't outsiders refrain from judging the ethical calibre of individual actions too harshly? Or is it more a matter of principle?

This is an important focal point in the study of financial ethics. We are all part of the global market. We compete for the same products, regardless of whether they are made in the US, Europe or Hong Kong. Our competitive edge consists of doing things just a bit differently from our rivals. The concept of 'doing things differently' may involve actions that one party regards as ethical, but which others may find unacceptable. In fact, a supplier's competitive position can be strengthened by 'unethical' practices, for example, by using child labour to price competitors out of the market. The issue of ecological damage produces similar inequalities. Some companies pay no attention to the issue, while others invest a great deal of money in preventing damage. This affects costs and therefore competitiveness. The issue is an important one because if we place no restraints on the competitive forces of the international market, there is a very real danger that unethical practices will be encouraged and ethical behaviour will be punished. Gresham's law – bad money always drives out good money – can also be applied to ethics. Bad practices will drive the good out of the system. In order to judge the impact of the products we buy in the international market we certainly need to look at the ethical aspects of the process that led to the manufacture of the product. That includes financial products. We cannot afford to be as naive as we were before the 2008 crisis, bestowing trust without verification. In other words, we have to unpack the product, literally and figuratively.

If cultural diversity plays a role in behaviour and actions, then it is important to be familiar with it and understand it. Let us take a closer look at some cultural differences, starting with a comparison of Germany and the Netherlands. The two countries have a long history of social interaction as well as major differences in culture and behavioural norms. To illustrate this point I will use a fictitious example that shows just how different Dutch and German behaviours are. The differences also highlight national strengths. In this example, a group of Dutch workers and a group of German workers are asked to move from A to B as quickly as possible. The groups cannot see each other, and have to complete the task independently. They receive instructions from their managers before departure and can consult them during the process. After the starting signal, the Germans immediately consult their manager. A briefing follows, and the team starts out. The Dutch team also consult their boss, but they decide not to follow up on his advice right away. They first consult with one another. This takes time, and the Germans already have a head start. After a while the Dutch reach a consensus and start out, but within half an hour they run into an obstacle. The Dutch are shocked: there is a problem and they have failed to heed their boss's advice. They have another discussion, adjust the plan quickly, and are soon on their way once more. The Germans are far ahead of them but they too encounter an obstacle.

They respond with irritation: why didn't their boss anticipate this and give them alternative instructions? His incompetence makes the German team angry and upset. After a brief intermission they resentfully put their heads together. No one is willing to pull the chestnuts out of the fire for the boss. It's his problem, and he will have to deal with it. However, the Germans finally conquer their aversion, and start out again.

We never find out who wins, but that is not important. The moral of the story is that a command culture is better at solving structured problems than a liberal culture. In unstructured situations, however, both group and individual responsibility are important, and a creative culture is more effective in this context.

There are also major differences between the Dutch and the French. French managers are terrified of being asked a question they cannot answer. During the merger process between the Dutch and French stock exchanges, Dutch bankers joked about the trolley loads of files the French dragged around. Dutch bosses are not bothered about not knowing the answer. They simply call an employee, ask for the information, and that is the end of it. In the eyes of the French (as well as the Belgians), asking for information is a sign of weakness, but the Dutch see them as unable to delegate work. But the French can delegate: when they organise an event together, the Dutch ensure that it is well-organised and the French make sure they have front row seats. During the merger process I attended a meeting about the cultural differences between the Dutch and the French. The participants were asked to name a national hero. Almost all of the French mentioned Charles de Gaulle, not someone whom the Dutch regard as a hero. The Dutch thought long and hard before eventually admitting that they could not name anyone. Their response highlights the cultural differences.

Continuing my cultural journey I move on to Hungary, where, owing to historical circumstances, dodging the rules has become culturally ingrained. Hungary was part of the Austro-Hungarian Empire, and was later subject to the political domination of the Soviet Union. Circumventing rules imposed from above became the norm. Their past history ensures that Hungarians are good at recognising problems – a necessary survival tactic – but less adept at solving those problems. Their rulers never gave them the opportunity to do so.

There are, of course, Dutch people who ignore the rules, but their motivation is opportunistic. Who knows when the wind will change direction? Americans never cease to be amazed by the Dutch passion for drawing up rules, and their lack of regard for compliance with those rules. The Dutch find the Americans bureaucratic and wonder why they are still required, on arriving in the US, to fill out a form asking them if they were a member of the SS or a similar organisation between 1922 and 1945. Anyone to whom this applies is either long dead or almost certainly too old to travel. The Dutch find this bureaucratic and unnecessary, but it is culture. Dutch identity is linked to the sea and the wind. It is opportunistic and manoeuvrable. Because the Netherlands is a small country it has no military tradition, but it does have a structure in which opportunity and questioning authority have become the greatest virtues (this is quite ironic when we consider that the word 'boss' is actually derived from a Dutch word, 'baas'). Dutch society is result-oriented because the wind, the water and the sea are relentless. The US is big and strong. Its military tradition means that its citizens have more respect for authority, and managing a large country always involves more bureaucracy. In short, the wind, the sea, the temperature and historical destiny makes us who we are. That, too, is culture. In fact, that is exactly what culture is.

Although these anecdotes about cultural differences can be entertaining, they can easily take on slightly more troubling forms. Corruption is one example of this. There are cultural differences when it comes to the scale of corruption in a country, and the extent to which it is tolerated. This is where questions of universal morality come into play. They apply to all forms of corruption, discrimination, racism, child labour, money laundering and abuse of power. We all know very well that these differences in behaviour should not be swept under the carpet of cultural diversity, and yet it does happen. Many things can be explained from the perspective of cultural relativism, but sometimes we require an absolute normative standard. There has to be accountability when universal norms are breached. The world of football offers a good example. In November 2011, a controversy arose after Sepp Blatter, the head of the international football association FIFA, claimed racism was not really an issue in the sport and suggested that problems could be solved with a handshake after a match. His comments were met with outrage. It was argued that racism, forbidden by law in many countries, is far too common in the world of sport and should not be downplayed, which is exactly what Blatter appeared to be doing. The British, who had a bone to pick with FIFA after losing their bid to host the World Cup finals in 2018 in questionable circumstances, demanded his resignation. Blatter had been tripped up by a universal norm, one that he had not anticipated, and from his point of view the scorn he received was probably undeserved. One week later he offered an unreserved apology; even Blatter had no other choice.

One reflection of cultural differences that has a major impact on the financial world is tax morality. The Dutch, who do not always observe the letter of the law, generally understand the need to pay taxes and regard it as a necessary evil. In some other countries in the eurozone – Greece and Italy in particular – only the poor pay taxes. Tax evasion is also something of a national sport in Belgium. Not paying is the norm, especially in Berlusconi's Italy, where the prime minister himself set a bad example and offered protection to his wealthy friends. That is why I am still so surprised to hear talk of the introduction of a European tax regime as a way of solving the crisis in the eurozone. I would not call it a solution, but a guarantee for a further escalation of tensions. The problem is not equal rules, but equal compliance with the rules, and that is a question of culture. In my view, tax systems may differ from one another as long as they are equitable. The real answer to the euro crisis is the creation of a single tax paying morality. If that existed, many more people would be willing to help euro countries achieve economic recovery. The absence of a uniform morality undermines solidarity. European solidarity has to begin with solidarity among citizens of the member states where the problems arose. A precondition for cross-cultural solidarity is that the recipients of solidarity did not get into trouble through any fault of their own, and that the donors are considerably better off than the recipients. The Czechs, who have a relatively low average income, still pay their taxes and have a comparatively low level of government debt. They cannot be expected to come to the aid of the Greeks and the Italians. Based on these arguments, the International Monetary Fund is of the opinion that wealthy Europe should solve its own problems. This brings us back to the question of norms and values, which we talk about all the time but do not always live by.

Norms are imposed from outside. Societies create them, externalise them and then formalise them as laws, rules or codes. Values tend to be internalised, but they have an important influence on the formulation of norms. Norms are rules (thou shalt not this, thou shalt not that) while values are more general principles. Every norm should be based on a value, but in practice that is not always the case. I refer here to moral values that are derived from the basic human objectives mentioned earlier: security and the survival instinct. There is an ongoing debate in the study of ethics about which values should rank more highly: vital values (those which are related to life itself, such as vigour, happiness and power) or moral values. To some extent, this is also determined by culture. Most of the rebels who were prepared to die during the Arabic Spring for ideals such as freedom and the elimination of oppression placed moral values above vital values. Nevertheless, a great many people are prepared to accept their fate, to be a communist among the communists, or a capitalist among the capitalists. These are the people who place vital values above moral values, and who are willing to compromise in order to survive. They look the other way, or worse, they collaborate.

The financial world can now be divided along two important fault lines. One of these relates to the main values or hard-wired norms, the other concerns whether transparency is considered good or evil. This is a matter of culture and cultural differences. The first fault line concerns the extent to which people allow themselves to be governed by principles or rules, while the second (which is in a sense linked to the first) relates to the degree of transparency people are willing to offer or accept. In general, we can say that the Anglo-Saxon countries are much more rule-oriented, but they are also more open to scrutiny when it comes to compliance with the rules. Other countries, including those of continental Europe, are more principle-based and see transparency as more of a threat. For many people, not being transparent is an important defence mechanism ('it's no one's business but my own'). Even worse is the attitude of 'ask me no questions, then I'll tell you no lies'.

In this chapter I have described some of the differences between Anglo-Saxon countries and other cultures. I would like to add another difference to the list, one that is related to the ethics of honour and of conscience (see Chapter 15). The ethics of honour is based on external norms, the ethics of conscience on internal norms. For most employees, good behaviour is determined by the conditions laid down in the company's code of conduct. It is enforced using the company's internal instruments. In countries where the ethics of honour play an important role, people tend to be guided by external norms. Public perception is an external norm. In other words, not being transparent becomes a very important tool for concealing unethical behaviour. After all, transparency can damage one's honour and ego. Such damage is experienced as a defeat, which is a high price to pay. In the Anglo-Saxon cultures, damage to one's reputation is shed more easily. If we go bankrupt, we start again. If we are sent to prison, we serve our sentence and after that our friends welcome us back into the fold. By contrast, in some cultures people bow their heads to the floor in apology and commit suicide if the personal scandal can no longer be contained. In other cultures, while people are troubled by the punishment itself, they manage to pick up their lives again once it is over. It is interesting to note that regulators, including those in the Western world, rely on both concepts when it comes to enforcement. They mete out punishment for violations of the rules, sometimes in the form of fines. These are a blow to the ethics of conscience, because they hit where it hurts – in the wallet. Regulators also publish details of violations, naming the perpetrators. This policy of naming and shaming is more painful for those for whom ethics of honour are more important, because it damages their reputation. They may well prefer a larger fine to this form of punishment.

Let us conclude this chapter on cultural relativism with another example of how some cultures are guided by principles while others rely more heavily on rules. In other words, how they take a deontological or consequential approach to problems. The anecdote, which is taken from real life (although told with a bit of literary licence), dates back to my time as the CEO of Robeco. A wholly-owned subsidiary of Rabobank, Robeco is run as an independent asset management company with its own international network of branches and subsidiaries. At least, that is how we perceived it. The US regulators, however, had no sympathy for subsidiaries of parent companies that claimed a right to self-determination, as we shall soon see. Until November 2011, Rabobank was one of the few banking institutions in the world with a generic Triple A rating. Earlier this century it acquired a bank in the US as part of its strategy of becoming the world's largest agricultural bank. This relatively small bank had many agricultural clients in rural areas of California but it had no financial expertise. It was particularly lacking in knowledge of financial supervision. After the initial euphoria of the takeover, Rabobank paid little attention to its acquisition. Negligence can lead to accidents, and that is exactly what happened. Employees at the bank acted in breach of the rules as a result of an intrinsic weakness in their compliance system. The California Superintendent of Banks alerted them to the problem, and when this did not help issued a written warning. The bank's reply failed to satisfy the Superintendent, who sent an angry letter to Rabobank's holding company in New York and also notified the Federal Reserve. As this letter also failed to elicit a satisfactory response, an even angrier letter was sent to Rabobank's headquarters in the Netherlands. After receiving another disappointing reply, the Federal Reserve lost its patience. The regulator decided to play hardball and threatened to rescind the holding company's licence to operate in the US. The head office in the Netherlands saw this as a problem, but it did not consider it a threat. After all, it was only a minor matter, involving a minor acquisition, and the compliance situation at the California-based subsidiary had already improved considerably. However, the situation was much more urgent for Robeco. Without a licence for Rabobank's holding company in the US, life would also be very difficult for all of Robeco's subsidiaries in that country. The leasing company De Lage Landen, another Rabobank subsidiary, was in the same boat. By the time Rabobank's Executive Board fully appreciated the scale of their problem, it had become 10 times larger. The Executive Board took action and alerted the Supervisory Board. It was agreed that a delegation would be sent to the Federal Reserve Bank in Washington to explain the measures that had been taken and discuss how the problem could be solved. However, we also had a question for the regulators regarding the status of the holding company. It was not clear from the letter whether it had been suspended or not. Perhaps they just wanted us to eat a bit of humble pie.

I went along to represent the interests of Robeco. We had drawn up a plan with a structural solution for the problems, including a time line, a financial plan, and a list of the people at Rabobank who were responsible for solving the problem. The evening before our meeting with the Federal Reserve we discussed our strategy for the next day at a restaurant. Our US lawyer was also present. The plan was a simple one: apologise, be humble, point out the measures already in place and explain what further steps would be taken. We would also casually mention that Rabobank was a Triple A rated bank with a commitment to the US market. How serious could the problem be? After all, the problem existed even before the takeover. It could, we thought, also be regarded as a bit of overdue maintenance on the part of the regulator. In short, we were full of confidence. Our visit would be a turning point, and above all, we had our principles, and we were virtuous. At least, that is what we thought.

That is not how the meeting went. We were shown to a large table where an inordinate number of representatives of the Federal Reserve were seated. They made no contribution to the discussion at all – on the contrary. They stared straight ahead, and were clearly there just to make up the numbers. Living wallpaper. It was obvious from the start that only one person from the Federal Reserve would speak. It turned out to be a very one-sided conversation. 'You are not here to ask questions or receive favours. You must realise that you have violated the rules. The Federal Reserve will take appropriate action.' That was the opening line of the leader of their delegation, and it set the tone. I asked myself what this was really all about. What was the problem?

It was the summer of 2008 and a number of historical developments had taken the Federal Reserve completely by surprise. That same month saw the last-minute rescue of Bear Stearns, and within two months Lehman Brothers had collapsed, the US government had been forced to bail out AIG, Merrill Lynch was in trouble, and Morgan Stanley was on the brink of collapse. There was no end to the misery. American financial institutions were guilty of practices that were not forbidden at the time but which are now regarded as criminal. Clients were robbed and some were even made destitute. In Europe, it was mostly German banks that succumbed to toxic US mortgage loans.

Again I wondered what this was really all about. What was the underlying problem here? Suddenly, among all those silent faces across the table, I saw Immanuel Kant, listening intently. He looked at me as if to say, 'You see, my theory about the categorical imperative is not so bad. And it works here, in the US.' I disagreed and tried to make this clear by shaking my heading and whispering, 'I'm more convinced by consequentialism and the ethics of virtue.' The message did not get through. Kant did not hear me, and he looked away.

Two months later Rabobank had solved its compliance problems in California. The US financial system, however, was still staring into the abyss.

Chapter 8

Where are the customers' yachts?

What moral dilemmas does a broker face when preparing advice for customers in his capacity as an agent? Is he intellectually and emotionally free to give the best advice, or is he compromised by his own interests and the producer's incentives? Is the broker bound to the producer by family ties or linked through lucrative agreements? And does the producer know what he is doing? Is the customer's money segregated, or does it disappear into the large pool of the bank's money? Are transactions executed as the bank sees fit or in the best interest of the customer? When we live in a bunker, it is constantly dark, even at noon.

The tale behind the question that forms the title to this chapter has taken on a mythical dimension. It is not entirely clear what its precise roots are, although the most reliable account dates back to 1870. The story goes that some people were watching boats sailing off the coast of Rhode Island. One of the observers asked who all the beautiful sailing boats belonged to. He was told that they belonged to brokers. In response to this, he asked, 'Where are the customers' yachts, then?' This innocent question was elevated to a question of conscience. It was selected as the title of the 1950 bestseller by Fred Schwed Jr on malpractices in the financial world, to which customers continue to fall victim time and again. The readers of his book doubtlessly include people who have helped pay for the yachts. The practices described by Schwed have existed for centuries and have withstood the test of time, so well in fact that the original text of his book hardly required any revision when it was reissued at the end of the 1990s. If time has changed anything about human behaviour, it is that it has become even worse. So I will reiterate the question: where are the customers' yachts?

This question has its origins in a very basic concept in our society. Customers and suppliers do business, including financial business, in order to achieve personal goals. However, customers know little or nothing about financial matters and are not experts when it comes to entering into contracts. By contrast, the professionals with whom they do business are experts who have made financial services their career. Customers who do business with professionals without using some form of protection will come a cropper sooner or later. This is because the game is not fair. The parties are not well-matched, and so the strongest party will abuse its position, perhaps after exercising some self-control. The underdog – the customer – is the obvious victim. This is not right. At a social level, we strive for equal opportunities for all. The structure of our economy ought to be a reflection of this social order. This means that if we want equal opportunities to exist in our economic structure as well, we need to do something to rectify the difference in the skills that customers and professionals have, just as someone accused of a crime hires a solicitor. An obvious solution would be for the customer to engage a professional who would focus solely on promoting the customer's interests. In other words, the customer would hire the professional to act as an adviser, in other words as his agent. This would appear to solve the problem, but a crucial transformation takes place within what starts out as a sound concept. Advisers cannot live off the fee alone, and so they combine their advisory activities with the provision of the same services they are supposed to be advising the customer on. In this way, the adviser becomes a broker, and somewhere along the way he becomes conflicted – one of those people with the yachts.

On 23 August 2011, the *Financial Times* published details of the heart-rending story of a British couple, Anna and Geffrey Quick from East Preston. In 2007 they invested more than £100,000 in a fund that Barclays had sold as a 'balanced fund', investing in a mix of asset classes. At the same time, the couple informed the bank what they wanted to achieve by investing. When the stock market collapsed later that year, Mr and Mrs Quick were in Australia, visiting their daughter. They desperately tried to call someone at the branch of Barclays in their home town, but they could not get through to anyone. On their return to England, the value of their investment had fallen to £60,000. 'We knew nothing about investment,' Mrs Quick explained. 'We just wanted a monthly income in retirement.' Clearly things did not go according to plan. In the same year, a Dutch entrepreneur sold his business. The proceeds were transferred to a pension product that was supposed to enable him to enjoy a carefree retirement. This entrepreneur had asked his adviser to put half of the proceeds into 'secure' investments and to invest the other half a little more speculatively. The adviser purchased two notes: one with a fixed coupon and a guaranteed principle, and one with more market risk. Both notes were issued by Lehman Brothers, which would get into serious trouble shortly afterwards. You can guess the rest.

Another example concerns payment protection insurance (PPI) policies, which many people in Britain took out when they concluded their mortgages. This form of insurance pays out if the borrower is unable to generate any income to repay the mortgage. In such constructions, it is often the case that the interest rate on the mortgage seems to be in line with the market, but the invisible costs (that is, the costs of the insurance) are in no way proportionate in view of their added value. Similar practices also took place in the Netherlands, most notoriously at DSB Bank. DSB sold mortgages with very appealing interest rates, but the borrowers were required to take out insurance. They generally had no choice about this, as they were restricted to the options on offer. Even when they did have a choice, they were not informed that insurance was compulsory until late in the process when there was only one offer left that could be accepted. The total insurance premium for the whole term of the policy had to be paid upfront as a lump sum. DSB calculated the amount payable by discounting all the annual premiums. Because this was a huge sum that most customers were unable to pay in one go. This was not a problem; the amount was added to the mortgage debt. In this way, apparently cheap mortgages led to very high levels of debt. These were extremely expensive solutions with useless insurance policies which were not priced in line with the market and which were discounted against an unfavourable rate. The unhappy result was over-indebtedness, hanging like a noose around the necks of innocent customers.

The above are just a few of the many examples of incidents in the financial industry. In each case the customer got into difficulties as a result of the wrong decision being made, and sometimes as a result of bad advice. However, things go really badly only in a relatively small number of instances. After all, anyone could take the wrong exit on a very busy road. Then again, what exactly is a relatively small number? Does it even matter? However many it is, it makes no difference in terms of what the victims suffer. This is something that those working in financial services should stop to consider. We need to be much less tolerant of mistakes.

The above examples are representative of a more general impression that exists, that advisers acting as brokers abuse their position of power or fail to provide expert advice. Experience has shown that some people are simply dishonest or display criminal behaviour. The sad truth is that even honest brokers may become less honest over time owing to force of habit, temptation and the erosion of the normative framework. Advisers are independent from an economic perspective, and they know instinctively that they have to take good care of themselves. Their only source of income is their customers, and that is why customers who have placed themselves in the 'caring' hands of advisers are in a vulnerable position. Importantly, customers often do not pay a fee for advice provided by brokers, and instead brokers receive a fee deducted from the proceeds of sales provided to them by the producer. The fee is ultimately paid by the customer, but any awareness he has of this payment will be indirect, since the producer is the one granting the fee. This inverted commission structure constitutes a threat to independent advice. This is because whoever pays the piper calls the tune, and when advisers are looking to promote their own economic interests they turn their focus towards the producer and away from the customer. But surely I have not told you anything you do not already know.

In this structure, brokers have shifted from acting as the customer's agent to serving as the agent of the producer, and advice from independent brokers is determined by the highest retrocession commission. Some brokers are part of an integrated financial conglomerate and are restricted to selling in-house products only, while others are part of a large conglomerate but are free to sell other products too (known as open or guided architecture). Other brokers are independent and are free to provide any product they consider the best for their customers. But high commissions based on lucrative arrangements can make even independent brokers dishonest.

Advisers want to earn money, especially for themselves, which makes fees for selling products a dangerous weapon. Acting like backseat drivers, producers can dictate how advice is given by varying the level of return commission. The adviser-producer relationship needs to be scrutinised to ensure that the broker does not have any motive to palm off the wrong product on the customer. If they do, this could have far-reaching negative implications. What are the products brokers are asked to advise on? Brokers can provide advice on products for customers who need to invest, as stockbrokers do, and also to customers who want to borrow. Mortgage broking is a whole other line of business, and what a business it is.

One of the main causes of the 2007–2008 crisis was irresponsible behaviour on the part of brokers in the US, who misled customers when selling mortgages. They told customers that they could afford the home of their dreams, something they had previously thought was out of their reach. Mortgage loans were arranged in situations where it was clear in advance that the borrowers did not have the means to make the repayments. That did not matter, since the initial interest rate was below the market rate. The problem was put off in the hope that the price of the property would rise, enabling the loan to be repaid by selling the house. But what happened if property prices refused to play the game and headed in the opposite direction? Brokers in many Western markets are very actively involved in arranging loans and finance. They earn income from all the intermediary services they offer. The financial institutions to which the mortgages were transferred were only too happy to pay for this. The market for arranging loans is vast, and it has frequently been the cause of misery and personal suffering. Credit addiction is a huge problem within society. The practice of loading unsuspecting consumers with debt has been around for centuries. The recipe is a very simple one: just tell consumers what they can buy with a loan and they are sold. Another concern is that the mortgages they arranged were placed with third parties, and so the risk of default was passed on. That made mortgage arrangers very careless, since they would not be on the hook if the loans went bad. The principle of passing the parcel applied particularly in the case of mortgage loans that were securitised. In many instances criminal behaviour was involved, a combination of unethical behaviour and the provision of inaccurate information on the borrower's income and the value of the property. All this was done purely for the sake of fee income.

Brokers in investment products suffer from the same disease. In the case of investment products, brokers mediated in services either produced by themselves (if they are part of an integrated financial institution) or provided by third parties. Many financial products are assembled in a similar way to physically manufactured goods. Individual parts (such as various services provided by third parties) are bundled together to create the end product. Once again, we need to consider whether the relationship between main contractors (often brokers) and their subcontractors is a pure one that is always entered into with the aim of offering the best possible service to the customer. Or are the customer's interests subordinate to other interests? Later on we will consider the difference between producing an ordinary household item, specifically a refrigerator, and producing a structured financial product. But first let us look at 'soft dollars', a concept whose mere name made me suspicious.

I gained my first professional experience of the securities industry in London in 1987. Prior to that time I knew little about the rules, regulations and ways of the industry, but that was not a barrier. In those days you did not need any experience to set up a securities institution with a licence, and no one thought this was a problem at the time. And for those of us who were not exactly sure what to do, there was always the TSA rulebook. The Securities Authority (TSA) was one part of a self-regulating regime, in which the Securities Investment Board (SIB) was the highest authority. The TSA rulebook was based on a loose-leaf system to which new rules and regulations could easily be added. It might have looked very convenient, but the contents were unfathomable. In fact, they were unreadable! I was struggling after just one page, so it was a pretty useless endeavour. However, there was nothing else to go by apart from practices passed on by older colleagues, and they were not very adept at explaining what they were doing. I therefore only had my own intuition to help me make my way through the jungle of rules. And who could object to that? Fortunately, one of the first practices that my intuition warned me about was covered by the TSA rules. Although the mere name of the concept – soft dollars – made me feel uneasy, the language said such arrangements were permitted.

Soft dollar arrangements were first seen in the US in the 1960s, following the abolition of the fixed commission system for securities transactions. Under the fixed commission system competing on price was impossible, and so competition was based on quality and the range of additional services provided. The practice of charging high, fixed commissions for securities transactions (referred to euphemistically as 'full commission') came in for a great deal of criticism. It was considered price fixing, which is why it was ultimately abolished. The abolition of the practice in the 1960s created opportunities for discount brokers – brokers who charged lower, more competitive prices for executing orders for securities. They offered a no-frills service and charged commission that was fully negotiated. However, old practices tend to die hard, and the old-style brokers do not want to perish either. They were dependent on the fixed commission system and had structured their organisations to provide 'frills', and this was something they were good at. These brokers asked the regulator, the SEC, whether they could carry on charging higher fees if they provided additional services. More than anything else, they wanted to be able to continue to fund their securities research activities and cover the costs of advice provided to customers from commission income. The SEC agreed to this, albeit under strict conditions. Funding securities research by charging more in the way of transaction execution fees is permitted under safe-harbour provisions. The following example illustrates this.

An asset manager is mandated to manage the assets of customers, who pay management fees in exchange for the service. The commission paid on the purchase or disposal of financial assets is, of course, deducted from the investment proceeds and therefore paid for by the customer. Prior to making investment decisions, the asset manager has to conduct research (securities research). He will have at his disposal a team of in-house researchers and numerous proprietary systems that provide a constant supply of information and relevant alerts. The asset manager can either conduct research internally or purchase information from third parties, or use a combination of the two approaches. Internal investment costs are borne only by the asset manager, but if the research is purchased from third parties, who pays? Preferably the customer, but is that fair? The securities trades are executed through a broker charging full commission. In exchange for paying this high level of commission, the broker provides the asset manager with additional services. For example, the broker might install free screens to provide the asset manager with research. The asset manager achieves major savings because the customer ultimately foots the bill by paying more in the way of commission. This is how softing works. Soft commission arrangements involving some services other than securities research, which do not fall under the safe-harbour provisions, are not necessarily illegal. The condition specified by the SEC, which has to be satisfied for such arrangements to be legal, is that the bundled services must provide an exclusive benefit for the customer. The burden of proof is on the broker. The caveat is that the SEC protection for using soft dollar arrangements only applies to registered operations. The world beyond registered operations is free to do as it wishes. As long as hedge funds do not need to be registered, the provisions of soft dollar restrictions will not apply to them, and so softing can be extended to include unnecessary services, leaving customers with no choice. Customers think that all services are covered by the management fee charged by the manager, but the reality is different. They most certainly do not want to have to pay for any services twice. Soft dollars has been a major cause of unethical behaviour in the opaque world of funds (including hedge funds).

There is another argument that can be put forward against the use soft dollar arrangements that is just as relevant as the one given above. This has to do with the lack of choice. Full commission means purchasing a bundle of services, but are all the components of that bundle the best available in the market? Asset managers fail to make optimum decisions when it comes to order execution on behalf of their customers, and the same problem may arise with respect to securities research purchased from a broker as part of a bundle of services. When selecting a broker, the customer's interest may not always be the first priority. Other considerations play a role that might be connected to the asset manager's own self-interest. An asset manager may be tempted to pick a broker for the wrong reasons. Not because the broker provides the best execution, but because it offers the best softing conditions. And even if the broker is the best at execution, is he the best at research too? Or could the money be better spent on unbundled services? Is the broker that is best in terms of execution also the best when it comes to research? Is the money the customer pays well spent? Linking two or more services is reminiscent of an earlier example in which consumers that took on a mortgage were required to take out insurance at the same time. The sting is always in the cost of the bundled product.

When the dotcom bubble burst in 2000, there was a great deal of criticism of the securities research published by financial institutions. Were the reports honest, and did they reflect the sincere, professional opinion of the relevant analysts? Or were they designed to be marketing materials? Merrill Lynch's internet guru, Henry Blodget, admitted in an e-mail that a company he had just recommended was, in his assessment, a 'piece of junk'. Internal documents came to light in which he described another company that he had heartily recommended as garbage. Eliot Spitzer, the then New York Attorney General, managed to get his hands on a huge amount of highly revealing material about analysts, which he published. When investors realised they had been lied to they were furious. However, that was not all. Companies that switched from one securities institution to another investment bank would suddenly be given negative appraisals by analysts who worked for the institution they had left. Analysts' reports had therefore become a tool for acquiring customers for the investment bank and punishing them if they left. Evidence emerged that analysts had a share in the profits their employers earned from investment banking. Analysts were therefore incentivised to help generate trade. Chinese walls may have existed on paper, but the reality was very different. A huge number of revelations concerning Merrill Lynch came to light, and its share price went into free fall as the threat of legal action loomed. In 2002 Merrill Lynch was forced to make a US$100 million settlement in order to avoid further legal proceedings. Steps were also taken to separate securities research from general banking operations.

In the US, the proceeds of the settlement were used to finance an initiative for independent securities research. In 2004, Europe followed with a similar move, which was chiefly initiated by the British. In contrast to the US, however, Europe was unable to raise funds as they had not imposed similar fines. Independent securities research had to be funded in some other way, and that way was known as commission sharing. Basically, commission sharing arrangements amounted to a reversal of softing, and hence the unbundling of services and therefore the unbundling of commission payments. This meant that an order for securities could be executed by a securities institution (let us call it A), which would withhold some of the high commission it charged to pay – as directed by the customer or asset manager

– securities institution (which we call B). Company A was the best in terms of order execution, while company B generated the better research or ideas for investment. At the end of a year, the pot of commissions retained at company A was redistributed, at the behest of the customer, to companies including company B for its advisory services. Unfortunately, this noble attempt to reassemble the financial services industry came to very little. Suppliers had problems kicking their old habits, and so did customers. They had issues with paying for securities research, and when they were charged with full commissions they could count on receiving research as free advice. Nevertheless, the separation of order execution and research is a very worthwhile objective because it adds value. It is the equivalent of an open architecture.

Should we require brokers to focus more on the interests of the customer? Most regulators do believe that brokers should prioritise the interests of the customer. But a much more fundamental question needs to be answered first. Are companies right in making their own interests subordinate to those of others? From the perspective of an organisation's statutory responsibilities, the answer to this question is a resounding no. Just as any other organisation, the broker's organisation, together with all its stakeholders, comes first. Yes, customers are stakeholders too, but they represent only one group of stakeholders and they cannot demand preferential treatment. However, brokers will take the view that promoting the interests of customers is fully in line with their own interests, since a happy customer is more likely to introduce new customers and this is in their interests. So there should not be a problem. However, what happens if these interests are conflicting, which they sometimes are?

In extreme circumstances, the interests diverge, and it is at such times that most accidents happen. To illustrate this point let us consider the case of Fortis Bank, where a dilemma took on excessive proportions. In the months running up to the start of the 2008 liquidity crisis, raising finance in the interbank market was very difficult and there was a great need for financial stability. One form of stable finance is customer deposits. Customers that received advice from private bankers at Fortis had several options: they could place their money on deposit at Fortis and receive a good rate of interest, they could place their money on deposit at another bank, or they could invest in investment funds. What were the private bankers at Fortis supposed to advise their customers to do? They knew that the bank needed to boost its deposit base and that investing in funds would not do anything to help the situation, and placing money on deposit at another bank would be even less useful for Fortis. What should the private bankers have done? The situation in this example is not a particularly extreme one. As a bank, Fortis was right to pursue its own interests first and attract customers' deposits, but it left its advisers facing a personal dilemma. Could the advisers look angry customers in the face following a bank default? The crisis currently affecting eurozone countries has led to another loss of confidence in the banks. Bankers are once again facing the same stark choice as Fortis. In the end self-interest comes first, which is entirely justifiable given the mission set out in the bank's articles of association, but it is not justifiable from the perspective of the customer's interests. Nevertheless, this conduct on the part of banks has never been subject to much criticism. A large number of brokers are teetering on the edge of ruin and they desperately need money and commission from customers in order to survive. There is overwhelming pressure to generate sales, which does not normally serve the interests of the customer. It also indicates that brokers are very receptive to the commission they receive from producers, and dance to the tune of the producer that pays the most return commission. This kind of behaviour is frequently associated with excessive bonuses, but it is more often motivated by a battle for survival.

The British financial regulator, the FSA, developed its Treating Customers Fairly (TCF) concept before the 2008 credit crunch. The use of the word 'fairly' is an indication it was accepted that conflicts of interest exist and that advisers can act in their own interests provided the customer does a fair trade. Fairness is an important concept in ethics. The book *Ethics in Finance* (1999, edited by John R Boatright) contains a chapter by Eugene Heath (professor of philosophy at the State University of New York) on fairness in financial markets. His definition of fair treatment can be summed up as follows.

> Fairness is a moral principle that involves treating or judging people (or a group) in the same way. Being treated fairly means being treated in the same way as other people when it comes to a rule, a contract or an acknowledged expectation... A rule can be unfair if it does not require someone to act in the same way as others who are of equal relevance.

The FSA fleshed out the TCF concept and decided that brokers needed to achieve at least six outcomes in order to treat customers fairly. Standards were set to make these outcomes measurable. I shall take the liberty of formulating the outcomes in my own words without detracting from their essence. First, however, I would like to add something to my earlier discussion of the distinction between providing advice and selling a product or financial service and the production of that product or service. We have already seen how advisers can also be producers too, but sometimes products are purchased from third parties. The combination of advice, sales and production determines whether the customer is treated fairly and is therefore likely to determine whether the customer is happy. Production and sales are complementary activities. If we assume an open architecture, at least two parties contribute to the happiness of the customer. The customer may be happy with the quality of advice or with the quality of the product. Unhappy customers do not usually care where the problem originated. A mutual dependence forms between parties in the business column, leading to supply chain responsibility. The adviser and the seller are responsible for providing sound advice and a good range of products, while the producer is responsible for the quality of the product. However, as they all need to ensure the customer is happy, they have overlapping responsibilities. Dissatisfied clients know exactly how they can best exploit this supply chain responsibility, and so they should. Private bankers who invested in funds managed by the fraudster Bernie Madoff were held liable, and there are countless other examples in which the fates of producers and sellers are tied. Producers can also be held responsible for the fact that good products are mis-sold or are sold to the wrong customers.

Returning to the subject of the FSA's six criteria for fair treatment, the regulator's first consideration is that brokers must be able to demonstrate that the fair treatment of customers is central to their corporate culture. In other words, brokers need to make a conscious effort to exhibit customer-focused behaviour. The customer must be provided with sound information regarding advice and the product before, during and after the sale. Moreover, the advice must be suitable and actually cater to the needs of the customer. In addition, a good service must be provided before, and particularly after, the sale of a product. Once a transaction has been done, the customer must be able to come back and must continue to have insight into the value of the product and any changes to the product. Neither the broker nor the producer should abandon the product until it has come to the end of its lifecycle. There also has to be a good complaints procedure. Finally, the FSA set a criteria concerning product quality. Products must comply with the quality requirements and standards in the market, and more than anything else they must do what they promise.

Products often fall short of their promise. In most cases, this is mainly down to the misleading names they are given. For example, customers who bought the '*winstvertiendub-belaar*' ('profit up ten-fold'), a product issued by Dexia's Legio Lease in the Netherlands, suffered heavy losses. The 'ten-fold' did work, only it created leveraged losses. Many financial products have names that include words such as 'guarantee' or 'insurance' even though they do not actually provide any guarantee or cover. Funds that had the word 'balanced' in their name were not balanced at all, and some 'absolute return' products produced nominal losses. 'Sustainable' is another term that is frequently abused. Finally, the word 'star' is used a great deal. Unfortunately, stars have a tendency to fall, especially in the financial world. It is all just hype. In the US, the SEC started to monitor whether products were appropriately named back in 2003, but the 2007 crisis showed that the naming problem had not been solved. If this all seems to be delving too much into semantics for your taste, and if you believe that names are irrelevant, I would like to ask you to consider the following. The term 'sub-prime' suggests that a mortgage is only slightly worse than a prime mortgage, not that it is rubbish. If a more accurate term, such as junk mortgages, or exploding, had been used, the crisis may have been averted. Appropriate names can help prevent a systemic risk from unfolding.

Besides naming something appropriately, it is also essential that the marketing material produced for a financial product is consistent with reality. This is most important when it comes to the prospects for future returns. These are usually spoken of in glowing terms, and future returns are simulated on the basis of historical data, a technique known as backtesting. However, there are a number of methodological problems associated with backtesting that cause indications of future returns to be far too high almost by definition. Backtesting replays the past using what we know now. It is highly unlikely that a product developed now would have come a cropper in the last crisis, and this is how the distortion starts, with a bias in the product selection process. In addition, the historical data is purged of all the companies that went under. Securities issued by Lehman Brothers and Madoff funds, for instance, are not included in historical data series. This survivor bias results in estimates that are excessively optimistic. According to the FSA's TCF rules, producers need to be much clearer about the actual returns, and these must not contain as many surprises in future.

As thorough as they are, the criteria set out by the FSA are lacking in some areas. The TCF concept does not pay anywhere near enough attention to the transparency of products, especially during their lifecycle, and that aspect is, in my view, of particular relevance when it comes to investment products and the interests of customers. The key question here is whether the assets are kept segregated from the company's assets as well as any other form of toxic waste, or if they are co-mingled instead. Separation provides for an easier audit trail and so sheds more light on the money flows and the fairness of the transactions. It enables the management of the product to be followed, which ensures honesty. Some investment products, such as deposits or different types of notes (structured products), are nothing more than amounts owed to clients by a financial institution. They are monetary claims on a company. The value of each claim is calculated on the basis of formulae, and the result of the calculation by no means certain. They are literally products that are issued by the financial institution itself and backed by nothing more than words. If the institution becomes insolvent and cannot pay the claim, the customer stands to lose some or all of the investment, just like the Dutch entrepreneur who lost his pension by investing in Lehman notes. Many investors in Hong Kong had a similar experience, as demonstrated by public anger. Customers are exposed to counterparty risk, which is always seriously underestimated. But even if matters do not get that far, there is cause for concern. Once the customer has purchased a product, deposit or note, the money disappears into a pool is where it is mingled with the bank's own funds and it is difficult to see what is going on. In the context of transparency, and in order to clarify my point, I shall briefly digress and look at investment products that have a specific legal structure, such as mutual funds established in accordance with the UCITS rules.

Undertakings for collective investment in transferable securities (UCITS) were created by a European directive adopted in 1985 and are designed for the collective management of assets entrusted by customers. The customers' assets are combined, but at the same time they are kept separate from the assets of the financial institution in a legal structure with a personality of its own. UCITS structures have become hugely popular, particularly since the introduction of the euro. Their popularity has spread beyond Europe, the product concept has survived every crisis that has taken place since its introduction, and UCITS has become a global brand and a worldwide standard. According to this concept, the financial institutions that create such products are in effect suppliers of a facility or service, but they are not the counterparty in any legal sense. As the service providers are no longer counterparties but parties with mandates to manage assets, they are referred to as advisers. The term is somewhat euphemistic since it creates the impression that the service providers only provide advice and the customers can then make a decision on the basis of this advice. However, these advisers operate on the basis of irrevocable mandates. They can change the way in which the combined assets are invested, although the assets will always be segregated. This makes trading transparent. All the transactions executed for a UCITS fund by an adviser are recorded and can be traced. This means the adviser's activities are visible and conflicts of interest can be clearly identified. If the adviser goes out of business, the customers' assets are not affected as they do not form part of the adviser's assets. A UCITS fund from Lehman Brothers would therefore have survived the company's collapse with no intervention apart from the appointment of a new adviser.

It seems fitting at this point to include a brief anecdote about something that happened to me while dealing with a case study as part of the Comenius course on financial ethics, which I teach. I refer to this case study as the difference between a refrigerator and a structured financial product. Both are products a customer can purchase if he wishes. I put forward a convincing argument that financial institutions which issued structured products had a duty to comply with the principle of best execution while entering into transactions and managing the product after the point of sale. In other words, transactions that are executed by the issuing bank during the lifetime of the product may only be concluded with divisions at that same bank if they happen to offer the best price, and not just a market price. I had expected that the students would immediately start nodding approvingly, but to my surprise most of them disagreed with me. One of the students summed up their view as follows. 'If you buy a fridge made by Zanussi or Bosch, you don't make any demands about how the manufacturer handles the purchasing of the materials, do you? That's the manufacturer's job.' I was quite surprised, although I thought the example was a convincing one. If the example of the fridge and the analogy were correct, what was wrong with my own reasoning? Where had I made an error? I needed to think about this for a while.

The student's reasoning was flawed, and slowly I regained my self-confidence. The two products represent two quite different concepts, and this difference goes to the heart of what financial products actually are. Financial products are not like fridges. When we buy a fridge, we know what we are buying. All a fridge needs to do is last for a good many years, and if it does not it will be repaired or replaced under the terms of the guarantee. Many financial products promise to generate value (that is, returns) for customers, but it is nothing more than a promise. It is often not a very firm promise either. Even guaranteed products are not certain to generate returns, as guarantees are often conditional. In the final analysis, financial products are not finished products at the time they are sold. Actions performed subsequently as part of the management of the product are of crucial importance when determining the quality and the final outcome of the product. This requires customers to have confidence in the professionalism and integrity of the product and, more importantly, the producer. It is not an equal exchange, because the customer pays now for something the bank delivers at a later date. The returns achieved are sometimes good, but more often than not they fall short of expectations.

Unexpected external factors may have an adverse impact on returns, and that is not at issue. A perfect excuse is always available. But as a promise of future returns is a soft promise, the customer becomes a stakeholder in the management process of the product. It is not acceptable that the interests of the customer are compromised during the management process and not dealt with in an efficient, competitive way. One such unacceptable practice is in-house order execution at prices that are favourable to the house executing the transactions. This is an unfair practice because the customers are trapped and have no choice. It is a pure betrayal of trust.

Who is responsible within the organisation for ensuring that all transactions done as part of product management operations are executed at fair market prices? Who ensures they comply with the best execution requirement? And who monitors whether the customers' assets are used purely for the purposes for which they were intended? Managers can gain additional benefits that are not visible to customers by failing to manage the customers' assets in the best possible way and using them for other purposes. They may also use soft dollar arrangements to cover operating expenses improperly, use the equity portfolio to provide security as part of the bank's other operations, or lend the equities to hedge funds. These borrowers pay a fee for this. Is this fee added to the return that customers achieve as indirect lenders? This is a simple question, and perhaps it is unnecessary. Transparency has disappeared, as has accountability. The moral of this story is that products in which the customers' assets are kept separate are better than products that are structured as amounts receivable from a bank. That said, buyers should always beware.

The financial world is full of wolves in sheep's clothing. As I said before, I believe that products that are structured in a way that segregates investors' assets (such as UCITS) are better products by far. The assets that are held in such structures are often securities in their own right, such as equities, bonds and securitised mortgage loans. Within the legal structure of a fund, these assets held are clearly identifiable, and they are secured in their own right. They are not, for instance, vague claims on major financial conglomerates, that can be tempered as described above. There were two types of products or structures at the heart of the 2007–2008 crisis: collateralised debt obligations (CDOs) and credit default swaps (CDSs). A CDO is an independent legal structure, as described above, that holds securitised debts, either in the form of corporate bonds or securitised mortgage debt. The structure of a CDO segregates customers' assets. No problem so far. A CDS is an agreement with a counterparty that pays out money in the event of a predefined credit event, such as debt rescheduling, at a particular debtor. As it provides compensation if a credit event occurs, a CDS is essentially a standard insurance policy with an upfront premium. In contrast to a CDO, a CDS is a claim on a financial institution, as described previously, and the money paid as premium disappears in the dark pool of co-mingled monies. So where did things go wrong in 2007? CDSs were included in CDOs. And as a CDS is a contract with a bank or insurance company, this meant that claims on financial parties started to sneak into what was otherwise a basket of real, identifiable securities and cash instruments. A clean product structure was poisoned by direct claims on banks. It was a real Trojan Horse.

As clean as these products were in the early days, CDOs were polluted with all kinds of derivatives that were issued and managed by the banks and security houses. These sleeping monsters were given the harmless-sounding name of synthetic CDOs. The derivatives were contractual agreements with counterparties to settle differences in cash. The difference could be between the value of an actual security and the level of an index, or involve several indices or baskets of mortgages. Such contracts are known as 'absolute return swaps' because they involve swapping investment returns. Something very important happens at this point. The swap undoes the entire process of separating asset components in a CDO structure. The swap is essentially a contract with a counterparty, and so the CDO now has a claim on the counterparty to the swap. There is no longer any segregation. The previous assets of the CDO – the clearly identifiable securities – vanish. The CDO contains a claim on a banking institution, or, more accurately, a claim on the Trojan Horse. As a consequence, the CDO structure that was meant to keep clearly identifiable securities together becomes nothing more than a front. Introducing counterparty claims into the CDO structure is tantamount to closing the curtains so that robbers are not disturbed while they work. And this is, in effect what, happened.

What kind of game is this? In his book, *Too Big to Fail* (2010), Andrew Ross Sorkin refers to one form of misconduct in particular. A customer that concludes a swap contract to settle cash differences (such as the difference from a specified index) needs to know for sure that the other party to the swap is not the compiler of the index. If it is, the setup is rigged. This happened time and time again. We are now close to the epicentre of financial ingenuity, and at this point it is worth having a close look at the real monster – the assassin – which is the pledging of security. Sometimes there is a huge amount of leverage concealed behind opaque swaps, which is supposedly designed to boost returns. Macho bankers call this construction a turbo. As we saw above, swaps are claims on other financial institutions that pay out in the event that a particular scenario occurs. This payout profile might have the same structure as an aggressively leveraged financial future. But if the market moves in the wrong direction, the swap can lead to unexpected losses. Security is provided because the counterparty needs to be certain that the CDO will make up the difference. The danger is that the structure of the product may lead to the innocent, neatly segregated asset components being pledged as security for the swap or turbo. And if the turbo does not lead to a good outcome, this creates a quandary. The assassin strikes without mercy and appropriates the security. The segregated assets in the CDO are seized by the holder of the pledge. Can you still follow? Do not be embarrassed if you feel a bit lost, because I am unable keep up too by this point. But what really is shameful is that the producers lost their way as well. In the end, many producers lost track of the side effects of the CDOs they sold. No one understood the contents of these products any longer. They were medicines with disproportionate side effects. The buyers were baffled. What is much worse, the producers were too. The leading investor, Warren Buffett referred in this context to weapons of mass destruction, drawing an analogy with the war in Iraq.

The issues that affected CDOs a number of years ago are now affecting UCITS. The UCITS rules now permit counterparty exposure up to a limit of 10%, and many market players use the scope this provides to enter into total return swaps. We are repeating the mistakes we made with CDOs. A curtain is being drawn within a structure that became popular owing to its transparency and simplicity. This is a real strategic error.

Product governance is the way forward when it comes to overcoming the lack of insight into structured products and the associated lack of accountability. If customers are stuck with a product or service that they cannot get out of without incurring losses and service providers are not under an obligation to achieve a particular result but only to make efforts, the primacy of the producer's actions must be called into question. Consumers must be given control over the management of the product. To a certain extent, this is already the case when it comes to mutual funds. In the US, independent boards keep a close eye on the interests of investors in mutual funds, while Europe has codes that asset managers must comply with. Although a structure based on codes is less stringent, there are rules in force in Europe to ensure a better segregation of duties. These rules, taken in combination with the involvement of regulators, offer some protection. At an international level, many pension funds are structured in exactly the same way with a supervisory board. However, the best-laid plans often go awry, and this is something we need to deal with.

We have now reached the end of our exploration of products and how their structure can offer additional assurance with regard to fair treatment and avoiding the risk of the broker or bank going under. The latter can also be achieved if the customer does not buy any products that are separated by a legal structure but instead puts the money or assets in an account with a broker in which, under the terms of the account's conditions, the customer's money or assets are segregated from the broker's assets. Anglo-Saxon rules in particular provide opportunities for non-professional investors to segregate their assets from the broker's so they are not swept away in the event that the broker defaults.

This brings us to the scandals surrounding the collapses of Lehman Brothers and MF Global. Everyone has heard of Lehman, but MF Global is a little less well known. MF Global was a large global derivatives broker that was once known as Man Financial. Its CEO, Jon Corzine, used to be a partner at Goldman Sachs and in the intervening period he had been a politician for the Democratic Party, serving one term as the 54th Governor of New Jersey. MF Global changed its business model, with Corzine believing he could build a second Goldman Sachs. But on Sunday 30 October 2011, MF Global collapsed, largely because of its large, speculative position in European government bonds. It was quickly discovered that there was a substantial shortfall in the segregated customer funds. Monies were transferred days before the bankruptcy. The shortfall was initially US$600 million, but it soon soared to US$1.6 billion. Of this, US$900 million related to US accounts and US$700 million to accountholders in the UK. CEO Jon Corzine claimed he had no idea what had happened to the money. The question this raises is how the shortfall should be treated, since some of the customers' assets are still identifiable. How should different customers – the haves and the have-nots – be treated? At the time of writing the case had been brought before a court in the US, and the judge's opinion on how to deal with this shortfall was awaited with great anticipation.

This question has in fact already been answered in an identical case involving Lehman Brothers. The UK Supreme Court reached a historical verdict, finding that Lehman Brothers International Europe had been negligent when it came to separating client money correctly. Only £2 billion had been properly segregated; the rest was swept away at the time of the collapse. The Supreme Court ruled that customers, who had been entitled to have their assets segregated, which Lehman had failed to do, were entitled to a share of the pot of cash that remained. This created an intriguing dilemma. Some customers had been vigilant and had contacted the broker to check whether their assets were segregated. Others had been more negligent, or perhaps more gullible, and had simply assumed everything was fine. The Supreme Court ruling means that the cash needs to be shared among a larger number of parties, and so vigilant customers will not recover all of their assets either. And so we return to the essence of Eugene Heath's previously quoted definition of fair treatment. Should vigilant customers share equally in the fate of all customers and pay the price for other people's carelessness? Where, in fact, does fair treatment end? This story illustrates the real difference between regulatory and legal separation. Regulatory separation is an important line of defence, whereas legal separation is akin to an Atlantic wall.

Finally, I would like to briefly revisit the FSA's six outcomes and consider the culture surrounding client services as well as the duty to provide after sales service. Providers of financial services are under an obligation to provide after sales service, irrespective of whether the customer is tied to a product for a long period of time or is free to make different choices. However, we are not keen on treating existing customers as well as prospective customers. It is simply not in our nature. Special offers are used to entice new customers. Once they have been secured, the process of earning money, and in some cases big money, from the customer starts slowly and almost imperceptibly. Interest rates on deposits that are extended suddenly become less competitive, and when it comes to renewing mortgage interest rates the bank does not ignore the fact that the client is stuck. At the same time, money may be made because the customer has become less vigilant. While we should not abuse or exploit this situation, we should be able to demand that customers do take some care. Unfortunately, customers are not always careful, and that is why they are sometimes the cause of their own financial misery. The extent to which blame can be attributed to customers is considered in the next chapter.

Chapter 9

When the customer is to blame

Is it possible that customers can also be blamed for the fact that they have been fooled constantly? Do customers have a duty to take care of themselves that they fail to fulfil properly? In other words, are customers victims of their own actions? And if so, should we do more to protect them from themselves?

Customers are often the losers in the games played in the world of finance. However, this is not always solely due to the actions of their advisers or brokers. In many instances, customers are also the victims of their own actions. They are well-known for having unrealistic dreams. If, for instance, they see a nice house for sale, they want to do a deal quickly and press the bank for a high mortgage. And, of course, they start renovating straight away, even though they already decided to take a holiday in South Africa with the children. Which they refuse to cancel. After all, look on the bright side: the renovations could be carried out while they are away, and the loan from the bank can cover all costs. True? So, on the borrowing side, customers take on huge risk for a reward they cannot resist.

When it comes to savings, the reverse is true. They do not want to run any risk yet still want plenty of yield. Customers are unwilling to run any risk on their savings, but they still want to accumulate enough capital so that they can start taking things easy when they turn 55. They want to get an average return of 6% but ignore the associated risk, and become infuriated when things go wrong. This is just as unrealistic. In other words, customers are to blame as well. They are just like everyone else, and so they often act irrationally. Such irrational behaviour is also seen when they take financial decisions. They unintentionally become the victims of the 'animal spirit' and are often just as keen on making a profit as their brokers and advisers. Customers can also be greedy when it comes to money, and this creates problems.

Consumers suffer from nominalism, a form of variant behaviour mentioned in Chapter 5. Future returns are expressed as percentages, which are nominal units. The problem is that we tend to think in nominal terms. For example, we can see immediately that 5% is greater than 4%, so if we can choose between an investment with a return of 5% and one with a return of 4%, we will have a clear preference straight away. It is almost impossible to judge the difference in risk between the two investments at all, let alone quantify the risk differential. For this reason we tend to ignore the difference in risk at times when matters are relatively calm on the financial front. Risk is often considered to be 'theoretical'. One investment may entail more risk than another, but generally speaking people believe that the event that leads to the risk materialising will not occur. Greek debt, for example, carries sovereign risk but offers a higher effective return than German debt. Greece could not go bankrupt, surely? In such cases people look mainly at the absolute returns, and assume that even a bad credit name will honour its debts. And who would have expected a heavyweight such as Merrill Lynch to go under? Or a market player such as Lehman Brothers? A great many people based investment decisions on arguments of this kind, and this had major consequences. They ran risks they knew nothing about and which they could not assess. Moreover, all seemed well at a 'nominal' level. Besides this, their behaviour was also encouraged by monetary authorities, which kept interest rates artificially low. Money held in savings accounts did not earn enough interest to compensate for inflation. Investors who wanted to keep up with inflation created a demand for returns and were blind to risk.

Many parties made use (or perhaps took advantage) of the fact that investors failed to perceive risk. One well-known, legalised and socially accepted form of failure to perceive risk concerns games of chance, such as state lotteries:

> Often consumers do not have to stake a great deal of money. Each of them pays a small amount in absolute terms, but they have no idea whether this amount is in proportion to their chance of winning any of the prizes, let alone the jackpot. Consumers focus solely on the jackpot in absolute terms. This is their dream. If they do not win and the dream is over, they can buy another lottery ticket next week, for the following dream. The illusion of the jackpot is nominalism – a pure form of money illusion.

The animal spirit ensures that in periods of relative peace people fail to appreciate risk. The risk they run constantly increases for relatively little extra in the way of returns. People who do not believe that risks will occur also have a tendency to be open to financial products that involve borrowing money. This is what happens in the case of leverage, for example. Leverage ensures a certain return is obtained, which is exactly what investors are looking for. They are told more or less what the risks are, but they dismiss them. That is exactly what happened with CDOs in the period 2005–2008. These products, which are sound in their basic form, were structured more and more aggressively, and in the process slowly became ticking time bombs. The reverse is true as well. The animal spirit also emerges in relatively troubled times. When things go wrong on the financial markets, the animal spirit fuels the panic. People flee to the nearest emergency exit, avoiding all risk. In this case, they seriously overestimate the amount of risk. Risk becomes overpriced. When the price of risk is overestimated or underestimated, this tends to occur on a structural basis. Everyone does the same as everyone else, creating systemic risk.

One particularly interesting form of money illusion relates to what are called 'carry trades', in which money is borrowed in a low-interest-rate currency and lent on in a high-interest-rate currency. Carry trades are regularly performed by professional investors, but there is an equivalent that private individuals often use when taking out mortgages in low-interest currencies. In countries such as Poland, Hungary and, let us not forget, Iceland, for example, people took out mortgages in Swiss francs and euros en masse. Interest rates were so tantalisingly low that everyone wanted to take advantage. However, when the forint and the Icelandic krona collapsed in value during the credit crunch, the principal amount of their mortgage loans doubled. Or more accurately, they doubled in local currency, the frame of reference for the borrowers. All the benefits they had gained from the low interest rates had been cancelled out for decades. The joy of low interest rates suddenly morphed into the misery of negative equity. Since this form of home financing was used on a very large scale in countries such as Poland, Hungary and Iceland the risk became a systemic risk, and hence a social risk. That can have far-reaching consequences for other countries, as the following extract illustrates (taken from an article published in the *Financial Times* on 12 September 2011):

> The Austrian government attacked a plan by Hungary to allow its citizens to wind up Swiss franc-denominated mortgages at a preferential exchange rate, saying the Hungarian move posed an 'existential threat' to Austrian banks. Viktor Orban, the Hungarian prime minister, told parliament on Monday, that Budapest would press ahead with a proposal enabling Hungarians to close their burdensome Swiss-franc mortgages in a lump sum and at a rate of 180 forints to the franc (compared to the current market rate of around 234 forints), with the exchange rate loss falling on the banks…
>
> Two-thirds of Hungarian mortgages are in Swiss francs. Austrian banks have some €6 billion of foreign-currency loans outstanding in Hungary, according to Austrian officials.

In this way, a significant downward correction in a currency, which usually is due to the poor state of the country's economy, creates additional distress for the people of that country. This is a classic example of systemic risk. So, when it comes to prohibitions, borrowing in low-interest-rate foreign currencies is, in my view, something that regulators should ban. Moreover, the above shows that if customers en masse cannot make payments, the banks are at risk.

How far should intervention on the part of regulators and authorities be taken in an effort to protect consumers? Should those consumers also be protected against themselves? In connection with this I refer once again to two important philosophical theories on ethics. The first concept stems from the philosophy of Immanuel Kant and concerns autonomy. People have the ability to protect themselves from harm and destruction and make decisions for themselves, and their right to do so is fundamental. Utilitarianism is less explicit, but the need to take care of each other plays a greater role in this concept. This need to care can go against our sense of autonomy. The moral ambivalence in this situation is that we instinctively cling to the concept of autonomy, since we are, after all, articulate consumers. However, we behave differently in reality, and that has become much more apparent in the financial industry than anywhere else within society. Pensions form a good example. Participation in pension schemes is often mandatory. Participants have to put part of their income aside in a fund that pays out once their working days are over. The same is also true of health insurance in countries such as the Netherlands and other European countries. In these cases, society takes a paternalistic approach. The government wants everyone to be able to receive medical care when they are ill, and businesses do not want to have to deal with the problems of widows and orphans. We are forced to take out insurance or save up, whether we like it or not.

Should such a paternalistic attitude be condemned by definition? No, because consumers sometimes find it very difficult to work out what is good for them. When consumers behave in a way that society believes is not in their interests, they tend to continue to act unwisely. Warning them rarely helps. If an alien from outer space were to find itself in a cigarette shop on earth and see all the frightening warnings on packets of cigars and cigarettes, they would be surprised to see some people still smoking. Consumers do not heed warnings, however, because they are addicted. Some are addicted to smoking, but others may be addicted to eating, travelling or shopping. Addictions make people behave highly irrationally. There is something very elemental in the thought process that leads us to buy and use stimulants such as nicotine. As consumers we are entirely focused on today and disregard the future consequences. There is now an imbalance when it comes to the order in which we enjoy pleasure (the inverse in economics is low interest rates). We choose the pleasure of smoking now because the possible downside will not materialise for some time, if at all, so why worry about tomorrow? Here, too, people fail to appreciate the risk and the long-term picture. In the financial world, addiction to credit is a major problem. It leads people to make choices that provide greater pleasure in the short term but might not provide any benefit at all in the longer term. All in all, it can be argued that, in their desire for short-term pleasure and enjoyment over long-term effects, the 'pleasure discount factor' that customers apply is too high. The major negative consequences today's actions will have in the future are trivialised today by applying a pleasure discount yield that is way too high. This factor is not in synch with long-term interest rates, and as a consequence large numbers of consumers tend to use borrowed money to fund consumption. They enjoy today's pleasures, either forgoing the benefits of interest on savings or accepting the cost of borrowing. Bringing interest rates down makes the problem worse. Addiction to credit is a serious problem, and financial institutions are much to blame for this situation arising. In the US, for example, teaser rates were used to entice homebuyers to take on large mortgages. Teaser rates are low initial interest rates, but they are increased after a few years to a market rate or sometimes even higher. Customers looked at the initial rate and the home they had fallen in love with, and decided to get into debt. They knew that the interest rate they would have to pay in a few years' time would be higher, but they accepted this as the pleasure discount factor was greater than the expected increase in interest rates. A similar situation arose in the Netherlands owing to mortgages based on growth annuities, which also turned out to be a poor choice for the consumer.

It is hard for consumers to deal with credit addiction on their own. Consumer loans are sold by showing us pictures of beautiful new bathrooms and wonderful holidays that we can pay for with borrowed money. It is difficult to say no. In some cases, it is almost impossible not to make use of credit. In the Netherlands, for instance, a student loan is offered to, or more accurately foisted on, every student. The loan is automatically paid into the student's bank account. Students who would rather not take on a loan have to go to a great deal of effort to stop that process. It is no different from the government handing out free drugs to people who have not yet developed an addiction. Many people also complain about the high house prices in the Netherlands and the barrier this forms to those starting out on the housing ladder. However, the problems they face are not just down to high prices. Many people looking to buy their first home have a great deal of student debt. They want to be active on the housing market, but their debt makes it harder for them to afford their dream home. Interest rates have been very low for years, and borrowing is relatively cheap. This makes it appealing to borrow money to pay for something we consume now. Interest rates are determined partly by monetary authorities, central bankers and tax authorities. For these last two groups, low interest rates are of great social importance. You may therefore wonder how independent our central bankers are when it comes to setting socially acceptable interest rates (or interest rates that would make borrowers more cautious since credit would cost too much, and investors more cautious by giving them an accurate impression of the interest rate on risk-free investments). As for those private individuals who have savings to preserve, they will continue to be extremely worried as long as short-term interest rates remain lower than the rate of inflation.

However, addiction to credit is not the consumer's only problem. When it comes to financial services, a great deal of misery is caused by other factors, specifically brokers who chase after commission (whether they are tied to specific products or not) and the aggressive tactics used by producers of financial products, which attempt to increase sales by taking a product-push approach.

The fee the broker receives for its service to the customer is often a retrocession fee, which is paid by the producer. However, it is derived from the total price paid for the product. It is paid for by the customer without his knowledge but with his implicit consent. The producer can therefore bribe the broker into giving customers biased advice, making it a corruptive process. A ban on the payment of retrocession fee offers a way of solving this structural weakness.

This idea was incorporated in the Markets in Financial Instruments Directive (MiFID), the EU directive that provides for a harmonised regulatory framework for transactions in financial instruments. MiFID is currently being tested by the market. The European countries that had the greatest problems when it came to the mis-selling of financial products, such as the UK and the Netherlands, are now at the forefront of the debate on the ban on return commission. In the Netherlands, which has had to deal with scandals surrounding single-premium annuity policies and investment-based insurance policies, the ban on commission was supported by a large majority of MPs. However, if a ban on return commission is introduced, this could lead to major structural changes in the financial services sector. For this reason, some European countries, and France in particular, are not at all keen on the idea.

Are all the changes always for the better, or are we solving a problem by creating new ones? Before looking at two new problems that will be created by banning retrocession payments, let us first briefly consider how fee payments are supposed to work after the ban becomes effective. Producers will no longer be allowed to pay brokers a retrocession fee. The fees that a broker is entitled to will have to be paid by the customer, and he will only pay them if he is satisfied with the service he receives. From this it can be concluded that a customer will pay different fees for execution services from brokers combined with advice, and execution services without advice (that is, execution only). At present the retrocession fee for both services is the same, but that will change. The customer will only be prepared to pay if the existing product becomes cheaper, so producers that no longer have to pay retrocession fees should lower the overall price of the product. If they do not, the customer will be worse off. Will producers lower their prices, or will we be confronted with a de facto increase in the cost to the customer? The latter might prove to be the ultimate outcome. The customer may well decide that he is not prepared to pay the broker a fee; he had always considered the service to be free and it will be difficult to convince him that the product he buys now is cheaper than before the ban. As it is, customers never like to pay fees if the fact that they have to pay for them is made visible. So brokers will be squeezed in the middle and will have problems earning a decent living. As a consequence, their yachts will have to be put up for sale. Independent brokers will be particularly hard hit, while the brokerage arms of integrated financial services providers will be less concerned. For them there is always a way around the problem. The producer is an in-house entity, and it is irrelevant where the revenue is earned, as long as it still comes in. The use of internal debits and credits means the retrocession game can still go on. The ban will therefore affect independent brokers or suppliers and favour integrated houses, which are precisely the institutions that need to be changed. Open architecture and the open market will suffer, and free competition based on the best product will disappear. By hurting the independents, market pluriformity will suffer. Best execution will receive a further blow, which will affect all products available in the market. And there will also be a major shift towards in-house products. The brokers' yachts may indeed be up for sale, but will this benefit the end customer?

Chapter 10

Blind faith

Is it possible for an asset manager to serve the interests of customers exclusively, or do conflicts of interest always play a role? Does blind faith equate to asking for trouble?

In the spring of 2012, BlackRock, the world's largest asset manager, ran an advertising campaign about investing for a 'new world'. The advertisement asked, 'Are your reliable sources of income still reliable?' and showed a middle-aged man with grey hair and dark glasses looking straight into the camera. And through the lens of the camera into the world. With his left hand on his right forearm and his veins clearly visible, sporting a grey beard, a shirt and a tie with a star pattern, and carrying a coat over his arm, he struck a semi-informal note, but it was accompanied by a touch of formality. The advertisement was clearly designed to communicate trust. It focused on one question: what should an investor do with his money? *But who is this man?* These two questions are the focus of this chapter.

Not everyone understands investing. There are also some people who simply do not have the time or, worse, have no interest in the subject whatsoever, even when it comes to what they do with their own money. Others are not allowed to invest directly owing to their social position and the codes of conduct they have to adhere to. In short, for some people it is a good idea to hire a professional to take over the management of their assets. An important question in this context is whether the relevant professional focuses on one task or whether he or she wears a number of hats. In other words they are conflicted. Is the professional just an adviser, or perhaps also a broker? In the asset management sector tasks are sometimes combined, although the standard practice is to segregate duties. Generally speaking, advisers are specialised asset managers who are not connected to a particular company of brokers, because asset managers must be free when it comes to the execution of transactions they initiate. They have to have the freedom to select the broker as the quality of services can vary. Once brokers believe they have customers in their pocket, they soon become lazy. Besides, brokers earn money from executing transactions, not from achieving good returns. The temptation to execute inordinate numbers of management transactions can become too great if they manage assets too. In addition, brokers sometimes trade for their own account, and so before you know it they will be acting as the counterparty and paying hardly any attention to the interests of the customer. All in all, it is not a good idea to hire a broker to act as an asset manager. Sometimes an asset manager is part of a financial conglomerate but operates at arm's length. As it is, such 'segregation' is rather relative; it is a Chinese wall that can easily be peered over from the comfort of an office chair. There are therefore plenty of conflicts.

When someone hands over the management of their assets to a professional third party, the customer is supposed to take a step back. Although some customers may consult with their manager in-between times, the power to decide what action is taken has shifted. Asset managers cannot be held responsible if they are constantly hampered by customers. The relationship between the asset manager and its customer is therefore very vulnerable and delicate. The customer must be fully confident that the work will be done properly. It is a matter of blind faith. Faith in that the manager will not be promoted by conflicting interests. This is a major issue, and a great deal of space will be devoted to it in this chapter. But first, in order to gain a better understanding of the situation, let us start by looking at the different asset management models and the structure of the market, and consider the profile of the potential manager.

The management of assets can be done on an individual basis or for a number of customers by pooling their wealth. Customers with substantial assets, such as institutions, usually opt for individual, tailor-made service, based on clearly defined agreements (clear investment profiles and instructions). Smaller amounts of assets, which are usually held by private individuals, are managed according to a standard approach, often based on the manager following a model portfolio. In both cases, a structure is used whereby the money is kept in an account in the customer's name, and the asset manager is given a mandate. The asset manager effectively acts as an agent. But there is another structure that is used a great deal as well. Assets (usually, but not always, smaller amounts) may also be managed by being consolidated within a single legal structure. Money will therefore not be held in the name of the customer, since the structure has a legal personality of its own. The intention is to combine small amounts of assets to form an asset pool that has institutional scale and can therefore demand institutional services. This form of asset management offers all investors benefits of scale when it comes to costs and order execution. The most commonly used vehicle is the mutual fund. Mutual funds often have an open-ended structure, which means that investors can redeem their 'share' at the market value. This offers the best of both worlds: the benefit of scale, and the advantages of a personalised unit.

These days, asset management organisations are completely separate from the legal entity that represents the funds they manage, even though the names of these funds often include the name of the manager. Asset management operations are regulated and must comply with all kinds of statutory and other rules. Asset management organisations need to be structured in a way that safeguards the continuity of the performance of their duties. In addition, integrity needs to be ensured at all times. An important element in this respect is the segregation of duties both within and outside the organisation in order to create checks and balances. For example, the person (or department) who makes the investment decision must not be the same person (or department) responsible for measuring and reporting on investment returns. The front office must be separate from the back office, and within these departments certain duties may not be combined. For this reason, certain tasks may even be outsourced to third parties. Such work frequently involves duties in the area of safekeeping and record keeping in relation to securities, and the fund administration: the counting of units. In Europe outsourcing is standard practice, but this is not so much the case in the US.

In Europe, it is common for managers not to have customers' securities or money in their own custody but to entrust them to the safekeeping of others instead. Managers are in effect merely agents, and the securities are transferred to the care of others. Segregating duties is vital, and failures in this area created many catastrophes in the financial industry in recent years. If Bernard Madoff had outsourced his safekeeping function to an independent services provider, he would probably not have been able to defraud his customers of billions. As Madoff did not make any investments, there were no securities to be held in safekeeping, something an independent services provider would certainly have noticed.

Asset managers do not work for free, of course. They charge fees. This immediately raises a moral question. Should the management fee cover the asset manager's costs and perhaps include a small profit mark-up? Or should asset managers be allowed to inflate fees so that other costs are covered too? Most asset managers are commercial, for-profit businesses that spend money on non-investment related business, such as marketing and distribution. To put it plainly, should an existing customer pay for the acquisition of new customers? Asset management organisations advertise and take potential customers on trips to exotic locations in order to 'study new investment opportunities'. But marketing is not the only area in which substantial amounts are spent. With regard to remuneration, for instance, Stephen Schwarzman, the CEO of BlackRock, a US asset manager, earned US$213 million in income from employment and dividends. And managers work from beautiful offices since they want to impress foreign institutional investors and delegations from listed companies who come to visit. This all costs more than is strictly necessary. Is it right that existing customers pay these costs? After all, these costs do not relate to matters that provide much benefit for investors.

Let us take a closer look at the cost structure of asset managers. In the past, asset managers and funds were often one and the same, with a joint income statement. The rule that managers may only incur costs that directly benefit investors dates back to that period. The structure of most managers (with the exception of property investment companies) changed over the course of time, and today, as we have seen, managers and funds are separate entities. The manager stipulates in a contract what the customer has to pay in the way of a management fee, and ensures this is in line with market conditions. The money remaining after the operational costs of managing the fund are deducted accrues to the manager. Managers can do what they like with this money. They can spend it on excessive remuneration for the CEO, return it to shareholders, invest in advertising campaigns or organise lavish parties for potential customers. The market will take care of them; since there is sufficient competition the manager will not survive if he fails to deliver the goods and make customers happy. That is the safeguard against unprofessional behaviour or services which are not up to standard.

The total cost of a fund to an investor is known as the total expense ratio (TER) and it is made transparent. However, once again execution fees are not included, and sometimes some of the custody fee is left out as well. Blind faith requires that no hidden charges are levied, such as soft dollar arrangements or layered fees (extra fees payable because the asset manager invested in underlying funds). At one time that was normal practice, but opaque fee loading of this kind has now come to an end. Or has it?

Fees can be structured in various ways, often in a way that fulfils the needs of the manager and possibly the wishes of the customer. Sometimes the manager charges a one-off fee when the investment units are first purchased, and subsequently an annual fee. This annual fee may be a fixed sum or percentage (management fee) or a fee based on results (performance fee). Sometimes it is both a fixed fee and a variable top-up fee based on performance. This raises the question of what constitutes performance. Is it simply achieving normal returns, or does it denote something exceptional? In most cases, performance fees are based on a minimum annual return (hurdle rate). The return in excess of the hurdle rate is shared, and so the manager is only paid for achieving above-average returns. If the return for a year is negative, the manager must first make up the losses before it can share in the upside again. After a loss, the value of the assets must return to their previous 'high water mark' (highest previous level of performance) before the manager can share in the profits again. This is important, because without a high water mark a customer may have to pay more than once for the same fund performance. That would obviously be unacceptable.

Nevertheless, despite high water marks and effusive descriptions in prospectuses, the customer needs to be on the lookout for dodgy practices. Some asset managers do not apply a hurdle rate, and instead demand a performance fee for every increase in value. Moreover, if a fund has holdings of liquid assets, the value of these holdings may increase due to interest income. The manager will then demand a fee for interest income even though it did not do anything to achieve this return. The same situation applies with respect to normal stock market performance. Why should a manager be rewarded for keeping up with averages?

Matters can be even worse in the world of private equity (investments in unlisted companies), where management fees of 2% and performance fees of 20% are not uncommon. Private equity managers often take a very long time to invest all of the money that has been committed to the fund. This is because they have to identify and analyse various possibilities before allocating capital. However, some private equity managers charge management fees based on the committed capital, even if only a fraction has been invested. The consequence is that management fees are absurdly high compared to the amounts invested, at least in the initial phase, and this limits the fund's earning capacity. Private equity managers try to reassure customers by explaining that the returns curve is the shape of a hockey stick. They may incur a small loss now, but they have the prospect of a big gain in the future.

One of the questions raised at the beginning of this chapter still remains. *Who is the man in the BlackRock advertisement?* This person may well be middle-aged with grey hair, or it may be a young professional, or even somebody who, under normal circumstances, has long ago taken retirement. It could be a man, it could be a woman, but it could even be a computer instead. Perhaps he is an emotional person, but in any case he is likely to be rational or highly intelligent and most probably have a very good brain and be well-educated. Part of his education may have included the Chartered Financial Analyst (CFA) Programme – the stepping stone for any investment manager. In May 2012, the CFA Institute celebrated its 50th anniversary of the first CFA exam, which is now a global benchmark for professional analysts. But the CFA Programme is more than that. Its curriculum covers ethics and appropriate behaviour among those who handle other people's money. It is an introductory course to blind faith. On that day in May 2012, the opening ceremonies at five different exchanges around the world were conducted by the local chair of the CFA Institute, reflecting the fact that this really was a global effort. Ceremonies were held in New York, in London, in Singapore, Hong Kong and in the United Arab Emirates, where the Chairman of the local CFA Institute for that region was Yacoub Husein Nuseibeh. Born in Jerusalem of Palestinian parentage and educated in Boston, he now works for Abu Dhabi Investment Authority (ADIA). Yacoub Husein Nuseibeh gave the opening speech just before the bell rang and he was visibly proud – proud that his own local chapter of the CFA was growing rapidly, proud to be part of the CFA Institute, and proud of his profession. It exists, and it is right to exist. But besides pride there also needs to be vigilance, because bad practices lurk around every corner.

As mentioned previously, we will take a look at one of the big threats to ethical behaviour, namely conflicts of interest. Acting ethically and making the right choices, which means sometimes ignoring one's own interests, are crucial for retaining investor confidence. But it is not easy, and conflicts of interest can throw a spanner in the works without warning. We therefore need to be wary of certain practices. It is vitally important that customers investing in the same strategy receive equal treatment, even if the money invested in that strategy is spread across different investment vehicles. This is the same as the most favoured nation principle. Customers must receive the same services under the same terms and conditions, irrespective of their structure. However, this principle ignores the fact that tensions exist between the interests of new customers, existing customers and departing customers. Let us take a close look at these conflicts of interest.

Investors are able to join and leave investment funds at specified intervals. In the case of hedge funds this is about once a quarter, while in the case of mutual funds that invest in readily marketable securities (such as shares) they can do so on a daily basis. This means that, in the case of mutual funds, the value of all the underlying securities needs to be calculated at least once a day. This daily value determines the value of individual units, the sums that outgoing investors receive for their stakes and the price that those joining the fund have to pay to acquire units. The amounts represented by incoming and outgoing investors hardly ever match, and so the manager has to make adjustments for the net movements of funds. The manager therefore has to expand or reduce the portfolio to reflect the remainder, by either buying or selling securities on the market. It is important in this context that the manager keeps the integrity of the portfolio intact and does not pay outgoing investors more than he obtains when adjusting the portfolio. If he does pay more, there are unexpected additional costs, which the portfolio will have to bear. This means transferring the bill to existing investors, which is clearly unacceptable. Where the fund offers daily liquidity, it is important that the value of the portfolio is calculated extremely accurately, or else there will be trouble. No matter how hard a manager tries, such calculations can never be totally precise especially when it comes to global portfolios, because the valuation is a snapshot taken at different moments in time. After all, the day starts at different times in different parts of the world, and public holidays vary from one country to the next. If the value of the portfolio for settlement purposes is determined in the morning in Europe and prices on the Asian markets have already fallen sharply that day, the closing prices of the US equities on the previous day, as used in the portfolio, will no longer properly reflect the value of those equities at the time investors join or withdraw from the fund. This is not a theoretical scenario. The August 2011 stock market fall (which was partially caused by the Greek debt crisis) clearly demonstrated that using US closing prices to calculate the value at which investors could withdraw from the fund in the morning in Europe created a high risk of error. This could lead to investors receiving too good a price when they withdraw, which is to the detriment of other customers. In the past, arbitrageurs tried to profit from this anomaly, a practice known as market timing. Asset managers that tolerated this behaviour, or even contributed to it, paid a heavy price. It did great damage to their reputations, and it took them years to recover from this. Managers have a responsibility to ensure the interests of all their customers are given due weight, particularly in extreme market conditions, and this includes the interests of outgoing customers.

There are also funds that invest in underlying assets, such as property and private equity, for which prices are not calculated on a daily basis. In Germany, there are managed open-end funds offering daily liquidity that invest in property. That is not without serious risk. Besides the fact that land and buildings are difficult to value accurately, if a large number of investors want to withdraw from the fund it is impossible to sell off property in exact proportion to meet the redemption requests. Nevertheless, managers of open-end funds that include property must keep their promises and return the investment to the departing customer. The only way they can do this is by tapping in to their own cash balances or turning to a bank. Both actions have consequences. The investors who stay put are confronted with an increased risk profile owing to the fact that the same amount of property is shared between fewer unitholders. There is always a risk that investors might panic. If too many of them pull out, the fund may exceed the permitted level of financing. In that case the management will have to lock the stable door and close the fund. German regulations stipulate that a fund that has closed and is not reopened within a specific period of time has to be liquidated. Pity the poor investor who remained loyal. Sometimes it pays to panic.

During the 2007–2008 banking crisis, a different kind of open-end fund – money market funds – got into trouble. These are mutual fund constructions in which companies or institutional investors can park excess liquidity and receive an attractive rate of interest. The assets are repayable on demand. Money market funds were considered an alternative to bank deposits, and they enjoyed a rapid rise in popularity because banks were unable to offer competitive rates of interest owing to their banking liquidity requirements. Money market funds were in a position to offer appealing rates of interest, partly because they had no liquidity restrictions to comply with and partly because they rather naughtily exploited the interest rate curve, especially when the curve had a positive slope. The interest paid by the money market funds was inflated by borrowing short and lending long. They were climbing the yield curve – the classic gamble in banking. The risk that all the assets might be withdrawn at the same time is ignored. But 2007 was a strange year. Suddenly the market stopped trusting the banks. Money market funds were heavily exposed to certain banks, and the rumour was that these banks were the ones that had problems. Confidence in the opaque money market funds vanished into thin air. Major institutions withdrew their money en masse. The panic, and the fact that investors were offered daily liquidity, meant things soon went awry. As money managers were still sitting high (but not dry) on their yield curve, they could not satisfy the redemption requests. As a result, they had to close. Their goose had been cooked, and their credibility was lost forever.

A number of hedge funds suffered similar fates. They generally invest in assets that are difficult to liquidate, but once again that was not considered to constitute a real risk. Capital invested by incoming customers could be used to finance amounts payable to outgoing customers, and it was expected that this would keep things rolling. But once again insufficient attention was paid to the risk that panic might break out. In 2007, panic was sparked off by the Madoff scandal. Once that horror story broke, one investor after another withdrew from the hedge funds. The managers of the hedge funds tried to solve the problem by means of partial, rather than full, closure. The illiquid components of the hedge fund investments were kept separate in side pockets. The outgoing investors were now refunded partly in cash and partly in the form of a stake in the illiquid assets (the side pocket).

When considering the accurate calculation of the value at which investors can join and withdraw from a fund, there is one phenomenon in the investment world that cannot be avoided, namely Ponzi schemes. Often, Ponzi schemes are created by accident. They just happen. They are a consequence of lax morals and a few dishonest moments early on. Ponzi schemes come into being when an asset manager cannot realise the returns he promised, yet refuses to be honest about this. He lies, hoping that next month his luck will change. But instead of a return to fortune, he falls from grace permanently. Outgoing investors obtain too high a price when they leave the fund, while sitting customers are put at a disadvantage. The longer the lie continues, the more expensive it becomes. So, rather than investment, it becomes a game of keeping the lie alive for as long as possible.

Potential conflicts of interest between different customers also play a role when modifications are made to portfolios across different funds. In this situation, the asset manager actively manages the portfolios on the basis of the revised conclusions of analysts or on new insights. Such changing insights affect all the manager's investments, which he often holds in a number of funds. This raises the issue of allocation. How should the manager allocate transactions if the prices at which he trades in the market differ? This issue also arises if only a limited number of shares are allocated in an IPO in which there is plenty of investor interest. The manager has some discretion, and this has to be dealt with in a way that is in the interests of all the investors. However, it is very tempting not to do this. Let us consider the manager of an institutional fund that is not performing well at all. The manager is aware that the customer might decide to withdraw its mandate. As a consequence, the fund manager has an interest in beefing up performance by other means. One way in which this could be achieved is through a biased allocation, but tempting as this is it is totally unacceptable. Trades must be allocated according to a procedure in which no discretion is allowed. The same situation exists when allocations are made in IPOs that offer the possibility of sharp gains in value. Here, too, the asset manager needs to allocate the transactions properly and fairly, which is not always easy to do.

The investment mandate also stipulates who is to bear which costs and how any unforeseen costs are to be shared. But not everything that is unforeseen can be foreseen. Not every eventuality is set in stone, and so the mandate allows a great deal of room to manoeuvre. The question is how to resolve trading issues and their consequences, such as losses, if one of the parties is not at the table. This raises the issue of product governance again. If a manager makes a serious mistake when executing an order, for example, by executing a buy order rather than a sell order or by trading the wrong number of shares, the asset manager has to bear the loss. This is because the loss cannot be charged to the fund or to the customer. But who ensures this is done? And what happens if the manager invested the money in bonds that were issued by Lehman Brothers, which is no longer able to fulfil its obligations? Should this kind of risk be borne by the fund? Yes, unless the investment was in contravention of the mandate or can be considered a serious professional error. There are countless examples of 'unfortunate circumstances' in which it is difficult to determine immediately who is going to have to bear the loss. Consider the case of a bond fund that focuses on frontier market investing and gets into difficulties because money released by the sale of government bonds it holds is available in local currency but cannot be transferred due to currency restrictions. Who should bear the resulting loss? The asset manager will argue that this situation is inherent to the risk attached to the investment mandate and comes within the scope of the customer's risk. However, if the manager accepted the risk attached to a bond fund investing in global bonds, the above situation would be considered a serious professional error, in which case the manager would have to bear the loss. And since transparency is rare when such issues arise, there is an increased risk that the manager will act unethically. Investment instructions and risk profiles form the starting points for funds as well as for individually concluded management mandates.

Generally speaking, asset managers sit on vast amounts of securities. These securities lie idle, and it is very easy and tempting to do something with them. Securities lending is the real temptation. There are some players in the market that are prepared to pay in order to borrow securities from the manager. They are usually short sellers, which are parties that have an obligation to deliver securities they do not have in their possession. Hedge funds in particular follow unorthodox strategies that require them to borrow equities. Many asset managers have programmes for lending securities that are owned by customers and are to remain with custodians for a long period of time. The fees paid by hedge funds provide a welcome stream of income. The only issue concerns who the beneficiary is of the fee income. As it happens, this income is not solely the customer's income, as it is shared with the asset manager, who retains around 20%. What is not shared is the corresponding risk in the event that the party borrowing the securities, that is, the hedge fund, fails to return the securities. This means that the asset manager pockets a share of the fee but does not have to make any contribution if there is a loss. While the risk of losses is small, partly because cash is always provided as collateral in transactions of this kind, the allocation is still extremely asymmetric. Furthermore, the collapse of Lehman Brothers showed that such practices are not entirely without risk. For this reason, the interests of the customer require special attention when it comes to securities lending.

A second aspect of securities lending concerns a moral issue. This is related to the fact that hedge fund managers plan to sell the equities they borrow, in the expectation that he can buy them back at a later date at a lower price. Is that in the interests of the original owner? Artificially influencing the price is, of course, not in the interests of customers, who would certainly not be pleased to find out that their own shares are being used for this purpose. In view of this, there is a school of thought that refuses on principle to participate in securities lending programmes. Perhaps the merchant banks think along similar lines. During Facebook's IPO, shares were apparently borrowed for very high fees, and the borrowers used the shares to benefit from the price fall once the company went public. How these shares could have been borrowed prior to an IPO is a new mystery to many market participants. However, the mere fact it happened epitomises all the points made above.

Another matter that calls for attention relates to the frequent reorganisation of funds. When too many investors pull out of a fund, the fund can become too small. It may then merge with, or alternatively be taken over by, another fund. This must be done in a way that is fair. But who has responsibility for monitoring this? The same question applies to all of the examples given above. How does the system ensure that all the moral hurdles are cleared, so that if the mandate has shortcomings the customer's interests are represented? This is not up to the customer, as again he does not have a seat at the table. Customers are normally unable to check whether things have been done properly, even from a distance, unless things go so badly the whole story becomes front-page news. How can customers be confident that the asset manager has the discipline and decency to ensure the process is fair? This question strikes at the heart of blind trust. It is asking for trouble if no additional safeguards have been put in place. This brings us back to the issue of product governance. The US has tightened up the rules in this area substantially, partly in response to scandals involving mutual funds at the start of the 21st century. Boards of trustees have been introduced to safeguard the interests of customers and ensure proper, decent management on the part of asset managers.

In my capacity as the CEO of Robeco, I attended many meetings of the Board of Trustees of Harbor Capital Advisors, a Chicago-based Robeco subsidiary and a rapidly growing mutual fund manager. Harbor has a single board of trustees, on the lines of the US model, which monitors all of its funds. Having seen it from close quarters, I would describe it as a system that works well. The Board of Trustees and the additional disciplinary effect it has have helped Harbor avoid becoming embroiled in practices that discredited the US mutual fund sector at the start of this century. It provides further evidence that it pays to be ethical, even if the payoff is delayed in many cases. That said, I have also seen the downside of this system of supervision. A board of trustees is a separate tier of management that is accountable to no one. It may have a link to the asset manager, because the chairman of the board of trustees often works for the manager, but most of the trustees are independent. If a board of this kind does not function well, there is a real problem. This can create a huge burden in terms of costs and demands on management attention. It can lead to unfair competition, particularly in an environment where mutual funds have to compete against financial products that have the same goal but are much less sophisticated or may even have no governance structure at all.

Given the problems with mutual funds in the US, as well as other factors, at the start of this century a debate began on the merits of introducing the American board of trustees system in Europe. After all, the conflict of interest between the asset manager and the fund existed in Europe too. In the end, a less stringent, code-based regime was selected in Europe, partly because Europe is much more stringent when it comes to the concept of the segregation of duties. Many more critical functions were outsourced, creating more inherent checks and balances in the system. In the Netherlands, Robeco took the initiative to introduce a code aimed at improving the management of conflicts of interest. This code covers areas in which conflicts may arise and described the course of action to be taken in such situations. But that was not the end of the matter. What action should be taken if an unforeseen conflict arises, or perhaps a conflict that deviates, even by a small margin, from the situations set out in the code? The smallest deviation can prove dangerous. Putting the interests of the customer first is not necessarily the right approach. For example, it may be concluded, after ample consideration, that rightfully the customer should bear some or all of the loss. The customer is not always right, and while his interests come first this can be difficult to ensure if he is not at the table. It is therefore essential that every situation is assessed in a balanced way. For this reason, we introduced the concept of 'conscientious consideration' at Robeco, and this was also included in the Dutch code. It is very similar to Adam Smith's notion of the 'impartial spectator', as it involves stepping outside of one's self and considering one's own position and that of the customer without bias to either party. The concept needs to be given a place within the organisation, and this means that the organisation undertakes to report on all such considerations. At Robeco, for instance, we produced reports that could be assessed by members of the Supervisory Board. The file was also available for inspection by the auditors and regulators. In a sense, this is similar to the standard set by the British financial regulator, the FSA, in its policy, specifically that customers are to be treated fairly.

In Chapter 3 we looked at the economic theories on efficiency and rational markets. If these theories are correct, this means that investing – and certainly investing in equities – is not that hard. The markets are, after all, efficient, and so the special insights of talented managers cannot outperform the omniscience of the market. If an asset manager performs in a way that can be considered just above average achieves similar results, this is merely coincidence and is not something he will be able to reproduce on a systematic basis. As a matter of fact, according to the law of averages it is highly likely that he will at some point lose the money he earned. Do these theories reflect reality? Let us consider the following example. John Alfred Paulson, of the hedge fund Paulson & Co, became well known among the general public owing to his involvement with the Abacus products, the Goldman Sachs collateralised debt obligations (CDOs) that got into difficulties. During the 2008 crisis Paulson earned a great deal of money for himself and his customers. He became convinced early on that the structure of financing property purchases by means of securitisations wrapped up in CDOs was bound to collapse. During the crisis his remarkable view paid off. In his book *The Big Short: Inside the doomsday machine* (2011), Michael Lewis gives an account of a number of visionaries who also bet against the market.

Once again, we wonder *who this man is who stands so tall in BlackRock's advertising campaign*, ready to convince us to entrust our money to him, making a leap of faith. Is he a man who believes in efficient markets, or is he someone who believes more in animal spirits and hence is prepared for the unexpected? This man could well be Michael Burry, the subject of Michael Lewis's book, *The Big Short*. Michael Burry had lost the sight in one eye as a young boy following the removal of a tumour. His disability made him stand out at school, and this had an impact in terms of social contact. But he also saw the upside, as he was able to focus much more than his classmates, and later on his fellow students, and he was very good at being on his own. After studying medicine Burry took up a position at the St Thomas Hospital in Nashville, but his passion lay elsewhere. The young doctor was bursting with intellectual energy and did not 'waste' any time on having a social life, which meant that he could devote all of his free time to performing economic analyses of listed companies. In time, Burry started to write recommendations for investments in high-tech companies. He had noted that the market did not make good use of a great deal of information and that investors could profit from this if they were prepared to study the matter in depth. He put it all in his newsletter, which contained interesting recommendations and what turned out to be an above-average number of correct conclusions. Not long after this Burry was advised to set up his own investment fund, which is exactly what he did. One day, his attention was caught by some exotic products with names that were difficult to pronounce: CDOs containing MBSs (mortgage-backed securities). Burry asked the issuers of these products exactly which underlying securities the CDOs contained, but most of the time he was given a noncommittal explanation. He therefore decided to do his own research. He literally got in his car and drove past the houses encumbered by mortgages that had been chopped up and ended up in the CDOs. The more he saw, the more Burry became convinced it was a corrupt, criminal process. He knew that things would go wrong long before other analysts started to have doubts. Burry set up a fund in which he intended to go short in CDOs, using credit default swaps. Given his reputation and track record, people were prepared to invest. Unfortunately they had to wait a long time for Burry to be proved right, who at times had to contend with doubts and a lack of understanding on the part of investors. But he was eventually proved right, as we all now know. His story took a poignant turn when his wife asked him to come with her to see a child psychiatrist because their son, Nicholas, was exhibiting deviant behaviour at school and was having problems keeping up. Burry thought this was nonsense, and that his son was fine. His wife asked him why he thought this. 'Because I used to be just like that,' he answered. His son turned out to have Asperger's syndrome, a form of autism. And Michael Burry was quite right once again: he has the same syndrome. His poor vision was not the cause of his social isolation after all, and his exceptional ability to focus and immerse himself in the subject was due to something completely different. However, this ability had provided him with an understanding that was evidently lacking in the oh-so healthy financial world. The moral of this story is that we may indeed wonder how it was that an industry full of healthy minds was unable to see that the system was on the brink of collapse, yet this fact could be perceived by a one-eyed man. Was this failure down to intellectual sloth, dishonesty or gullibility?

As an investor, Michael Burry was able to achieve better results than the market on a systematic basis. His story shows that even if full information is available in the so-called efficient market, people cannot be forced to make an efficient analysis. This constitutes a serious threat to the efficient market hypothesis. Admittedly, Burry's story may simply be an exception that does not affect the general applicability of the economic theories. However, if this sole exception manifests itself in the eye of the storm, it forms a compelling precedent that makes current theory building falsifiable. There are other exceptions, too, such as the success achieved by Warren Buffett. Does he have the ability to be more efficient than the market on a systematic basis, or is there a theoretical chance that he has had lucky throws of the dice? It cannot be merely coincidence. John Alfred Paulson is easier to explain, as at least part of his success in 2008 was allegedly down to cheating. He may have had good insights, but he has not been able to repeat his success. His ability to beat the market has therefore been questioned. He was the worst performing hedge fund manager of 2011, and the amount of money he lost for his customers exceeded the total amount lost by the hedge fund LTCM.

So was it a matter of luck or skill, or was it rigged? There are countless examples of managers who have an edge over the competition because they have better information and better access to sources. Moreover, it seems that sections of the market are temporarily or permanently unable to be efficient, and asset managers can take advantage of this. The extent to which they can do so depends on the size of the anomaly. The more advantage that is taken of inefficiencies, the more efficient the market becomes, thus removing further opportunities. Asset managers therefore need to realise they should never gamble too much, otherwise they become their own worst enemy. What they need is internal discipline.

Those who do not believe that the efficient markets can be beaten on a systematic basis tend to be adherents of passive investing. One of the ways in which this can be done is by investing in indices that serve as a proxy for the market. The vast majority of global assets are invested in indices. Companies that are not included in an index are therefore not considered and become undervalued. At a certain point in time this undervaluation will become crystallised and it will be worth taking advantage of.

Investing in a listed company means that the fund or the individual investors become shareholders. As well as receiving healthy dividends, shareholders also have obligations. Shareholders are entitled to vote, and, within the context of corporate governance rules (the necessary checks and balances), shareholders have a certain duty to make their influence felt. Asset managers have set themselves up as the shareholders' agents, and they are often the parties that vote at general meetings. Although they exercise their mandate to the best of their ability, certain conflicts can arise in this area. For example, an asset manager may personally be very much against the hostile takeover of a company he has been following for years, has invested in and believes in. His confidence is personal and perhaps also professional, but he has to think whose interests he is really serving. Who has hired him to act as an agent? It is not the company. He has to always strike the best deal for his customers, and that might well mean agreeing to the takeover proposal. When it comes to voting, his self-interest and the interests of the company are irrelevant, because the interests of investors are what matter.

Such moral dilemmas also play a part when it comes to corporate social responsibility. Many customers have a conscience and moral convictions and find it difficult to depart from them, never mind delegate them to an agent or adviser. Managers are, of course, highly professional and when they take decisions they mostly use models, financial analyses and market instincts. However, they are unable to get inside the customer's conscience. Investors may have a certain sense of social engagement, convictions and emotions, and sometimes be outraged at investment decisions (such as the decision to invest in companies with unethical operations). There are two ways of dealing with such situations: either enter into dialogues with the aim of influencing policy, or exclude specific companies. Many investors focus on dialogue with a company, either directly or through representative organisations. This is a commonly used method, particularly when the company's corporate governance is not in order. The shareholders, or their agents, hold talks with the company's management before the meeting. If this does not produce the desired result, they vote against the relevant motions at the general meeting. This approach has, for instance, resulted in a number of proposals to modify executive remuneration being voted down. The method also works if improvements need to be made to the company's policy on sustainability. It is often accompanied by outside pressure, from society, the political world and the press. One of the best known examples of this concerns the incident involving Brent Spar, operated by Royal Dutch Shell. Sometimes, however, the criticism is simply too fundamental. Asking Philip Morris to end its tobacco activities or Beate Uhse to pull out of the sex industry is just not possible. In such cases, the asset manager has to make a decision. He can either accept the company's activities or exclude the company.

Incidentally, excluding a company is easier said than done. All kinds of problems may arise, particularly if the manager is responsible for global assets. To touch on cultural relativism, not everyone on earth is equally upset by the same conduct. The Dutch, for example, are very much against cluster bombs and the tobacco industry, but they are very tolerant in other areas. Americans, by contrast, do not want to invest in anything that has ties to the sex industry but think it is fine to sleep with a gun under the bed. Asset managers that operate internationally come up against different ethical perceptions that are culturally determined to a significant extent. It is therefore difficult to gain a consensus for the entire portfolio. And on top of this, consistency is important when it comes to sustainability policy.

In 2005, the Government Pension Fund of Norway caused a major stir when it proposed excluding a number of companies involved in making cluster bombs, including EADS and its sister company EADS Finance BV. EADS was created in 2000 as the result of the merger of several European defence companies, including France's Aerospatiale Mantra and Germany's DaimlerChrysler Aerospace. There were accusations that EADS produced vital parts that were used in the manufacture of cluster bombs. The criticism was aimed at TDA, a joint venture between EADS and Thales. TDA produced munitions for mortars, and these could be considered cluster bombs. However, EADS successfully challenged this definition of cluster bombs. Currently, the official line is that EADS complies with the terms of the Ottawa Treaty. Although this has taken the sting out of the debate, it raises interesting moral questions, mainly because EADS does not operate in isolation. Almost a quarter of its shares are held by the French state. Daimler, the parent company of Mercedes, may have a smaller stake, but it holds over 25% of the voting rights. Fewer than 50% of the shares are held by the public. If we are to punish EADS by refusing to invest in its shares, at the very least we need to be consistent. Does this mean we should be able to fly to New York in an Airbus? Should our conscience bother us if we drive a Mercedes? Should we continue to go to France on holiday? How consistent are we, and how far does our outrage extend?

Similar dilemmas arose at a meeting of Chinese and Dutch bankers during the Shanghai World Expo in 2010. I gave a presentation on sustainability and presented a number of dilemmas, such as whether it was desirable to finance a company that is involved in large-scale illegal logging in the jungles of Borneo. The Dutch bankers were totally against this, while their Chinese colleagues could not see the problem. I then asked the Dutch bankers whether they would be willing to finance Chinese banks if they knew they funded companies involved in large-scale logging in Borneo. They said that they would. This once again raises the question of how far our outrage goes. Clearly, it is very hard to be consistent.

In the case of shareholders who invest passively, voting has another dimension. Votes in favour of motions indicate that the management can count on those shareholders' support. Shareholders who disagree with the company's policy will cast dissenting votes. These shareholders may turn their back on the business if there is no change in policy. By contrast, the hands of passive investors are tied. If they cast dissenting votes but the company continues to be included in the relevant index, their voting behaviour will not lead to the usual consequences (that is, their departure). The opposite situation can also happen. Shareholders who agree with the policy may still end up pulling out if the company is removed from the index.

Generally a situation such as this could be considered a technical flaw in a perfect capitalist system, but as most of the world's assets are invested passively it is a moral dilemma of major proportions. How much attention should the management of listed companies pay to the opinions of passive investors? These investors are not at all interested in their specific company, and their reasons for investing somewhere are based on incorrect considerations. Passive investors have lost influence, yet passive investing represents the majority of global investments.

Chapter 11

Professional dishonesty – the gap between seeing and knowing

Professionals are not allowed to cheat retail customers, but are no holds barred when professionals do business with each other? Is the game played fairly? What role does information play? Is seeing the same as knowing? Manipulating information to manipulate the market.

Steyning lies in the south of England, just half an hour's drive from the seaside resort of Brighton and a stone's throw from the Chanctonbury Ring. It is a tiny village, peacefully nestled in the South Downs, where things move at their own pace. It is at least a half a century behind the rest of the world. Wiston House is a beautiful country estate located just outside Steyning. The manor is listed as Wistaneutun in the Domesday Book, the record of all English lands drawn up in 1086 at the behest of William the Conqueror. The first house built there dates back to the 14th century. Part of the present-day Wiston House was built in 1577. The magnificent central hall has a wooden ceiling that suggests Norman influence. Wiston House has been used for the Wilton Park conferences since 1951. The conference organisation was set up in 1947 to promote peace in war-torn Europe by means of democracy and dialogue. The original idea came from Britain's wartime Prime Minister, Winston Churchill, who wanted to bring leaders together in a secluded setting to discuss the future. The first Wilton Park meetings were held in a stately home bearing that name, but the organisation relocated to Wiston House four years later. The setting, at the foot of the South Downs, has a very English feel to it. The long history and the snug, traditional ambiance are as English as the big ideas discussed at the conferences. After midnight there is something enigmatic about the stately home. Everything creaks and groans, and it is as if you have stepped into an Agatha Christie mystery.

Based on the Wilton Park model, around the start of the new millennium Paul Arlman, a colleague of mine at the stock exchange in Amsterdam, took the initiative to set up a conference for discussing international financial relations. Paul had previously worked at the World Bank, where he had met many diplomats who ended up in the financial industry, as regulators, exchange executives or lobbyists. He invited them to take part in private discussions of financial topics, primarily from a policy-maker's perspective. Wilton Park was prepared to organise an annual conference, which would naturally be held at Wiston House. I attended the conference for the eighth time in 2008. I had a special interest in this particular conference as I had been asked by the organisers to invite Hans Hogervoorst, the chairman of the management group of the Dutch regulator, the AFM, to give a speech at the dinner on the Friday evening. The attendance list was impressive, and included policy-makers from the US, the CEOs of major players, and compliance managers. The discussions were led by Jochen Sanio, the chairman of Bafin, the German regulator. The Wilton Park conferences are subject to the Chatham House Rule, which stipulates that participants cannot be quoted in publications and reports, not even years later. Since I am not prepared to break the code, you will have to do without juicy stories about tempers flaring as we discussed who had caused the crisis and who should have to foot the bill for it. However, I can share the most relevant discussion of the conference with you without breaking the code. It took place outside the protective walls of Wiston House. I landed at London Gatwick at around 10 o' clock on Friday morning and hoped to be at the conference in time for lunch. I got into the first available taxi and asked the driver to take me to Wiston House. When he heard the name he immediately asked whether I was attending a conference. I said I was, and he boldly asked what the conference was about. 'It's about international finance and regulation,' I replied. 'Oh...you're a banker,' he said, somewhat witheringly. 'No, I work for an asset manager,' I said. The taxi driver considered the two to be interchangeable, and I rose to the bait. 'They are not the same at all,' I argued. 'Bankers lend and receive money and...' I started to explain, but the driver interrupted me. 'Bankers are all thieves. They don't earn money, they steal it. The government ought to lock them all up and replace them. Banking can't be all that difficult.' I tried to dissuade him from this radical standpoint by saying that there are many kind and honest bankers who have done a great deal to keep the economy going and create wealth. But the driver remained unconvinced. 'Nonsense,' he said, 'they are all criminals. The government should nationalise the banks, just like the National Health Service. If bankers earn money then it can go to the Treasury and not... are you one the speakers at the conference?' I asked him why he wanted to know. 'You look like you are.' I tried to explain to the driver that I had helped arrange the evening's speaker, but would otherwise just be listening. I took the opportunity to switch to a less defensive tactic. 'If I had met you sooner I would have asked you to be the evening's speaker. You appear to have a very original view of the financial world, just the kind of fresh approach we could use.' After that the driver warmed to me, and as we continued talking we came up with some extreme and highly creative ideas for dealing with the crisis. The driver was so engrossed in our discussion that he missed the turnoff for Wiston House. Fortunately he knew an alternative route. In Steyning he took a sharp turn right into Mouse Lane, which brought us to the side entrance of Wiston House. Halfway down the dark, narrow lane stood a large stone with a plaque engraved with a poem by a local boy, John Stanley Purvis, who had served as a lieutenant in the First World War. The poem was written under a pseudonym, which is why it was assumed for a long time that this poem was all that had survived the war. However, Purvis returned from the front and, with the scars of war on his soul, lived a peaceful life in York, where he died in 1968. The beauty of his poem seems to be in sharp contrast to the immoral acts of the war, and this is what makes these lines so intriguing.

> I can't forget the lane that goes from Steyning to the Ring
> In summer time, and on the downs how larks and linnets sing

High in the sun. The winds come off the sea, and, oh, the air!
I never knew till now that life in old days was so fair.
But now I know it in this filthy rat-infested ditch,
Where every shell must kill or spare – and God alone knows which,
And I am made a beast of prey, and this trench is my lair.
My God, I never knew till now that those days were so fair
And we assault in half-an-hour, and it is a silly thing:
I can't forget the lane that goes from Steyning to the Ring.

Written by John Stanley Purvis (under the pseudonym Philip Johnson) 5th Battalion, Yorkshire Regiment, on 2 December 1915, in a trench near the Somme.

The driver dropped me off at the main entrance to Wiston House. 'Are you sure you wouldn't like to speak tonight?' I asked him as I got out. He laughed but he did not answer my question. 'I hope you have a good meeting, sir, and that you solve the problems once and for all.' He handed me my luggage and drove away. My talk with the driver had been very educational because it gave me a better idea of what the man in the street thought of the crisis and of how, wrongly or rightly, bankers had fallen out of favour. On Friday and Saturday we held highly professional discussions in Wiston House. In spite of the realistic nature of the conclusions drawn by the professionals, none of us suspected that we were on the brink of a much more serious systemic crisis. The worst was yet to come. The damage had already been done; we were simply at that time in the incubation period, waiting for the final catastrophic blow. We did not see it coming. Nor at that point did any of the regulators. It took everyone by surprise – the retail investors and the professionals, the bankers and the regulators. The latter were shocked that professionals had cheated one another on such a large scale. Given this, an important moral question concerns whether professional parties also require protection if they are active on the financial markets. Or does anything go? Are professionals allowed to cheat one another, or are there limits to this kind of improper behaviour? Do we really live in a civilised world, or in the state of nature as described by Hobbes: nasty, brutish and short? Years later I came to the shameful conclusion that the taxi driver's judgment was better than the combined wisdom of the regulators attending the meeting, and that the most educational moment had been before rather than during the conference. So conferences can sometimes be useful after all.

The financial sector, like many other sectors of society, is a place where individuals take actions that are primarily for their own benefit. Sometimes it is a game, sometimes a competition, but all too often it is a war. And because it is all about winning, there is an obvious similarity to sports. If you look at retail investors, the financial game that is played can best be compared to golf. Not everyone plays the game equally well, but that is not a problem. The handicap system ensures that everyone has an equal chance of winning, in other words differences in skill are equalised. In a certain sense this is also what happens when retail investors become active on the financial markets. The difference in knowledge and expertise is compensated for by an agent who represents the interests of the retail investor, so everyone is equal. But what happens between professional parties? Do the same rules apply? If no allowances are made for differences in skill, the less capable professional is likely to have a difficult time. That, however, is the essence of the capitalist system. It is the same as in football: a team that loses too often will be relegated. It is a hard game. The successful coach Rinus Michaels, who led Ajax to glory, was right to say that football is war. But does that mean that everything is permissible? Is everything subordinate to the professional's desire to achieve better results?

Let us take the comparison with football a step further. The French international footballer, Thierry Henry was not in top form during a decisive match against Ireland, in which the two teams were competing for a place in the 2010 World Cup finals in South Africa. In fact, the entire French team was playing badly and the former world champions were in trouble. Surely *Les Bleus* were not going to be knocked out of the competition in the qualifying round? No, but the decisive goal was scored following a handball by Henry. He moved the ball with his hand, and this enabled a teammate to score. Since neither the referee nor the linesman saw it, the goal was allowed. Ireland was knocked out of the competition and felt sorely aggrieved. Emotions ran high, and not only within the sport. The incident was even discussed during a meeting between the French and Irish prime ministers. Henry knew full well that he had handled the ball, just as Maradona had done during the World Cup in Mexico in 1986. Was the outcome of the game fraudulent? Neither Henry nor Maradona was ever tried for fraud. No one expected either of them to go over to the linesman and own up to the handball. Apparently the players' consciences were untroubled. This raises a crucial moral question. In the professional world, is it permissible to violate the interest of others, provided that the regulator does not see it? In other words, does the eye of the regulator determine the boundary?

In 2006 the German bank IKB bought US$150 million of bonds using CDOs from Goldman Sachs (Abacus 2007-AC1) as collateral. Within less than a month the bonds began to lose value, rapidly and unexpectedly. This was one of the reasons why IKB got into serious trouble in the summer of 2007. Its losses rose to €8.5 billion and the bank had to be bailed out by KFW, one of its shareholders. In 2010 the SEC took action against Goldman Sachs, accusing it of deliberately misleading its clients. The evidence included e-mails from Fabrice Tourre, a Frenchman who was responsible for developing the Abacus products at Goldman Sachs. Tourre, also known as Fabulous Fab, described the products in his e-mails as 'monstrosities'. The Abacus CDOs were made up of mortgages selected for Goldman Sachs by the hedge fund Paulson & Co. The hedge fund was not only involved in compiling the underlying mortgages, it also traded them. Paulson & Co wanted to earn money by going short, in other words by speculating on a decline in the value of the Abacus CDOs. This provided a major reason to ensure the quality of the product was geared to that specific purpose. It now seems probable that John Paulson, the founder of Paulson & Co., selected the mortgage loans for the Abacus portfolio on the basis of the likelihood of default. And it is precisely that information that future investors in Abacus failed to receive. It was withheld from IKB, as well as from ACA Capital Holding (ACA), the insurer that provided the protection for Abacus and took a large chunk of the issue on to its own books. One of ACA's shareholders was a private equity division of Bear Stearns, and so the deadly circle was almost complete.

Within a month the Abacus CDO lost 85% of its value. Goldman Sachs defended its actions in several ways. It claimed the timing was unfortunate. IKB had purchased the CDO just when – as it later transpired – the market was about to collapse. However, IKB's

CDO fell much more quickly than the market, and in the end it produced a much greater loss. The Abacus portfolio contained a relatively high number of mortgages from what the Americans call the sand states: California, Florida and Nevada. The housing market was in much worse shape in these states than in other parts of the country. During a hearing before the US senate, Lloyd Blankfein, the CEO of Goldman Sachs, offered two arguments as a defence. The first was that in his view the professional market is a world in which the parties know exactly what they are getting into. They do not need to take each other by the hand. Blankfein's second argument was based on a comparison with the money and currency markets. Goldman Sachs had indeed gone short, but rather than speculating it had been hedging existing positions. Who would deny Goldman Sachs that right? In 2010 and 2011, other similar practices were made public as a result of measures taken by various regulators and liability suits lodged by victims. JPMorgan was accused of providing misleading information at the time of the issue of a mortgage-based CDO. This product was put together by the American hedge fund Magnetar, which, like Paulson & Co, had gone short. Magnetar had also been instrumental in selecting the mortgages included in the CDO. JPMorgan eventually settled for nearly US$154 million with the complainants, which included the pension fund of General Motors. In Great Britain, the national regulator, the FSA, took measures against UBS because of products produced in a similar corrupt manner.

Do the arguments that Blankfein put forward as a defence have any moral substance? Can we assume that everyone in the professional world does their homework? Was Goldman Sachs' behaviour justifiable because they were hedging positions instead of speculating? Is there a moral difference between the two? Let us start with Blankfein's second argument. In comparison with its competitors, Goldman Sachs was a late starter when it came to creating CDOs. The bank did not build up its own position in these loans until after 2005. But Goldman Sachs was one of the first to realise that things would go terribly wrong with these products. Once they had that insight, the bank's only option was to turn all of its own positions around by executing opposite transactions on a massive scale. All actions up to this point were permissible. But when a party selects innocent, unsuspecting customers for these transactions, this constitutes a serious transgression of a moral boundary. Speculation involves making a profit at the expense of the profession. This case involved risk avoidance at the expense of customers, and there is little difference between the two. So the argument put forward by Blankfein does not hold water. His other justification was that professionals are all big boys who do not require protection. That sounds Darwinian: the strong survive while the weak do not. How much truth is there in this argument? The comparison with currencies does not hold, because currencies are a standard financial product and familiar to everyone, whereas his CDO was secretly flawed. This touches on the key concept of morality in the financial world. Although parties such as IKB and the General Motors pension fund are professionals, they are not in the same category as Goldman Sachs. They remain customers, not counterparties. But even if they were, and the parties are declared absolutely equal on the basis of objective criteria, it is impossible to avoid the conclusion that Goldman Sachs acted amorally. The SEC ruled that professional clients also have the right to the truth, and that parties cannot hide behind behaviour that involves the deliberate circulation of false information for the purposes of personal gain. In 2012, Goldman Sachs became embroiled in controversy again, this time as a result of a letter written by Greg Smith, a mid-level manager who had worked at Goldman Sachs' equity derivatives arm for 12 years. The letter was published in *The New York Times*. Smith felt he could no longer remain silent about the toxic culture in which the customers – professional counterparties – were given the lowest priority. Customers were still being cheated and milked in order to achieve maximum profits. Smith saw e-mails from some of Goldman's managing directors referring to their customers as 'muppets'. The letter was proof that Goldman Sachs had learned nothing from the crisis of 2008; in fact the situation had only got worse. The monster was still on the rampage.

We may have to take into account the cultural difference between Anglo-Saxon customs and practices in continental Europe. Both the US and the UK have a strong tradition of *caveat emptor*: buyer beware. The mentality in continental Europe leans more towards acting transparently and in good faith. A seller of products that withholds information about their negative aspects is more likely to be held liable and charged with fraud. And this brings us back to Thierry Henry and his handball.

Deliberately withholding information which could later result in considerable damage being done to the counterparty is considered fraudulent behaviour, not evidence one is smarter than the other party. Henry should have gone to the linesman and told him that he had handled the ball, and that the protests of the Irish were justified. Of course, that never happens in football. Not being seen by the referee is to the guilty party's gain. And not being seen was to Goldman Sachs' gain. And yet, this argument is troubling. Goldman Sachs did not act in good faith, and it withheld information that was crucial to the investment decision. You might call it a fixed game. It goes straight to the heart of professional credibility, and to the heart of professional decency: it is pure fraud. In my view, there are times when parties in the professional arena need to sacrifice their own interests in the name of fair play, even if the referee is not paying attention.

Another example of how professional parties can abuse their position is Libya. The Libyan investment Authority (LIA) was founded in 2007 by Saif al-Islam, the second son of Muammar Gaddafi. It was given start-up capital of US$65 billion, and positioned itself as an extremely professional player, employing the brightest and best talent in the country and active in the top category of sovereign wealth funds. Any banker would be keen to do business with a party like this, but only a handful got the chance. The hall of the LIA's spacious offices in the centre of Tripoli was invariably full of waiting bankers. They soon learned that it was better to stay away until they were invited. The LIA was no ordinary investor, and it showed considerable interest in alternative investment products. That made sense because only bankers who had an exceptional case to make were admitted to the boardroom. This also meant that the investments often involved exceptional products. In September 2010, the LIA had almost US$7 billion invested in alternative products. The remarkable thing was that those products came in through the back entrance instead of through the front door. Some of the money was outsourced to hedge fund managers who had ties to the Libyan elite. For example, US$300 million dollars went to Palladyne Asset Management, a hedge fund manager which knew very few of the players in the global financial markets. One of Palladyne's directors is Ismail Abudher, the son-in-law of the former chairman of the Libyan state-owned oil company, NOC. At the time of the LIA investments, Palladyne was operating at a substantial loss. It later emerged that 70% of the loss was attributable to exorbitant fees. The fund was also being plundered from the outside.

International financial institutions hired agents to secure an introduction to the LIA. The fund's real business was conducted with parties who had sneaked in through the servants' entrance. Société Générale, for example, did a deal with Leinada, an offshore entity based in Panama, which arranged a US$1 billion mandate from the LIA for the bank. The French bank paid the introductory-fee for the transaction directly to Leinada, a company owned by Walid al-Giahmi, a businessman and childhood friend of Saif al-Islam, the most high-profile of Gaddafi's sons. And the investment mandate from LIA came with higher fees so that the introductory-fee paid by the bank was well covered. With so many conflicts of interest at play it is not surprising that the transactions were seldom intended to achieve a good investment return for the fund. The fees the LIA had to pay were too high, there were too many parties with a finger in the pie, and those involved were too greedy. In 2010, KPMG issued a harsh judgment: the company was in serious trouble and unable to implement its own ambitious investment strategy. This is another case of an ostensibly professional party being reduced to ruins by internal corruption and the willingness of major, internationally respected financial institutions to take advantage of the situation. And again, we need to ask ourselves whether the relevant international institutions should not have intervened and challenged the corruption. Or perhaps it is acceptable to get caught up in the moment even if you think the game is not being played by the rules?

I have described two instances of abuse by professional parties, but there are many more. We can conclude that a transaction between strictly professional parties – even if they call each other customers, or in the case of Goldman Sachs, 'muppets' – is not by definition fair and honest. Private investors are not the only ones who are deceived; it happens to professional parties as well.

The examples above show that, without the help of a third party, professional counter-parties are often unable to conclude transactions whose outcomes are equally satisfactory to all of the parties concerned. The complex financial world affords too many opportunities for a distorted outcome in which one party takes advantage of the weaknesses of another. There is trickery and deceit, and the betrayal of confidence, because monetary gain makes up for trust. These situations usually involve fraud and misinformation, and sometimes the payment of bribes to corrupt officials who subsequently take poor decisions on the company's behalf in return for money. In some cases, market manipulation and insider trading are also involved. These are all methods used to secure monetary gain at the expense of third parties, or the entire financial community. Information is a very important instrument in this game. It can be presented selectively or incorrectly, it can be withheld altogether or it can be distorted beyond recognition.

It is worth taking a closer look at some of these practices to analyse them. I will draw comparisons with the non-financial world to determine whether the mores of the financial world really are different. I will start with another comparison with football. One important tactic that nearly every football player uses is the feint, sometimes in combination with a bit of intimidation aimed at wrong-footing their opponent. It is interesting to observe how mastering this skill can turn a good player into a star player. It gets the supporters up on their feet, and makes them wildly enthusiastic. The same happens in other sports such as basketball and rugby. The feint serves the same purpose as misinformation, misleading one party and benefiting the other. The equivalent of the feint in the financial world is market manipulation, and it is strictly forbidden. Let us take a closer look at market manipulation and insider trading. Market parties trade on the basis of information. It may be general information that affects price formation in the financial assets being invested in or traded. But it may also be specific market information which, if it were available to the general public, would have such an impact on the supply of or demand for the assets that it would change the price. In fact, supply and demand do not even have to change because perception alone may be enough to cause the price to fluctuate. Information is money, and that makes it the most important instrument of manipulation and abuse in financial world, and perhaps in the rest of the world as well. I noted earlier that equal opportunities for all market participants and the perception of fairness are crucial for trust. This raises the concept of honesty again. A casino where you are allowed to bet but where the chances of winning are skewed will eventually lose its clients' trust. As will a casino that gives all the prizes to a small group of insiders. Trust is crucial for the continued existence of the casino, and the financial world is no different. Giving one party information that is price sensitive (that is, money) is tantamount to giving them the opportunity to rob the uninformed party. A market which allows that to happen is corrupt, as are the professionals who take advantage of the situation. Yet it happens every day, and it always has. In the 1970s, Lloyds of London, the market for underwriting insurance risk, was involved in a major scandal. Rich, and sometimes not so rich, private individuals participated in syndicates that shared insurance risk. The participants were known as names. But there were insiders and outsiders; some participants had more information than others. In the 1980s, the outside names were sometimes literally recruited on the golf course. Then the losses started to mount, partly due to claims related to asbestos and environmental pollution. The outsiders suffered the heaviest losses, and many of them were forced into bankruptcy. Some golf clubs were disproportionately affected and their membership was decimated. Many insiders were a little bit more aware of the risk and had invested proportionately more in the better syndicates. It became painfully obvious that Lloyds' processes were corrupt to the core, and trust in the organisation evaporated. Lloyds was doomed to extinction unless it could it could restore trust in its honesty. Have wisdom and experience now liberated us from this type of behaviour? In 2012, more than 10 regulators instituted investigations into the manipulation of interbank settlement prices, Libor, Euribor and Tibor. These are the rates fixed every day for interbank deposits in pounds sterling, euros and Japanese yen, on the basis of which interest is settled – interest settlements involving billions in interbank balances. There is a suspicion that in 2007 and 2008 the banks allowed their own business interests to prevail over the accuracy of the benchmark. Insiders are thought to have kept rates artificially low to mask their own financing problems. Barclays became the prime example of unethical behaviour, to widespread scorn. In response, chairman Marcus Agius resigned on Monday 2 July 2012, and his departure was swiftly followed by that of CEO Bob Diamond. Public anger was unprecedented. But why was this? After all, Barclays had only tampered with a settlement price. Why was it such a big deal? The fact is that the settlement price is so widely used that a systematic deviation of just one basis point over a three month period represents a wealth transfer of huge proportions. In this case, manipulation took place over a period of years, not three months, and the rate deviated by much more than one basis point. Even if the motives that drove the behaviour were, in a sense, understandable, since the manipulation was aimed at protecting the public image of Barclays during the financial crisis, in its naked form it represents theft. And as in the case of Lloyds of London, the matter destroyed trust, this time in the Libor, Euribor and Tibor mechanism. The guardian of the Libor concept, the British Bankers' Association (BBA), was taken off the case. The FSA, under the leadership of Martin Wheatley, was given the mandate to repair the broken system. And there are many more opportunities for manipulation of the market and insider trading.

A second example relates to derivative products. Derivative contracts end in one of two ways. The first method involves the physical delivery of the underlying value after the contract expires. The other method, contract for difference (CFD), is based on settlement of the difference in the price of the derivative and the price of the physical product. The price difference is settled in cash on the basis of an objectively calculated price for the product underlying the derivative. The best example of this is a futures contract on a share index. The owner of the derivative does not receive a basket of shares. Instead, the difference between the price of the derivative contract and the value of the index is settled when the contract expires. Like Libor, share indices are so widely used that every basis point deviation from the actual settlement price represents a substantial sum of money. This provides market participants holding significant sway in the market with a motive for acting dishonestly. And just as in the case of Libor, manipulating the settlement price only slightly can generate considerable income yet go undetected for a long time. The risk of price manipulation is inherent to all derivative contracts which are settled in cash. The less liquid the market is in the derivative's underlying financial instrument, the easier it is to manipulate.

A very special form of market abuse involves the use of price-sensitive information that is not widely available in the market. Insider trading is against the law. The most famous example of insider trading, which also bears a strong semblance to market manipulation, one that has now taken on mythical proportions, relates to the history of the Rothschild family. The influential Nathan Rothschild was one of the first to hear that the British had defeated Napoleon at the battle of Waterloo. He had this information long before the public did, and he decided to use it to his advantage. He spread the rumour that Napoleon had won. The English stock market plummeted and Rothschild bought up large quantities of shares. When the news broke of the real outcome of the battle, he sold his shares at a huge profit. That is the story anyway; there is no proof it actually happened. It does, however, indicate how important the age-old game of insider trading can be. It is still true today, even though the way in which we view the use of price-sensitive information has changed considerably over the years. Practices that were once entirely acceptable are now considered a crime. Price sensitive information has to be released simultaneously and not selectively. Oddly enough, the practice of selectively disclosing information lasted the longest in the world's biggest capital market, the US. Arthur Levitt, a former chairman of the SEC, discussed this in detail in his book *Take on the Street* (2002). After long discussions, and an equally long period spent formulating and reformulating, the SEC adopted the Fair Disclosure (FD) rule in the summer of 2000. Levitt recounts how just before the vote he received a note from Hank Paulson, the CEO of Goldman Sachs, who was travelling in China at the time. Levitt was not as surprised by the timing of the note as by its contents: *'I strongly urge you to vote no.'*

Until then, selective disclosure was common practice. Companies were allowed to disclose information at their own discretion, even if the information was price sensitive, and they often did so. The disclosure of important information was frequently preceded by a price movement, simply because the information had been distributed selectively. That made the investment adviser's job a lot easier, but it also resulted in great injustice. The selective disclosure of information could be used to buy favours. Companies listed on the public market were primarily interested in the favours of analysts. Favourable reports about the company in question were traded for inside information. The analysts were able to earn money on the side by taking positions themselves, and they were able to satisfy their big clients with almost certain profits earned on the strength of tip-offs (they called it advice). There was a rule covering insider trading, but it stated that the SEC had to prove the insider had used the information for personal gain. The burden of proof was so great it created a grey area in which the parties basically went their merry way. The new FD rule was meant to put an end to such practices. Analysts were to become analysts again instead of traders of inside knowledge. The FD rule unleashed a frenzy of lobbying. Drastic changes were made to the rules governing how companies in the US are required to handle price-sensitive information. Of course, technology played an important role in this. Information now travels around the globe so quickly that the difference between selective and full disclosure is barely visible. We now talk about information provided a few milliseconds in advance, rather than a few hours.

Which price-sensitive information is included in the ban on selective disclosure? The concept may vary slightly from one jurisdiction to another, but in general it refers to information about a traded security which is not available to the public, and the disclosure of which could bring about a price change. That definition includes the concept of expectation. We cannot know whether the new information will cause prices to change unless we know what the market expects. When a company announces that its profit will be the same as in the previous year, the market might have had such high profit expectations that its share price actually falls when the announcement is made. In other words, an unchanged profit forecast can be price sensitive. Companies must therefore be extremely careful about commenting on their expectations. It may not be the company's management who is expressing an expectation; analysts and journalists can also spread this information. Price-sensitive information does not have to originate with the company. The planning of a hostile takeover takes place in the enemy camp. The decision to arrest the CEO of a company is taken by the public prosecutor. Even the comments of meteorologists can be price sensitive. In October 2011, British weather experts predicted a very cold winter. Energy prices rose in response and that had consequences for the prices of certain shares. In short, anyone participating in social and economic life in the broadest sense can be the source of price-sensitive information, and if they use that information they may be committing a crime. Analysts are a particularly vulnerable group. It is their job to translate analyses into insights, and then into investment advice using only information that is available to the public. But during this process public information becomes private information, and it is therefore potentially price sensitive. How should such information be treated? Should analysts be allowed to use it? Some people think they should. They believe that conclusions reached by means of the clever analysis of public information should not be included in the ban on selective disclosure. The fact that some analysts are better than others is due to their personal skills, and it should be possible to use these skills as long as the public has access to the source of the information. This argument does not apply if the analyst has created market power on the basis of earlier advice and statements. That kind of power should be exercised with extreme caution.

In 2009 there was a scare in the US involving the hedge fund Galleon, which had everything to do with insider trading. It is an interesting case because many hedge funds face similar problems, and it illustrates the difference between selective disclosure and full disclosure. Galleon was set up by Raj Rajaratnam (1957), an immigrant who embodied the American dream. Born in Sri Lanka, he built up an enormous fortune as a self-made man. He began his career on Wall Street as a specialist in semi-conductors. Rajaratnam set up his hedge fund in 1997, and by October 2009, when he was arrested by the FBI, he was managing assets valued at over US$9 billion. During his time on Wall Street, Rajaratnam formed valuable relationships with consultants and advisers, and with the senior executives of listed companies. His most famous connection was Rajat Gupta, a former partner at McKinsey and a board member at Goldman Sachs. On 23 October 2008, Gupta heard during a board meeting that Goldman Sachs was about to announce its first quarterly loss since its IPO. Gupta called Raj Rajaratnam precisely 23 seconds after the meeting adjourned. The next morning Rajaratnam sold 120,000 shares in Goldman Sachs. We have no record of what was said in that telephone conversation, but subsequent phone taps revealed many more instances of the abuse of price-sensitive information. Confidential information about company results and takeover plans were systematically passed on to Rajaratnam. He amassed over US$72 million thanks to this inside information. That money was taken out of the market and stolen from a large number of anonymous investors. There was no fair play in this casino. Rajaratnam paid a high price for his crimes. He was sentenced to eleven years in prison (one of the longest sentences ever imposed for this type of crime) and fined US$92.8 billion. Things certainly have changed.

However, market abuse is viewed differently in other markets around the world, and the punishable act is interpreted differently as well. Investigative methods and sentences also tend to vary. In the US it is assumed that an act is unlawful if it is based on information which not only has the potential to influence the market, but was also acquired or leaked in spite of an express obligation to respect the confidentiality of that information. European legislation, which perhaps takes its lead from the UK, places much more emphasis on the investors' obligation not to act on any price-sensitive information they may have received. In the US, abuse is a very narrowly defined concept, and infringement of the confidentiality requirement is regarded as a violation of the rules. In Europe there is more concern about avoiding any semblance of an infringement, and semblance is a much broader concept than the simple fact of a rule violation. The American hedge fund manager David Einhorn, CEO of Greenlight Capital, found this out the hard way. Einhorn is a very successful manager who likes to be photographed with his baseball cap on back to front like a rapper, or perhaps more like Nick Leeson when he was arrested. The FSA fined Einhorn £7.2 million for insider trading. What had happened? Greenlight Capital had a large holding in Punch Taverns, a company operating a chain of pubs. In a telephone conversation with his broker Andrew Osborne, Einhorn learned that there was good chance that Punch Taverns would have to announce a new, substantial share issue within a week. Einhorn asked for, and received, additional information. On the tape of the conversation subsequently released by the FSA, Einhorn said, 'Wow that would be shockingly horrifying.' The management of Punch told Einhorn that if he wanted more information he would have to sign a nondisclosure agreement. Hoping to preserve his freedom, he declined. In the following days, Einhorn sold 12 million shares, reducing his holding from 13.3% to 9%. When the news of the share issue became public, the share price fell by 29%. Einhorn swore blind that he had acted in accordance with the rules because he had very explicitly asked not to be dragged over the Chinese Wall. In his opinion, his actions would not have been punishable in the US. His defence was that he was apparently insufficiently aware of the rules in the UK.

Price-sensitive information is not limited to information that influences investors' opinions about the value of a company that issues shares. It may also be information that is entirely market-related. A very sizeable transaction being presented to the market all at once will influence the market price. It is therefore profitable to do some active trading in the market in anticipation of that transaction. The practice of buying and selling securities on the basis of prior knowledge of a large transaction is called front-running. This type of market abuse is banned, but anticipating future supply and demand can take many forms. An analyst who adjusts his evaluation of a company can cause a surge in buying or selling. In effect, anticipating an adjustment in that evaluation is also a form of front-running prior to the publication of news. All of the examples given here amount to abusing information that is not publicly available. And because information can influence the price of financial assets, manipulation is profitable. That makes information a powerful instrument, and misinformation a significant source of systemic risk. Failing to provide proper information is essentially an ethical matter, particularly if it is done deliberately in order to influence the behaviour of other market parties. The source of the 2007 banking crisis was the failure to provide investors with solid information about the quality of the securities they were being offered. Many investors thought that securities with an AAA rating were a sure thing and did not need to be re-evaluated. But misinformation can go beyond even this. Greece wormed its way into the single European currency on the basis of financial information, which may have looked all right on the surface but was intrinsically flawed. Goldman Sachs played a crucial role in this affair by helping Greece to meet the admission criteria. Misinformation subsequently created a smoke screen that obscured the real state of Greek finances for a very long time. Facts and figures are not the only things that can influence prices. Wars are lost and won on the basis of information and how it is manipulated. Have we finally arrived at the source of all evil, and therefore the beginnings of a solution?

Let us return to one of the themes of this chapter, specifically seeing and knowing. Once again it took place at a meeting. In the spring of 2011, I attended a conference in Florida organised by ISEEE, a group of former exchange CEOs who meet once a year. I had been asked to speak, and I was looking forward to the opportunity to catch up with old acquaintances I had not seen for years. One of the other speakers was Harvey Pitt. He was Arthur Levitt's successor at the SEC, but the dotcom crisis in 2000 was his downfall. Naturally, his presentation touched on the 2008 banking crisis. Pitt's analysis was clear and simple. According to him, the problem arose because 'we lacked the data'. He implied that if we had had more information it would not have happened. I was astonished by this explanation, but it resonated with Greenspan's own arguments. Chapter 10 dealt in detail with Michael Burry, the man who combed through all of the available documentation on the CDOs he had invested in. He knew what was happening because he looked for the facts, and he looked for facts because he grew suspicious of what he saw and what everyone else could see. I surmise that he would heartily disagree with Pitt. We knew, but we refused to see. And our refusal to see consisted of a moral failing. We assumed everything was all right, and that is what we chose to believe. Information is essential of course, but Pitt's explanation ignores the fact that people will always hide their sins. We have to seek out the genuine facts as they will not be presented to us in an official book full on statistics. It is a reflexive process; manipulation is used to colour the truth and to alter it. Seeing involves reinterpreting the altered truth, while knowing involves letting the results of that transition sink in and facing up to the consequences. Goldman Sachs gave Greece a shaky leg up into the eurozone, but even without their help Greece would have been admitted. Instinctively, we knew back then that Greece was not ready. Government leaders were aware of the situation, but they did not think it was relevant, and certainly not a deal breaker. Greece was to be given the opportunity to continue developing within the eurozone. Looking the other way when the information is not to our liking is an all too human form of variant behaviour. So better information is not the answer to a lack of information or incorrect information. The real problem is that information is a tool, not an end in itself; the real problem is the failure of many, including the German bank IKB, to see information as an instrument used in the quest for personal gain. Thierry Henry used the lack of information about his handball to influence the outcome of the game. Incorrect information was at the heart of the CDO fiasco at Goldman Sachs and the decision to admit Greece to the euro. Such information is, however, provided by people, members of society and the financial system, with a view to defending, protecting and justifying the interests of a group. They defend the indefensible. The purpose of ethics is to cut through this smoke screen in order to make the right judgments.

In January 2008, John Bird and John Fortune, better known as the Long Johns, gave a comic interview on ITV's *South Bank Show*. In just three minutes they gave a concise, humorous exposé of the problems surrounding structured products and the entire sub-prime mortgage crisis. It is very funny and revealing, but above all it is true. The interview is one of the most popular videos on YouTube. The broadcast did not stop the practices it described. If a couple of British comedians can dissect the situation so accurately, then the fact that the regulators did not know what was happening had little to do with lack of information, and everything to do with how information is interpreted. The sketch appeared two months after the Wilton Park conference at Wiston House. Those attending the conference also had insufficient information, but if they had read between the lines they would have realised what was going on. Apparently the taxi driver was more attuned to reality than they were.

I would like to end with an anecdote befitting a chapter dealing with misinformation and manipulative misuse. Reality is misrepresented every day, and many of those lies end up being immortalised as history. He who wields the pen controls the truth, and the victors write history. That is what happened in Fremantle, a port just south of the Australian city of Perth. There is a beautiful park near the old harbour, where the residents go during their lunch hour to walk or escape the heat. There is an attractive but misunderstood statue in the middle of the park. It is a statue of a man with a sturdy, invincible air about him, recognisable from a distance as one of Australia's first colonists. The text at the base of the statue explains why he deserved this monument. According to the plaque he led a group of men who after a brief but fierce battle, defeated 'bandits' who had been spreading death and destruction. This is exactly the kind of courage and strength that merits a statue. However, a second plaque has been placed under the first, with the following text:

> This plaque was erected by people who found the monument before you offensive. The monument described the events at La Grange from one perspective only; the viewpoint of the white 'settlers'. No mention is made of the right of aboriginal people to defend their land or of the history of provocation which led to the explorers' deaths. The 'punitive party' mentioned here ended in the deaths of somewhere around twenty aboriginal people. The whites were well-armed and equipped and none of their party was killed or wounded. This plaque is in memory of the aboriginal people killed at La Grange. It also commemorates all other aboriginal people who died during the invasion of their country.
>
> Lest we forget.

Clearly not all of the 'bandits' were wiped out.

Chapter 12

The lady with the soft voice

How do stock markets work and how have they developed over the years? How honest and transparent are they? Which of today's ongoing debates affect the morality of these markets?

Events in the securities markets are the subject of both media and public debate. The focus of these discussions is on the continuous changes in and evolution of the capital markets. This chapter describes some of the changes of the past few decades, and provides insight into the issues at play, many of which have a strong moral component. The timeline of my narrative is random, and starts with the year 2002, when discussions arose about the need to harmonise the rules in Europe that govern securities transactions in public markets as part of MiFID. This debate focused primarily on the possible abolition of the concentration rule requiring investment companies to route all their orders through the stock exchange. The US and most European countries, including France, Italy and the Netherlands, had such a rule. There was no concentration rule in the UK, where investors had long been allowed to trade outside of the exchange. It was also claimed that abolishing the rule would create more competition for the exchanges. The Federation of European Stock Exchanges (FESE) opposed abolition. In an open letter to Frits Bolkestein, who was at the time the European Commissioner for Internal Markets, it argued in favour of the preservation of the last separation of functions in the financial markets. The letter, entitled 'Horses for Courses', also contained a plea for the actors in the capital markets to stick to their roles, to challenge the unlevel playing field resulting from actors exercising more than one capacity, and to preserve the system of complete transparency in the execution of securities transactions. The FESE also stood up for what it regarded as the most important value of the public market: equal access for everyone.

A war broke out over the contents of the letter, but it was a war conducted away from the public eye. The major banks and integrated brokerage companies were well aware of the historical opportunity to change course and they took advantage of it. The exchange operators looked on in dismay at the erosion of their franchise; they had no opportunity to put on a different hat and play another role. The matter was hotly debated in the press, and even more hotly among the parties concerned. Discussions raged in European capitals, particularly in London, and in Brussels lobbyists on both sides of the argument were dispatched to win over policy-makers. Bolkestein later admitted he had never seen such an enormous effort to influence policy-making. There were huge interests at stake, and those concerned evidently had the means to defend them at all costs. The battle for the structure of the markets was in full swing. The main players were the big banks, integrated brokers, smaller brokers, exchange operators and professional traders, to the exclusion of retail investors. The prize was preferential access regarding the execution of orders for customers.

The second event I would like to describe is one that is representative of the debate. There are hundreds of other comparable incidents that could be included but this particular incident took place in January 2011. That was when the US regulator, the SEC, announced it had imposed a US$10 million fine on Merrill Lynch, one of the world's biggest brokerage companies. Merrill Lynch was fined because it had done nothing to stop improper practices surrounding the execution of customer orders in the period between 2002 and 2007. What had happened? Merrill Lynch's professional traders and those responsible for filling customer orders had their offices on the same floor. Text messages were used to circumvent the last vestiges of the crumbling Chinese Wall set up to prevent such practices. They passed information to one another, fixed prices, manipulated and traded entirely in their own interests. Merrill Lynch failed to intervene, and as is so often the case, the customers were the victims. The SEC took stringent measures.

A little later, in the spring of 2011, the exchange giants Deutsche Börse and NYSE Euronext announced merger plans. It was implied that the reason for the merger was their vulnerability in the face of the growing number of transactions conducted away from the exchange using multilateral trading facilities (MTFs), opaque trading platforms (dark pools) and internal order matching systems at brokers and major banks. Deutsche Börse and NYSE Euronext wanted to reinstate the silo structure, giving them greater influence over the settlement of securities transactions. That was a remarkable standpoint, particularly for Euronext. Earlier in the century, under pressure from the major banks and brokers, the exchange operator had agreed to dilute its holding in LCH Clearnet, an important player in the settlement of securities transactions. The wishes of Deutsche Börse and NYSE Euronext would not be fulfilled. In February 2012 the European Commission announced that it would not approve the merger. It would, according to Brussels, leave too little competition in the market.

At first glance this impression of the public stock market may seem straightforward, but these developments are part of a highly complex world. It is the world of big money, big interests, power, personal ambition, dirty tricks and intrigue. It is a fascinating world where innovation often gets the better of the establishment. Make no mistake: there is a great deal at stake here. What makes this world so difficult to comprehend? To begin with, the term 'financial markets' is fairly abstract. The abstraction challenges the imagination of every policy-maker and gives market players plenty of scope for creating confusion. If you ask a trader what he is doing you will get an incomprehensible answer. Sometimes the smokescreen he throws up is a deliberate tactical move. But usually the trader cannot understand the big picture himself. He is just doing his thing. The players in the financial markets are often guilty of inconsistent thinking, and policy-makers clearly have a hard time interpreting all of the abstract terms. As a result, the public becomes entangled in fuzzy, poorly formulated concepts. Add to this the fact the regulators tend to cling to principles, which in reality are difficult to enforce, such as 'best order execution' and 'fair treatment of customers'. When courts are asked to pass judgment on conflicts, they avoid questions of substance and take refuge in procedures. That is why the financial world continues to be a source of strife and conflict. The parties are courteous in their dealings with the outside world, but it is all a show. In the harsh reality of the almost invisible side of this world, they are at each other's throats.

To understand how the game is played in the financial public market, and why it is played in this manner, we need to examine the structure of the market and the development of that structure over the years. There are many misunderstandings about this, which is why I want to make the abstract more concrete by telling the stories of some of the people who symbolise the development of the financial markets. I will also discuss one of the most important questions in the market: the professional traders' eternal quest for public orders. The similarity to foxes is striking. Just like professional traders, foxes are only interested in their prey, in this case the public orders of retail customers. Naturally they also want to trade with one another, just as foxes like to play with one another, but only as a means of rebalancing their positions and hedging their risks. Customer orders are their real food. When food is scarce, foxes encroach on residential areas and they become bolder. Some come right into their customers' gardens and lift the lids off dustbins seeking something to assuage their hunger. The tug of war in the financial markets masks moral dilemmas. It is important to identify these dilemmas and understand the compromises and sacrifices they entail. I will start with a brief explanation of how the market works, and how it has developed over the years.

Financial markets exist by the grace of the supply of and demand for financial assets. Those who have a surplus of assets make them available to parties who need them in order carry out certain social or economic duties. If those assets are available for a longer period of time, they are referred to as capital. People who lend money expect to get something in return, such as interest or dividend. Loans are not forever; the lender will eventually want the money back. Agreements about compensation and repayment help determine a loan's risk-return profile. The rights are legally structured as the standardised conditions that we know as securities, which include shares, bonds, options and warrants. The time when a provider of capital wants its money back does not always coincide with when the user of that capital has access to other funds that are released by means of free cash flow or disposals. The difference in availability is particularly visible in the case of shares. For the recipient (the company) this form of capital provision is permanent, with the exception of share buybacks, while the capital provider goes his merry way, hoping for an increase in the value of the investment or a nice dividend. The provider assumes he can get the capital back whenever he wants. He eventually plans to buy a bigger house, pay off the mortgage and save for his retirement, and that will require liquid assets. For him, capital provision is not permanent. That becomes even clearer when the investor dies. Heirs tend to make different financial choices, preferring money to shares. That is why it is so important to have a market where the securities can be sold. Securities with different maturities are traded in this second-hand market (the secondary market). The equity and bond markets have become an essential part of our economy. They play a pivotal role in the capital market and are a key measure of the level of confidence in the global economy.

The foundations of the modern stock market were laid in the Netherlands in the 17th century. The exclusion of the right of recourse was an important legal innovation, and it had a significant effect on stock market trading. The reasoning was as follows: if the purchaser has the right of recourse and the securities turn out to have some hidden defect that was not visible at the time of purchase, this would have a negative effect on the willingness of market players to buy and sell securities. The party selling the security on to others (the professional trader) would be reluctant to engage in active trading if it resulted in too many latent obligations. Abolishing the right of recourse paved the way for the active, and in a sense unencumbered, trading of securities. During Amsterdam's Golden Age, buyers and sellers met on the city's bridges to trade without the right of recourse. The buyer and seller agreed on a price, the seller exchanged his security for money, and this created liquidity. The stock market was born. The next problem was the regulation of the trading process and how to ensure the process optimally benefits all parties concerned. The aim of the public market is to ensure that all parties achieve the best possible results, in an honest manner. Honesty is not only a virtue; it is a necessity. A market that is not honest quickly loses the trust of its participants and is doomed to failure.

Like other public markets, public stock markets operate on the basis of important principles and concepts. They have values and this is a key aspect of the morality of stock markets. The most important principle is that two competing buyers or two competing sellers are always treated equally. They are separated only by the price difference. If a buyer is prepared to pay more for a security than a competitor, his offer takes precedence. The same applies to sellers. Equality comes into play when two potential buyers are willing to enter into an agreement at the same price, and likewise when two potential sellers are willing to dispose of the shares at the same price. Who comes first? The principle involved is simple, and it is the same principle that applies to queuing for a bus, at council offices or in a busy bakery. The one who arrives first on the market takes priority. Everyone has to wait his or her turn. Buying more than someone else does not provide entitlement to preferential treatment, even if you are a hedge fund. In the public markets, all securities orders are equal, regardless of their size or the importance of the person placing the order. Priority is determined purely on the basis of price and time. No queue jumping is allowed, no matter how important you are. If you want to be served earlier you have to show up earlier, or bid a better price than the others.

Another important principle is transparency. It is closely tied to the decency rule, especially where pre-trade transparency is concerned. If you do not know whether a party wants to buy or sell at a better price, it is impossible to tell whether he is jumping the queue. The market can have insight into the size of buy and sell orders both before and after the transaction. Public markets, which are accessible to everyone, have to be transparent. If the market price changes, potential buyers and sellers who have not yet announced their intentions can stay informed and anticipate changes in the market. A third crucial principle is that of immediacy. Sellers have a choice: they can have the transaction executed as soon as the order reaches the market, or they can wait for a better execution price. This mostly applies to orders that are large in relation to the market.

The three basic principles are supplemented by the trade-through rule, which ensures that orders are executed at the best possible price. In a trade through, the order of the customers is ignored. The market price moves even though the customer order could have been executed and improved the price formation process. Public exchanges all have rules on trade throughs, and in the US trade-through rules apply in full to all official trading platforms where the security is traded. Under new market regulations introduced by the SEC (Regulation NMS, which is identical to Europe's MiFID), the trade-through rule remains an important aspect of the structure supporting market integrity. The trade-through rule is essentially the same as the best execution rule. If the market trades through my price, I will not get the best price, and neither will the counterparty. This is not just a technical detail. It is a moral issue involving the institutionalisation of the concept of honesty.

Exactly what is the 'best price'? How is it established? These questions are dealt with in detail in the draft version of the SEC's evaluation of the structure of the equity markets (January 2010). The SEC's objective is to ensure the system offers the most willing seller and the most willing buyer the opportunity to achieve an optimum outcome. The price at which a transaction is possible is the best price. One notable aspect of the SEC's definition is that the parties have to be willing. Naturally, parties who wish to improve on a price, but prefer to do so privately, cannot be forced to participate in the process simply to make the public stock market efficient. Consequently, the best share price is the price at which parties in the global market have indicated they are prepared to enter into a transaction to buy or sell a security. Around the world there are many platforms where securities are traded, and securities are often sold outside of these platforms as well. Brokers therefore need to have insight into all of these prices and be able to use that insight to get the best possible price for their customers' transactions. The best price at which to sell is the other party's best bid, the best price at which to buy is the most favourable price at which a potential seller offers his securities, that is, the best offer. The best price is therefore a combination of the two: the best bid and offer (BBO). The assumption is that this is the very best price. In markets that are dominated by professional traders, the BBO is sometimes understood to mean the best prices quoted in professional circles. In the days of the stock exchange automated quotation (SEAQ), British exchanges displayed the professional BBOs on a screen and highlighted them in yellow. They were referred to as yellow strip prices. However, customer orders were excluded from improving the yellow strip prices, which raises the question of whether they were in fact the best prices.

Before continuing my discussion of the organisation of the market and price determination, I would like to take a closer look at the securities that are traded, using shares of the electronics group Philips as an example. This is very homogeneous security. There are large numbers of the same shares in circulation. If you bring all the buyers and sellers together, you have a market. However, matters are not always that simple, and the situation surrounding other securities may be very different. Take, for example, the Dutch government bond that matures in April 2023, of which there are far fewer in circulation. There are fewer bonds in general, and many of them are held in not very active portfolios. As a result, sellers of securities such as these are not always sure of finding an interested buyer when they want to sell. If the search for a buyer takes too long, and others get wind of the fact that the security is difficult to sell, the price may fall. Pre-trade transparency is not in the seller's interests and is something he would rather avoid. The broker representing the seller seizes the opportunity to provide an additional service by taking on the bond and holding it in his own account. He will eventually sell the bond, if possible at a profit. The broker is in effect taking over the role of the market, which may seem unobjectionable but in fact constitutes a very elementary conflict of interests. The broker who is meant to safeguard the customer's interests is also the counterparty to the transaction with the customer, and he is certainly not likely to lose sight of his own interests. If it takes too long to resell the bond, the broker may also be tempted to move things along using improper means. He may, for example, circulate documents among his customers urging them to buy this type of security. The research department of a brokerage company can be an invaluable tool in such cases.

The broker can avoid conflicts of interest and still help the customer by offering the securities to a professional trader. To ensure that there is no further conflict of interest, it is important to know whether the broker and the trader are economically independent of one another. In most cases the professional trader is part of the same company as the broker. Sometimes the broker receives so much commission income from the trader that he allows his interests to prevail over those of the customer. Choosing between two customers also involves weighing up interests. This issue is currently much debated in relation to hedge funds. They bring in a great deal of business for brokers, who stand to earn much more from them than from regular customers. Hedge funds are therefore in a position to demand preferential treatment, and they usually get it. Choosing the most lucrative customer is an indirect way of choosing one's self, and that is usually not a hard choice to make.

Let us return to Philips which is, as I said, a homogeneous share. What may be slightly less homogeneous is the size of the securities order. If an institutional investor decides to sell a 5% holding in Philips, it will probably not be able to get the same price as a normal-sized order. The seller realises that the sell order is so big the market will capitalise on the sale, causing the price to fall. This phenomenon is called market impact. The seller wants to ensure that the market impact is as limited as possible. This means that, as in the previous example, pre-trade transparency is not in its interests. This principle also applies after the seller has sold its position to a professional trader. He too has little interest in letting the market know he has acquired the securities, because the block of shares is in fact still looming over the market. The parties concerned will not be willing to give full disclosure until they have sold the entire block to another long-term investor, or sold it in pieces to the public market. The conclusion is that while Philips shares are homogeneous, differences in order size can shatter the homogeneity. In other words, it is not only the underlying security itself that determines the market, it is also the size of the order. This is an important factor for the regulator to take into consideration.

All of the above applies not just to stock markets, but also to trading venues for other products, such as derivatives markets, commodity markets and foreign exchange markets. The ideal market structure – the structure that delivers the optimum outcome for the willing buyer and the willing seller – depends on the extent to which the product (security/commodity) is standardised. But the ideal market structure cannot always be achieved, not by a long shot, because self-interest means that the parties involved cannot agree on what the most efficient system is. Vested interests stand in the way of the changes that would make the markets more efficient. Some parties are like foxes: they make their living out of inefficiency. Conservatism tends to prevail until the unstoppable force of innovation causes changes to be made. This is also true – perhaps uniquely so – of the financial markets.

Nevertheless, we can formulate some basic assumptions regarding the efficiency of a stock market. Highly standardised securities and commodities (such as shares and futures) are best traded in an order-driven market where all public and professional orders come together at a central point and price formation is efficient. Americans call this an auction market, while in Europe we refer to it as a public order book. Pluriform securities, such as bonds, some options series and warrants, need the help of a professional trader who is prepared to quote prices. As discussed above, the same is true of standardised securities if the order is large in comparison with the market and has to be executed in one go. Professional traders want to make money and they certainly want something in return for their services. It need not always be money. They will take privileges too, such as the right to be the counterparty to any public transactions. The best privilege of all is to have priority in the execution of the public order flow, preferably all orders, and if possible, to have this right in perpetuity. This may be contrary to the generic interests of the customer, but market operators are prepared to grant this privilege because it costs them nothing. In the end, the system finances itself. In addition, the professional trader often owns the exchange and the head of the exchange organisation is often willing to accommodate these wishes. The abuse is deep-rooted, as we can see.

Having discussed the best price, we also need to talk about the best market structure. Markets are organised differently in the US, the UK and continental Europe. Let us start with the American model. In the 1960s the US had several regional exchanges and two major, traditional exchanges in New York: the New York Stock Exchange (NYSE) and the American Stock Exchange (Amex). The NYSE was by far the most dominant market, and its power was respected by all and feared by many. The exchange had a whole laundry list of regulations. Number 390 banned members of the exchange from quoting prices for off-floor trading in shares listed on the NYSE during official exchange opening hours. This more or less gave the exchange a monopoly; the US version of the European concentration rule. The procedure for executing securities orders was even more objectionable. On the NYSE and the Amex, customer orders were brought to the floor by a floor broker and handed over to a specialist. The specialists controlled the order book and were responsible for ensuring that the customer's order was executed. If supply and demand were not in balance, specialists were permitted to act as the counterparty and execute the order themselves. In return for their services, they demanded unlimited insight into all incoming orders. It was a card game in which the specialists had the right to see all of the other players' cards and had no competition at all, although they naturally never lost sight of their own interests. In 2001, specialists accounted for 32% of all share transactions in the US.

In 1971, the National Association of Securities Dealers (NASD) set up a modest trading platform for small companies that the NYSE was not very interested in. These included Apple, Microsoft, Cisco Systems and Intel. They did not meet the stringent listing requirements of the NYSE, but they needed a place where their shares could be traded. The result was a platform with automated quotations, known as NASDAQ. For a long time it was not an exchange but a market where prices were established by competitive bidding among broker-dealers (a combination of a broker and a professional trader). It was a different kind of trading. There was competition, but only among professionals. Dealers on NASDAQ quoted their best bid and offer prices. It was not a monopoly because brokers could choose between prices from a range of dealers, which was very different from the NYSE system. The two market models, which had developed organically but in different ways, existed alongside one another. In the 1990s, NASDAQ experienced phenomenal growth thanks to the rise of high-tech shares. As the influence of the electronic exchange grew, it threatened the hegemony of the NYSE. It was more than just a battle between competitors. Two fundamentally different views about share trading degenerated into tribal warfare. The chiefs of the warring tribes were sworn enemies. There was hate, rumour mongering and mistrust. It was in fact the financial equivalent of the rivalry between Pepsi and Coca Cola.

Both trading systems were far from perfect, and various scandals and abuses brought them face to face with their own shortcomings, albeit at different points in time. The reputations of the professional traders at NASDAQ were tarnished when an SEC investigation revealed that they were guilty of making secret deals. The way in which bid and ask prices were established was unfair, and this corrupted the competitive process. The customers were the victims, and the management of NASDAQ had looked the other way. The SEC finally brought out the big guns and forced the market to clean up its act. In 1996 new rules were adopted. These stipulated that every order that improved prices had to be visible. The new rules for order handling forced the best execution issue by making brokers and dealers responsible for securing better prices for their customers' orders. But it was not only NASDAQ that had been in the wrong. The specialist system at NYSE proved highly vulnerable to human failing. Specialists were accused of hanging on to orders far too long. The time claimed by them was value they had appropriated from the customer. There was public outrage in response to this behaviour, and the voices calling for change became louder and louder. Hank Paulson, then CEO of Goldman Sachs, attempted to combine all execution systems in a single national system of order execution. He wanted to create an efficient system by routing all orders to one central point. It was a nice initiative, but it died without a whimper. In a country ruled by competition and vested interests, this was a bridge too far. The SEC kept looking for a solution. Over the course of several decades, the regulator developed the National Market System (NMS), a system in which prices in all markets were visible. There was no trading via the NMS as its only purpose was to enforce best execution.

In continental Europe the securities markets were essentially public markets comparable to the NYSE, to which orders from investors were routed for execution. Many European markets had their own equivalent of the specialist (the *hoekman* in the Netherlands, the *animateur* in France). They operated in a similar fashion, executing customer orders without competition in a market that was vital to investors. In the 1990s, the roles of the specialists and the animateurs were severely restricted, and they lost many of their privileges. Continental Europe eventually saw the creation of the kind of national system that the US regarded as the most efficient, albeit impossible to achieve: a system based on a central limit order book.

The securities markets in the UK were fundamentally different from those in continental Europe. They were much more oriented towards wholesale investors. Private capital was generally institutionalised, which means that retail investors in the UK usually sought out mutual funds and left it up to them to do the investing. Retail customers in the UK who wanted to invest directly in shares almost always did so within the confines of a local network. Sending private orders to the central market was the exception rather than the rule. In short, the UK did not have a central public market.

In October 1986, under pressure from Margaret Thatcher's government, the market was deregulated and this had a huge impact on the structure of the financial markets as we now know them. Because the move was so radical and the changes were introduced all at the same time, it became known as the Big Bang. Before the Big Bang roles were segregated:

one was either an agent or a principal. The Big Bang eliminated that distinction, and the roles of agent and principal were combined to create the function of broker-dealer. London was copying the now so successful NASDAQ. The Big Bang also put an end to the agents' system of fixed commissions. After the changeover, commission was determined by supply and demand in open competition. The Thatcher government was a proponent of free capital markets and especially of self-regulation for markets. The broker-dealer's two main activities – brokerage and trading – meant an inherent conflict of interest, but the liberals were convinced that self-regulation and accountability would prevent abuse. The free markets were also necessary because London had lost so much ground to New York. They wanted to follow the American example and replace floor trading at the London Stock Exchange with electronic trading. At least, that was the idea.

After the Big Bang the British financial market focused primarily on accommodating large orders, but things did not go according to plan. Floor trading did indeed disappear, but it relocated to the telephone instead of to electronic screens. The screen was simply a means of advertising. An actual transaction required a telephone call between the customer and the broker-dealer. The transaction was concluded bilaterally via the wire. The end of floor trading effectively meant that the entire stock market switched to over-the-counter transactions. The London Stock Exchange also took the name of its new trading system – SEAQ – from its US counterpart. As at NASDAQ, the SEAQ screens displayed only the prices at which professional traders were willing to trade. Although this made it possible for the London market to handle large orders, it involved some generally dubious trading practices and criticism of the trading system quickly grew. Professional traders were often unable to trade at the price shown on screen, and the market generated via the telephone reflected an entirely different economic reality. If a trader was unable to honour his quote, there was no certainty that another party would be willing to take up the slack. Calling another trader usually did not help, since most of them were in the same situation. On Black Monday, that fatal day in 1987, telephones went unanswered. The official version was that traders were too busy to answer them, but in fact they stood idly by while the system collapsed. There was a crisis and calls from panicking customers were the last thing they needed, especially if the customers wanted to sell. The traders refused to quote prices, and that is understandable. It was like asking someone to remain on the railway tracks as a train speeds towards them.

Michael Jenkins was a member of the board of the London Stock Exchange from 1971 until 1977 and was responsible for setting up Talisman, a new settlement system for shares. When the project was completed, the exchange's management felt it had done enough to computerise its systems. Jenkins saw things differently, fell out with the CEO and left. The Netherlands welcomed the Brit with open arms, just as it had Henry Hudson in the 17th century. In 1608, the British sea captain was under contract to the Moscovy Company, which financed explorations. However, his bosses were disappointed by the results of his long sea voyages. It is not clear whether they actually fired Hudson, but it is certain that financing for new expeditions was withdrawn and his ambitions were dashed. Even before Hudson had closed the door of the Muscovy Company behind him, representatives of the Dutch East India Company had a contract ready for him to sign. Hudson was encouraged to make his own plans and money was no object. The result was the discovery of New York in the name of the Netherlands. In that same tradition, the Dutch offered Michael Jenkins a contract to set up Europe's first options exchange in Amsterdam. This may not seem as significant as searching for the northern passage to the West Indies, but it certainly was a great strategic move. The options exchange was to be a joint venture between the Amsterdam Stock Exchange and the London Stock Exchange, and would be based in Amsterdam. Why not? The US options exchange was not based in New York, the country's financial centre, but in Chicago. This new exchange would be called the European Options Exchange.

Jenkins relocated to the Netherlands and moved into one of Amsterdam's typical, narrow streets, not far from the Rijksmuseum. Just when he had succeeded in getting the options exchange off the ground, the British got cold feet. Having decided that they would rather see the plan succeed in London, they pulled out of the deal and set up their own options exchange: the London Traded Options Market (LTOM), which became part of the London Stock Exchange. The Dutch were out of luck this time; they were left with a local market for equity options with a name that was a painful reminder of their original ambitions. Jenkins returned to the UK to accept an even greater challenge. He was to set up a futures exchange in London, based on the US model, which would be entirely independent of the London Stock Exchange. That was the start of Liffe, the London International Financial Futures and Options Exchange. After a few difficult years Liffe became a great success, as did the EOE, Amsterdam's options exchange. The LTOM continued to struggle, partly because private investors in the UK did much less direct trading on the stock markets than European and American investors. In addition, Britain's capital gains tax meant that trading options was less profitable than it was in the Netherlands. But the biggest obstacle was the structure of the market. The cartel of broker-dealers continued to wield a great deal of power. After the Big Bang, the uncontested king of the broker-dealers was Smith New Court. The equity market was extremely profitable for this broker-dealer, which had every intention of keeping it that way. Smith New Court was active in almost all of the shares listed on the London Stock Exchange, especially in large securities. Like other broker-dealers, Smith New Court was not a fan of the options market. There were defensive reasons for keeping the market afloat, but that was all.

In the meantime, independent traders had appeared on the LTOM, including O'Connor, CRT, Timber Hill and Hull Trading (all from the US), and various European trading groups, mostly from the Netherlands. The origins of these trading companies were remarkable. Their operations were based on the latest financial and academic insights, and they had been set up by young people whose commercial instincts were entirely different to those of the establishment. Blair Hull was one of these people. He had a fascination for probability calculations, and as a young man had travelled to the blackjack tables in Las Vegas to test his theories. He earned piles of money and in time he was no longer welcome at the casinos. It was a true victory for someone who believed in efficient markets. Hull decided to use his knowledge in a game where the stakes were even higher: the financial world. Option trading was similar to blackjack, and based on the same principles of probability distribution. Hull moved to Chicago, set up Hull Trading and became a member of the options exchange. According to the rules, traders had to be present on the exchange floor. Hull was slightly older than his competitors, and this did not work in his favour. Trading was not only a mental and intellectual game, on the floor of the exchange it was also about physical stamina. Being faster than the others was an advantage. It was a game in which risks were hedged by means of buying and selling replica portfolios. Complex formulas determined the number of shares needed for a perfect hedge. The most famous was the Black & Scholes model, which is based on the implied volatility of the share price. The replica portfolios were adjusted on the basis of price moves. This meant continuously buying and selling shares.

Hull traded index options, and with every sharp fluctuation in market prices he had to adjust his hedge. But other traders always beat him to the floor broker who traded the underlying shares. Hull could not win the game this way, and he was out to win. He was too much of an entrepreneur and optimist to accept his loss. His philosophy was that obstacles were there to be overcome. Hull was one of the first to use computers, and that made him a little faster. He also began to calculate cross correlations between all of the financial instruments included in the index. That gave him entirely new insights. If his competitors were crowded around a particular floor broker, Hull went off in the other direction. He hedged his investments with financial instruments that had a different correlation to the index. This led to the development of his concept of the least likely hedge, and eventually to the birth of the grand game of correlation matrixes. Techniques were developed that enabled investors to earn money by taking small risks. A large number of small risks can eventually generate big yields.

In 1989, Hull Trading started its London operations, under the management of the distracted mathematics professor Warren Langley, who was responsible for providing Hull with most of his academic knowledge. The London establishment wanted nothing to do with the newcomers. The independent derivatives traders and the broker-dealers, whose prices were determined by a simple process of supply and demand, made strange bedfellows. There was little sympathy and a great deal of animosity. There was a dependency, but it was one-sided. The professional traders on the LTOM needed a context in which to quote good option prices – reliable prices at which they could hedge risks on the stock market. Those reliable prices had to come from broker-dealers, who were more than willing to play the game. They did so primarily in response to large price fluctuations caused by major events, such as the announcement of a merger or takeover. The broker-dealers who knew of these events ahead of time took large positions in options on specific shares just before an announcement. They made use of intermediate brokers to ensure the option market makers did not suspect anything. If the option trader subsequently wanted to hedge the risk inherent in the acquired position by buying or selling shares, things took a rather nasty turn. The price disappeared from the SEAQ screen without warning. When the price was displayed again it had changed and a loss was certain. As a result, option traders became less willing to quote prices on the LTOM. The British options exchange became an empty exchange, a showcase of goods without price tags. This did little to encourage the public to become active in options. The LTOM had no future. It had been suffocated by the protective wings of the London Stock Exchange and by market abuses by broker-dealers.

A few parties, including MeesPierson (where I was general manager at the time) and James Capel, saw the storm clouds approaching. These parties were members of the LTOM, but they decided that enough was enough. Without the knowledge of the London Stock Exchange they submitted a plan to Michael Jenkins for the takeover of the LTOM by Liffe. The plan was carried out not long after that. When the board of the London Stock Exchange heard about this, they showed little interest. They reasoned that if necessary the initiative could still be quelled from a distance. And so in 1992 Liffe became a futures and options exchange.

After the takeover, the equity options division of Liffe needed a manager: an experienced professional, preferably someone from outside. Jenkins was strongly in favour of appointing a manager from continental Europe. He invited me, in my capacity as chairman of the member committee of Liffe, responsible for supporting and monitoring the overall development of equity option trading in London, to a meeting with Sweden's Karin Forseke. She was the dream candidate for the position, and it was hoped that she would breathe new life into the market. Ms Forseke worked for Westpac Banking Corporation at the time, but her knowledge of derivatives came from her time as Head of Business Development at the London branch of the Swedish options exchange OMX. We had agreed to meet at London's Savoy Hotel. The street in front of the hotel entrance is the only one in Great Britain where cars have to drive on the right. That says something about the Savoy: it is a unique hotel with its own personality and many traditions. We met in the main lobby of the hotel. The similarity to a trading floor was striking: nothing had changed for years and there was a great deal going on at the different tables. It was a perfect, symbolic location for a meeting with Ms Forseke. She turned out to be a woman with a soft voice. She spoke almost in a whisper, which forced us to listen even more carefully. We talked to her for over an hour, and at the end of our conversation Jenkins was convinced. He offered the position at Liffe to Ms Forseke. She had to give it some thought, as her partner still lived in Sweden, but in the end she accepted the job. New challenges awaited her as well as Liffe.

In the meantime, Bernard and Peter Madoff had gradually expanded their small brokerage company in the US into a broker-dealer organisation. The brothers had realised that there was good money to be made from placing customers' orders on their own books. They started with the shares of small companies mainly because they were not traded on official stock exchanges. In time they shifted their focus to larger companies. The Madoffs had one big advantage: they were not members of the NYSE and not part of the established order. The fact that rule 390 (the ban on quoting prices off the floor of the exchange floor) did not apply to them opened up possibilities. They were also clever and highly adept at sailing close to the wind. They made some key moves. The brothers were the first to understand the importance of computerising the order execution process, and not only did they understand this, they acted on it too. While it normally took a minute and a half to process an order on the floor of the NYSE, the Madoffs took only four seconds. They also had another trick that would later be adopted by operators of alternative platforms. They acquired the Cincinnati Stock Exchange, an entity which had an exchange licence but which was in fact an empty shell. The Madoff brothers had their own way of filling up that empty shell. They computerised the matching process for competing orders and turned the Cincinnati Stock Exchange into a computer console. Their exchange licence gave them access to the National Market System (NMS) which had been set up under the auspices of the SEC to ensure pre-trade price transparency for the entire US market.

However, the biggest innovation was yet to come. It was a bit dubious and not uncontroversial, but to their own surprise the Madoffs won the support of the SEC. What exactly did they do? They bought the order flow by paying everyone who brought orders to their platform one cent for each traded share. That was of course return commission in its purest form. The SEC approved this because at the time what really mattered to the regulator was breaking the power of the NYSE. The concept of paying for order flow let the genie out of the bottle, and to this day it has proved impossible to put it back in. The principle is that orders have to be executed at the best price, but paying for order flow creates a sharp contradiction. It encourages brokers to send their orders to the platform with the highest return commission, which ensures best execution for the broker delivering the order, not for the customer. As a result of this innovation, the big brokers began routing their transactions in NYSE shares through the Cincinnati Stock Exchange, and the Madoffs were eventually able to siphon off approximately 5% of the NYSE's trading volume. It also made the much criticised practice of preferencing popular. Because order processing was so fast – only four seconds – no one noticed if once in a while it took five seconds. That extra second was used to show the order flow to one or more big brokerage companies, such as Shearson Lehman. If they were interested in the orders, they took them onto their own books. All other orders went to the Cincinnati Stock Exchange. Naturally the Madoff brothers charged for this 'service'. It was a foretaste of what was to happen at the start of the new millennium with the advent of high frequency traders, which we will look at later.

Back in London, confidence in the fully broker-dealer oriented market was waning. Out of frustration at the failure to set up an equity options market, Liffe launched its attack. Karin Forseke took the lead. She had studied the success of the options markets in the Netherlands, Germany and Scandinavia, and concluded that it was the result of a different share trading structure. The structure created for the London stock market at the time of the Big Bang was outdated. She asked herself why private investors who bought and sold shares had to trade at the quotes given by professional traders. Why were private customers not trading among themselves if these prices were better? She talked to everyone, including market parties, politicians and managers. In continental Europe, unlike in the UK, the public order flow and orders from professional traders came together to generate a best bid and ask price. In Ms Forseke's opinion, that provided a much better basis for the prices of options traders. Professional share traders might withdraw their prices at the most inopportune moment, but customers did not and the market was for everyone. The London Stock Exchange appeared to be unconvinced, but slowly the British exchange's opposition began to crumble. This was the result of political pressure, changing circumstances in other markets and the scandals at NASDAQ, but above all it was down to the efforts of the woman with the soft voice. Another important factor in this process was the takeover of the most intransigent opponent to change, Smith New Court, by Merrill Lynch. The latter was known for its brokerage services and was much less entrenched in the debate than its new acquisition had been. In the end the London Stock Exchange decided to make the best of the situation and introduced a new electronic trading system (SETS). It was a victory for Liffe and Ms Forseke, who now thought her work was done. She returned to Sweden to become the CEO of the big brokerage company D. Carnegie & Co, and was later appointed to the board of the British financial regulator, the FSA.

With the arrival of SETS the London Stock Exchange became one of the last European exchanges to switch to a real electronic system. It had been a long road from the floor to the telephone, and finally to the screen. It was a typical case of a head start turning out to be a handicap. However, the same was also true of Liffe, which still had floor trading. Liffe had actively opposed the dealer system on the London Stock Exchange and been the driving force behind a new way of organising the market, but it soon got a taste of its own medicine. It had its own established order, one that was opposed to the further development of screen trading. Liffe, with one of its most successful products, the German Bund future, entered into a liquidity battle with the German electronic exchange DTB, which it lost. It marked the end of the struggle between floor and electronic trading, at least in Europe. The triumph of electronic trading settled another battle. Not only had Europe's securities markets switched to electronic trading, they had also adopted the concept of fully order-driven price formation. The professional traders, specialists, *animateurs* and *hoeklieden* lost their franchise. Some of them merged with brokers, a few became hedge fund managers, but most ceased to exist. Was this the final victory for the market purists who demanded an order-driven market? Was it the end of the professional traders, the foxes who owed their demise to their own greed and lack of compassion? Or was it just a temporary lull in the never-ending battle for the customer's orders? In fact, the tribal warfare continues. The key factor in the struggle is the equity trading model. Exchange organisations and private investors are best served by a central market and transparency. Their position is diametrically opposed to that of the brokers and professional traders (and the major banks) who want to trade large orders. Those parties gladly take advantage of transparency but do not want to be transparent themselves. The battle between the order-driven market and the dealer market still continues. Should retail investors and the exchanges sacrifice transparency to appease institutional parties? Or should institutional parties realise that transparency always triumphs in the end and is also in their best interests? It should be clear by now that I am in favour of transparency for everyone, before and after the transaction. If everyone – literally everyone – is transparent, the volume of information will be so big that there will be little reason to fear abuse of that information. It is time to make an irrevocable commitment to transparency.

In 2002, the internationalisation of the local European exchanges and the work on MiFID brought the concentration rule to Brussels' attention. The fact that many exchanges had transformed themselves into for-profit organisations intensified the debate. The concentration rule stipulated that public orders for securities had to be routed through the exchange's central market. That looked suspiciously like a monopoly, and in a free European market it could not be tolerated. The offensive launched by the major financial institutions targeted the concentration rule as well as the silo construction which gave exchanges ownership or control of the clearing houses that handle transaction settlement. The reasoning behind the position of the big banks and the integrated securities institutions was that the clearing houses should also be able to offer their services for off-exchange transactions. It was an unequal battle because the exchanges had to defend their franchise against the same big banks that supplied the order flow. Never bite the hand that feeds you. The London Stock Exchange lined up squarely on the side of the hand that fed it, and showed no inclination at all to join the resistance put up by the other exchange organisations. Euronext tried to run with the hare and hunt with the hounds. It did the politically correct thing and sold its clearing organisation. Deutsche Börse followed the most independent strategy, refusing to sell its clearing organisation, Clearstream, despite great political pressure. It declared itself an unashamed proponent of the silo concept.

> The role played by the London Stock Exchange is particularly notable when viewed in a historical context. Euronext sold its clearing organisation in 2004 and began one-sided preparations for a merger with an unwilling bride (who did not believe in the silo concept), only for the unwilling bride to buy the now independent clearing house, LCH Clearnet, eight years later.

The letter from the Federation of European Exchanges to the European FESE exchanges, which I referred to earlier in this chapter, should be seen in this perspective. The exchanges argued in their letter that they were not opposed to free competition, but what was good for the goose was good for the gander as well. They had noticed that since the Big Bang in the UK and the repeal of the Glass-Steagall Act in 1999 (which banned US retail banks from securities trading), the expansion of the activities of the major financial institutions had only resulted in a further accumulation of conflicts of interest. Why? Because they thought they could create value by keeping things in the family and partially excluding market competition. By this they meant value for the financial conglomerate. The parties who had objected to the silo constructions set up by exchanges brazenly created their own silos, unassailable bastions of conflicting interests that were resistant to the call for open architecture. Merrill Lynch, for example, took over Smith New Court and Mercury Asset Management. What kind of moral dilemmas does an integrated financial services provider face if it manages assets for customers but is also a broker trading for own account and risk? How many conflicts of interests can pile up before the whole construction gives way under the weight of moral objections? What should these companies do with positions that remain open after a public issue that they had underwritten? Should these institutions be allowed to execute customer orders internally, before the market has had the opportunity to participate in the process?

There were therefore quite a few moral arguments against the internalisation of the public order flow as proposed by MiFID. Large financial institutions are selective about the orders they accept from customers. A significant shadow market is created behind the front door, and if that door is not open to all parties, a large number of parties will be excluded from the market. This places those parties at a disadvantage. The transaction and price formation process becomes limited to the happy few, and the public nature of the market ceases to exist. Why do prestigious, high-profile companies continue to do business with Goldman Sachs even though the public is aware of how this bank treats the interests of its customers (who are disparagingly referred to as 'muppets')? The answer is simple: the 'muppets' do not want to lose access to the front door. Sheer market power that is.

Another moral objection to the internalisation of public orders relates to transparency. A customer who places a securities order with a large financial institution needs to know what the reference price is in the market. That is how the customer judges whether or not the financial institution has quoted a representative transaction price and hence whether that institution is a reliable party or a vulture. The diversion of an increasing numbers of orders away from the central marketplace has an adverse effect on the price formation process, and hence on the quality of the reference price. It gives integrated financial institutions more freedom to abuse their position, and that, as it turns out, is their objective. It becomes advantageous for the financial conglomerate to weaken the market. The FESE argued in its letter that while it had no objection to competition, it had to be on the basis of a level playing field. An institution that is only permitted to fulfil only one role will always lose out to other financial institutions that are allowed to act in all capacities and carry out exchange activities as well. It is comparable to supermarkets that place their own label products at eye level and relegate independent brands to the top and bottom shelves.

The points discussed in 2002 were implemented in 2007. MiFID was very ambitious. It was designed to make the European markets more competitive and create a European capital market. The compromise reached with regard to securities trading led to the creation of new multilateral platforms (MTFs) for the execution of securities orders. In addition, large securities companies could apply for systemic internal settlement status. The new rules recognised cross systems, which allowed brokers to cross their own customer orders, that is, to match opposite orders and execute them. The concept of dark pools came into being. This happened because some of the execution platforms, such as the cross systems, did not have to provide pre-trade transparency. Other platforms, such as MTFs, did have an obligation to do so, but they could apply for an exemption. The regulators had created scope for orders to be executed on a so-called public market without requiring transparency. Many market parties took advantage of this, and the result was the rapid growth of the number of securities transactions executed in dark pools. The market became increasingly opaque. Post-trade information is just as important as pre-trade information, but MiFID was soft on the newcomers in that area as well. According to the new directive, securities transactions had to be reported in real time, or within three minutes in any event. But in some cases, the delay could last for as much an hour, or even four days.

This was all part of the compromise between the parties in the tug of war. There was still a moral underpinning: best execution continued to be the central principle. Brokers had to guarantee that the customer's order would get the best possible execution price. There was just one hitch. Getting the best price for customers is not only dependent on the structure of the market, but also on the speed with which the transaction is executed. We have already seen that Blair Hull had a problem with being slower than the rest, and that he was able to turn that disadvantage into an advantage. The Madoff brothers also focused on speeding up the execution process, and on taking unfair advantage of the increased speed. Another good example of the speed issue is an incident that took place on the Amsterdam exchange at the end of the 1990s. It occurred during the switchover from the local trading system to the system developed by Paris Bourse after the merger that created Euronext. The technical infrastructure of the new platform was set up so that transaction and price data could be routed to the central market via satellite, while data relating to the execution of orders would be transmitted via an underground cable. Professional traders thought they had discovered that the two data flows were not synchronous. The cable was said to be faster, and there were suspicions that the situation was being abused. Parties who knew the prices because they were trading themselves could, via the cable, take advantage of parties who got their information one tenth of a second later via satellite. This was never proved, but perception is stronger than reality. Some people were convinced that the markets were unfair, protests were made, and the newspapers reported the story. True or not, abuse is definitely possible in such situations.

Blair Hull's speed deficit is now the high frequency trader's bread and butter: powerful, high speed computers use algorithms to scan the market for opportunities. Milliseconds matter in modern trading systems, and it makes sense to locate a trading system close to the exchange's central computer. High speed traders can make a living from their activities, and whole companies are built on being one millisecond faster than the competition. In these circumstances, not knowing in advance the price at which part of the market wants to execute its orders, and a period of three minutes in which to report a trade, provide considerable scope for abuse. They are the same forms of abuse that the specialists on the floor of the NYSE were guilty of eight years ago, only then it was a question of minutes instead of milliseconds. The counterparty is free to choose the best transaction price. It is the customer who provides the leeway, but no one has asked their permission, and they are unaware of it. It all happens too quickly.

MiFID's premise is that it does not matter if a market is fragmented, provided that the publication of price and volume data after the transaction is done immediately. That means it is possible to check whether the price is the best one extremely quickly. In industry jargon, this is known as creating a consolidated tape. But what information does the tape contain? The National Market System (NMS) in the US has a tape with both pre-trade and post-trade information, and that makes sense. In Europe, only post-trade information is available. You might ask yourself how useful that is for determining the best price. It is, after all, old news, provided after the fact. In the world of milliseconds, three-minute old information is a bit like medieval history. But post-trade information offers no protection at all beyond a false sense of security. In effect, the best execution principle, which was meant to protect retail investors, has become a paper tiger. Regulators rarely take action because of a failure to provide the best price. The victim is usually none the wiser, but enormous profits are earned in this way. The speed of execution is one reason why few victims notice they did not get the best price. The Madoffs taught the industry how to do this.

The failed merger between NYSE Euronext and Deutsche Börse brought these facts home again. NYSE Euronext in particular has seen a dramatic decline in executed volume. Only small transactions still take place on NYSE Euronext's central market, since high-volume trades now use other routes. Under pressure from competition from integrated financial institutions and other platforms, the exchange has had to adapt its business model. Exchanges are no longer the organisers of the market. Instead, they have formulated new objectives, such as operating major data centres and accommodating the competition. If you cannot beat them, join them. They provide sub-platforms where brokers can find a counterparty for their own customer orders in a secluded environment. Those orders have to be executed within the margins of the official exchange, the BBO. However, the spread between the best bid and best offer will be so wide that it gives all of the brokers in the sub-markets a mandate to earn a good profit on their customers. If this process continues, eventually, the real public market that is accessible to all and has high-minded principles will cease to exist. It is already rapidly becoming the waste pipe for the capital market. Having been institutionalised, the process of fragmentation will then be complete.

In 2010 another incident took place in the US which was to have major consequences for regulators and policy-makers. This was the Flash Crash. The incident illustrated once again

121

how important the organisation of the securities market is for our economic wellbeing. As the name indicates, the Flash Crash was a rapid market collapse. For no apparent reason, the Dow Jones Industrial Index lost hundreds of points in less than 20 minutes before recovering again. The index opened at 10,787, dipped to 9,982 and closed at 10,520. Panicking investors who sold at the lowest point felt the market had taken them for a ride. They asked themselves how it had happened. The regulators opened an investigation, the most remarkable aspect of which was the amount of time it took for the conclusions to be reported. Gathering data took so long that the media suggested that the regulators were responsible for maintaining an IT museum. The answer to the Flash Crash clearly could not be provided in a flash. The explanation finally published by the Commodity Futures Trading Commission (CFTC) and the SEC was complicated and immediately challenged by the market parties. Then academic researchers got involved. Amid the uproar, only one cause seemed plausible: the vulnerable market structure. As a result of the sudden fall in prices, the dark pools and the internal matching systems of broker-dealers lost their capacity to function. All the 'subterranean' volume surfaced. Buckets of orders from alternative trading systems were emptied into a public market already weakened by ruthless exploitation. This provides further evidence of the parasitical behaviour of the internal matching systems and the dark pools. Moreover, it highlights real concerns about the structure of the market and the consequences for price formation.

The draft version of the 2010 SEC evaluation contains a number of remarkable observations. The SEC is also concerned about the quality of reference prices, and links this to an even more worrying suspicion. The SEC thinks it is possible that professional parties in a dark pool will temporarily emerge from the darkness and move into the public market in order to trade within the BBO. Not with a view to increasing liquidity, but to influence the reference price. A big transaction in the dark might make this worthwhile. In other words, if there is a profit to be made in the dark, influencing the price in the public market is an easy choice, even if it costs money. It could be money well spent. However, the potential for market abuse in the event of a weakened reference price is even greater. The majority of the world's financial assets are passively managed or invested in indices. The price formation of these assets is extremely important, but it is based solely on published volume. While there are some honest foxes, there are also an awful lot of chickens. We therefore need a solution for the problem. The SEC's concept of *at market* is an interesting suggestion for dealing with dark liquidity. At market implies that if the price in the dark pool is the same as the public price, the transaction has to be executed in the daylight. There is considerable opposition to this idea in the US. Thomas M Joyce, chairman and CEO of Knight Capital Group, has called it an insane idea. In the 20th century the SEC's greatest fear was the power of the NYSE. Its fears now focus on the erosion of the public market.

MiFID paved the way for the establishment of new trading platforms. The idea was that the platforms would give the end investor more choice. The result is that the costs of executing a transaction on these platforms have in fact decreased substantially. The exchanges and the MTFs have had to make enormous gains in efficiency. Unfortunately, that is not the whole story. Brokers charge their customers an integral fee for executing an order, which includes the costs of the platform. So, initially, it is the broker, and not the customer, who benefits. Customers do not benefit unless they can negotiate a lower brokerage fee. But the benefits of an efficient market as a result of ensuring the order gets the best execution price are for the customer. A slightly better price can compensate for a major proportion of the costs, particularly if it is a large order. However, the question is whether the price formation process really has improved. Fragmentation suggests the opposite is true. With lower fees concealing the fact that the execution price has become worse, are we really better off?

And what has happened to the foxes? Have they died out? Far from it. The professional traders who were deprived of their food (the public order flow) understood all too well that they needed to go in search of well-stocked houses: the big banks and the integrated brokerage companies. That is exactly what they did. Blair Hull sold his company to Goldman Sachs for over US$1 billion. Swiss Banking Corporation, the bank that later merged with UBS, took over O'Connor. Once the foxes had forced their way in, and MiFID had given them free rein, the food was there for the taking. Once again, they were closing in on the public order flow. The story about Merrill Lynch at the beginning of this chapter symbolises this. The foxes lifted the lids of the food bins and emptied them. And so the game could begin again.

The smartest foxes are gaining more and more ground. Every MTF, dark pool or organiser of an internal network is fully aware of the fact that price formation in this segment of the market cannot differ too much from the BBO. If it does, the platform cannot claim to provide best execution and it will risk losing its *raison d'être*. Exchanges and platform operators are very apprehensive of this. And who can guarantee that BBO? The foxes naturally, which is why they have been invited back. Professional traders have been asked to help various platforms ensure that transactions are settled at the BBO. Even the exchanges have introduced a system that involves services provided by professional traders, for example, when the reference price is weakened and the spreads are too wide. With the advent of competition between trading platforms and the fragmentation of the public order flow, the order-driven market has disappeared and the dealer market has been reborn. We have returned to the situation that existed at the end of the 20th century.

The sciences are based on certain axioms, or universally recognised truths. For example, the shortest distance between two points is a straight line. That is true until proven false. The same principle can be applied to the financial markets. It is preferable that transactions are conducted by daylight and not in the dark. There are arguments in favour of the latter, but that does not detract from the obligation of regulators and supervisors to encourage transparency. Openness, in combination with free competition, is a great asset, one that discourages abuse, whereas abuses flourish in the dark. There is one further a priori axiom: a global system of bringing together all buy and sell orders for a given security represents the best price formation process. There is no better method, because sweeping everything together into one big pot, known as the central order book, allows us to make optimum use of global liquidity. It is the best place for willing buyers from around the world to meet willing sellers and achieve a price that both are happy with. Fragmentation makes that process inefficient. Individual parties with an institutional order flow may benefit from diverting a large order away from the central market, but this is not in their collective interests. However, the markets are now on an irreversible path towards a decentralised model and having to deal with the consequences of an inefficient solution.

The decision by Deutsche Börse and NYSE Euronext to set up sub-markets seems like the desperate cry for help of those abandoned to their fate. On 4 April 2011, almost 10 years after the first letter, the FESE wrote another letter to the European Internal Markets Commissioner, a position now held by a Frenchman, Michael Barnier. The letter accompanied an extensive response to the consultation on the MiFID review. The cry for help was reflected in the statement that the European capital market was speeding towards a system of non-communicating sub-markets. The letter argued that studies had indicated that less than only a quarter of the volume traded outside the regulatory system met MiFID's volume requirements. The remainder were transactions that actually belonged in the public market and had been wrongly diverted away from it. The message of the letter was not only that the rules needed to be more stringent, but also that compliance with the rules needed to be improved.

I started my story by defining honest markets as transparent markets in which all players are equal and all have equal access. How have we drifted so far away from this definition? The financial market is one big game of valuable marbles. That means that those who play the game do so with complete dedication and using all available means, regardless of whether the means are permissible or not. The market is huge and anonymous, and parties will always be inclined to choose their own interests above the common good. This raises an important human dilemma: one person's truth is the collective's lie. When taking individual decisions, people will use any available leeway to pursue their own interests. The financial world is full of examples of this. We want to trade ahead of a big order, yet if others do the same they spoil the party. We want to trade on the basis of privileged information, but if others receive that information we lose our advantage. We want to avoid paying our taxes, but all the while expect others to pay theirs. If the behaviour of one individual becomes common practice, it disrupts society. Markets are a form of society and there are many examples of individuals carving out behaviour that would destroy the market if adopted collectively. In the financial world, the reference price is used by parties who need it to protect themselves from the dishonesty of the counterparty, but in doing so they do not contribute to the making of the reference price. That behaviour is, in essence, parasitic. Just how vulnerable is a big institutional order if there is no reference price to determine whether or not a fair transaction has taken place? What the individual gains, society loses.

This is the opposite of what the Utilitarians had in mind for their perfect society, and it is the opposite of John Rawls's theory of justice:

> Social and economic equalities should be organised to provide the greatest benefit to the least-advantaged members of society.

For the purposes of this chapter, the theory of justice can be reformulated to state that the greatest benefit should serve public instead of individual interests, and that attention should focus not on the power of a rich and highly vocal lobby, but on words spoken with a soft voice. Where can that voice be heard?

There is a reason why traders in 17th century Amsterdam chose bridges as their place of business. The bridges were highly visible, but the merchants were pretty certain that trades would be shielded from public view. Talk about transparency. The discussion has been going on for centuries, so perhaps it is best not to harbour any illusions about the chances of finding a solution any time soon.

Chapter 13

Selling an empty promise

What are the pitfalls that need to be avoided when a company decides to obtain a stock-exchange listing? Which parties are involved? How can we ensure that the process leading up to and following the IPO is honest? And what about investors? They would rather be given a lie for free than pay to discover the truth.

Not many processes in the financial world are as full of intrigue and fraught with moral dilemmas as an initial public offering (IPO). An IPO is essentially the sale of a promise that a company makes to its future investors. A company may decide to access the capital market and offer its shares to the public for the first time for any of a number of reasons. The most obvious reason is that the company's owners or founders (or providers of private equity, as the case may be) want to convert their stakes in the business into cash. Alternatively, an IPO may be the result of the spin-off of a division from a larger conglomerate, which often occurs as part of a strategic reorientation. The state is also a major potential source of IPOs, as the financial institutions forced into state ownership during and after the credit crunch illustrate. Governments will, in due course, have to dispose of such investments, which were forced upon them by the social situation, at which point the public will be relied on to provide the capital. However, the desire to achieve a sale is not always the primary reason for an IPO. Sometimes a company decides to go public with a view to raising fresh capital, so that it can finance new initiatives or perhaps simply pay off some of its bank loans, for example. If a share issue is initiated by a company that is already listed on the stock market, this is known as a secondary offering, as opposed to an IPO.

The intriguing thing about IPOs is that they are the culmination of various events that are out of the ordinary. A great many activities coalesce at the same time and place, creating a kind of atomic reaction that generates new energy. The birth of a public-listed company is like the creation of new corporate life. It suddenly emerges into this world, with all of its fingers and toes, and is held up for all to admire. It has a face and personality of its own, and also its own quirks. From the moment of its birth, the 'corporate being' is public property, and its beating heart can be measured from one hour to the next. When the new life appears, the first questions that onlookers ask are whether it is healthy and how much it weighs. Sound health is an absolute prerequisite for entering the public market, and the weight corresponds to the value in the eyes of potential investors. Bankers, accountants and valuation specialists are able to discount all expected profits or future cash flows, but the valuation still remains theoretical, and matters do not always go according to plan. Moreover, many companies that decide to go public do not even have positive cash flows. The value of a company that is to be listed on the stock market is therefore highly subjective. The value is calculated, considered and anticipated, and promises are made to a certain extent. The company's actual value is determined when its opening price is established, after the global supply of and demand for its shares have been matched. The selling shareholders experience similar elation to new parents, and the world listens to the baby's first sounds, but soon the crying and wailing starts. Before the bursting of the dotcom bubble at the start of the 21st century, most businesses offered their shares at a discount in order to be certain that the share price would rise after the IPO. Even if the share price did happen to fall below the issue price, the general expectation was that the situation was merely temporary. As it was, most of the babies were back up to their birth weight within 10 days.

The almost systematic expectation that the share price would rise following the issue made the allocation of shares in IPOs an exceptional situation. Certainty that the price of a share one holds will rise is a form of free money, and that is something everybody wants. Shares tend to be placed with institutional and private investors using the market mechanism. Since the end of the 20th century, book building has become almost standard. In book building, all the parties interested in the IPO enter their orders (stating the number of shares they want and the price they are willing to pay) in an order book, rendering the level interest in the IPO and the potential issue price visible. The party that submits the first price or the best price is not by definition given priority. Shares are allocated at the seller's discretion, since the seller is free to decide who it prefers in the way of buyers. This creates a great deal of scope for doing favours and demanding privileges. When state-owned companies were privatised in Europe in the 1980s and 1990s, a policy of encouraging share ownership among the general public – a new form of popular capitalism – was deliberately pursued. To encourage people to invest, state-owned companies were sold at a relatively high discount, giving investors in the IPO a premium. The public snapped up the shares. Some people sold them quickly at a profit, while others held off, confident that the future would be even brighter. Of course, matters did not always go smoothly. For example, the sale of the state holding in the British oil conglomerate BP in 1987 coincided with Black Monday. What should have been an IPO offering a good premium nearly did not go ahead at all.

The discounts at which shares were sold meant that the allocation process was very susceptible to sharp practices, and even fraud. Retail investors were tempted with attractive discounts and assured of profits, making them almost feel as though they had won the lottery. They started to oversubscribe, applying for more shares than they really wanted, as they believed they would only receive a limited allocation. By oversubscribing, they expected to increase their share allocation and win a larger share of the jackpot. The commission houses and merchant banks involved in the IPO were happy to go along with this. In Hong Kong efforts were made to put a stop to the practice by requiring investors to prove that they would in fact be able to pay for the shares if they were allocated the full number for which they had subscribed. In order to be eligible for allocation, investors needed to prove there was a bank that was willing to finance the purchase. But this requirement had no effect. Greedy bankers had no problem guaranteeing 10 times the sum involved in a possible issue as they knew the shares would only ever be issued once. Guaranteeing 10 times over the sum meant they would earn 10 times more in fees.

The merchant banks that handled IPOs and were responsible for allocation soon came to realise that their right of allocation represented a bonus, one which they could use at their own discretion. And their discretion was guided by self-interest. This led to a rapid, sharp rise in the number of conflicts of interest, and meant that the motives underlying the allocation of shares were compromised. All these methods of non-selective allocation were given striking names. There were quid pro quo arrangements, in which favours were exchanged. For example, an institutional investor might be awarded extra shares, in exchange for which it had to supply more commission income in future. In laddering, by contrast, customers were asked to agree to make additional share purchases on the aftermarket, and in return were allocated extra shares. And in spinning, certain parties were allocated shares so that they would vote in favour of awarding future contracts to the merchant bank handling the allocation. A classic example of spinning is described in a report written by former US Attorney General Richard Thornburgh, who was appointed by the bankruptcy court to investigate WorldCom. This telecom company went bust in 2002, not long after it was floated on the stock market. In his report, which focused primarily on the relationship between WorldCom and the underwriting bank Citigroup, Thornburgh concluded that Citigroup:

> 'gave extraordinary financial favours and assistance to Mr Ebbers (the CEO of World Com)...to award WorldCom investment business...'
> The report also noted that the first financial favours provided to Mr Ebbers were in the form of large IPO allocations on which large gains could generally be made.

Formal arrangements also existed under which people involved in an IPO could reserve shares for members of their close personal circle (known as friends and family shares). It would be difficult to find a more perfect example of tribal culture within the financial sector. Finally, there was of course the standard tranche for options awarded to management. All of these practices have largely disappeared thanks to stricter monitoring by regulators and fewer opportunities. The 'free money' is largely gone, and IPOs are much less popular these days. The bursting of the dotcom bubble marked a sudden change in mood. The supposed entitlement to a profit after a few days of trading made way for the phenomenon of evaporation. Using book building for IPO allocations contributed to the crushing feeling that followed the first day of trading. The issue price produced by a book building procedure comes very close to the full market price, and therefore less and less scope is available for discounts. The removal of the illusion of free money and the propping up of the issue price makes disappointment in the aftermarket more likely, particularly in a bear market. Matters started to go wrong at the start of the 21st century. The public, left with losses, began to wail. At the same time, the financial regulations also came in for criticism. What exactly had been sold on the public market? A company or a promise? Or was it in fact an empty promise?

Although internet companies in particular failed to live up to expectations, and some of them were even fraudulent, they were not the only ones. The hype on the markets at the end of the 20th century actually extended much further. The major European privatisations that took place in the last two decades of that century created unrealistic expectations when it came to the future performance of lacklustre state enterprises. Investors thought that these companies would make waves as soon as they were freed from their stifling, bureaucratic shareholders and the management was rewarded in line with the market. The CEOs, some of whom were rather hoary, felt they had been reborn as entrepreneurs and set to work. They certainly made waves, although perhaps not in the way they had intended as the businesses almost went under. A good example of this is provided by Spain's Telefónica, which wanted to expand beyond the mere transportation of data by supplying content as well, and decided to purchase Endemol, the Dutch television production and distribution giant. How far can a company move from its core business before it runs the risk of collapsing under its own weight? Something similar happened at the Dutch telecom company PTT, which paid far too much when it acquired Germany's E-Plus and choked on the initial costs of broadband, as did many of its competitors. Vivendi, however, is a somewhat different story. The simple, dull utility company was transformed into a modern entertainment group as a result of its merger with Canal Plus and Seagram. The man who accomplished this was the CEO, Jean-Marie Messier, who was once a partner at the merchant bank Lazard Frères. Messier acted as if he was the Sun King, adopted all of his American colleagues' bad habits, and used Vivendi's money to buy himself an apartment on New York's Park Avenue. Messier gave his autobiography the revealing title *J6M*, which stands for Jean-Marie Messier Moi-Même Maître du Monde (master of the world). He thought he was invincible and would be able to remain at Vivendi's helm for a very long time. But it did not turn out that way. In 2002 he was forced to resign after Vivendi reported a loss of €13.6 billion. He then tried in vain to have his New York apartment included as part of his severance package.

But this was not the only example of emotion and grandeur. Many British and French people decided, with a sense of history, to invest in the Channel Tunnel. Although the financial value of this huge project had not yet been demonstrated, it did have emotional value. As it was, the first investors were given the lifelong right to travel through the tunnel for free. This was especially appealing to the British, who could take advantage of this to pick up much cheaper alcohol in France. Unfortunately, this would be their only dividend.

Was it all just hype, with no actual economic or social substance? The Channel Tunnel was eventually built, but under very different terms and conditions and following numerous refinancings. And broadband was introduced, albeit with very different economic prospects than originally envisaged. And rather than turning out to be hype, the internet was a technological revolution of historic proportions. That said, only a small portion of the growth in its value has been shared via the public markets. There have, of course, been some success stories, such as Apple, Google, Intel and Microsoft, and at one time Cisco could be included in this group too. Nevertheless, the public markets have had to deal with a disproportionately large share of the disappointments. Given this, it is legitimate to ask whether the IPO process was sufficiently honest in each of these cases. When it is possible to raise billions with a story that unleashes many healthy emotions but cannot be fully verified, there is great pressure to proceed with the process without being entirely honest. This pressure is intensified because there is information asymmetry; the seller knows literally everything about the business, while the buyer knows almost nothing. Given this, how can we ensure the game is played fairly? What conditions does a business have to satisfy before and, even more importantly, after it is listed on the public market?

An IPO that is aimed primarily at the retail market, and not just at institutional investors, needs to be handled with extra care, and the rules have been designed to take account of this. This applies in particular to the prospectus and the marketing material, all of which must be intelligible and readable. We will return to this topic further on in this chapter. But first, let us consider the admission criteria, which form the other line of defence against the misery.

There are two basic philosophies that underlie policy on admission to the public market. Europe has traditionally had policies that concentrate on quality, whereas policy in the US focuses more on disclosure. Investors have greater protection under the European system and a greater right to self-determination under the US system. The European system specifies explicit conditions in respect of the quality of the company seeking an exchange listing. Many of these conditions relate to the financial soundness of the company. There are often minimum requirements when it comes to their market capitalisation, and sometimes for their track record of profitability too. In addition, market criteria are set for matters such as the free float (the percentage of outstanding shares that can be freely traded on the market) and the number of shareholders to which the shares will be distributed. These criteria are designed to ensure liquidity following the IPO.

The system used in the US places less importance on minimum requirements for admission, although a number of the aforementioned conditions applying in Europe are also standard conditions in the US. Instead, there is much more emphasis on the quality and detail of the information provided by the company seeking a listing. The idea behind this is that investors who are well-informed should be in a very good position to take their own decisions. In this case, the market determines the value of the company. If the market is prepared to pay billions, what right do the regulators have to say that the company is not welcome in the public domain? Investor autonomy is given precedence over excessively restrictive rules designed from a historical perspective.

Markets operating under the European and US systems will require more time to assess the new proposition. For this reason, it is crucial that there is a pre-marketing period in which the market can prepare for the IPO and check the price level. This is initially done using a preliminary prospectus, also known as a red herring. In the US, the SEC reviews the red herring and releases it for distribution, while the exchanges handle the listing process. In Europe, the implementation of MiFID resulted in the introduction of a system in which the regulator not only reviews the prospectus but is also authorised to admit the shares to the official list, provided its conditions are satisfied. Once the shares have been listed, they can be traded on one or more exchange platforms. In practice, they are often traded on the platform of the country of the competent authority that gave its approval. The exchange and the regulator are therefore somewhat like Siamese twins.

How can we tell whether the seller of the shares has good intentions, or whether the contents of the prospectus are in any way accurate? How can we ensure that there are no abuses in terms of conflicts of interest? This is, of course, the responsibility of the sponsors, that is, the banks underwriting the issue. But that is not all. It is important that all interests are kept separate. The sellers in the IPO must not be given the opportunity to fill their bank accounts and then abscond. This can be achieved by means of a lockup agreement, under which the parties are prohibited from selling their shares for a period of time. Usually, the people who are subject to a lockup agreement determine whether or not the IPO's promise is fulfilled. It goes without saying that new shareholders do not want such people to leave before they have delivered the goods. The lockup agreement may apply for a fixed period or until such time as certain conditions have been met. This may mean achieving a certain level of profitability, but other conditions can also apply, as explained in an article on LinkedIn published in *Het Financieele Dagblad* on 16 November 2011:

> The management of LinkedIn may pocket up to US$164 million from the upcoming sale of shares in the exchange-listed networking site. CEO Jeffrey Weiner, CFO Steven Sordello, three other senior vice presidents and a vice president are offering 2,151,947 shares between them for up to US$76.44 a share, according to a document LinkedIn filed with the SEC, the US exchange regulator. The company's senior executives are taking advantage of the sharp increase seen in the price of LinkedIn shares, which have increased in value by some 70% since the IPO in May. In New York yesterday, LinkedIn shares fell several percentage points to under the US$75 mark. Each of the senior executives is offering approximately 10% of their stake in the online network that puts professionals in touch with each other. However, Bain Capital has decided to pull out of LinkedIn completely. The document reveals that founder Reid Hofmann, who still owns nearly 22% of LinkedIn, will not be participating.

The main complaint today is the inverse of the above; the current complaint is that the stakes floated on the public market are too small and too many shares are subject to lockup rules. As a consequence, the stake held by the old elite will hang over the market, potentially putting the share price under pressure. LinkedIn shares suffered this fate in November 2011, when it was announced that the existing shareholders would sell more of their shares. Zynga, another successful IPO, faced the same problem. Clearly a balance needs to be found between offering too few shares (which pushes the share price down) and too many shares (which creates the impression the old guard is no longer committed) in one go.

Very strict rules apply to prospectuses. The sponsor bank supporting the issue makes a significant contribution and checks the contents, particularly the predictive information. Approval also has to be obtained from various third parties, including auditors, who check the financial data, and lawyers (if, for example, certain rights or licences are involved). Next, the regulator, in its capacity as the 'competent authority', has to approve the prospectus. Nevertheless, prospective investors need to be aware that investing in companies with little in the way of a prior history is a matter of blind faith. For some companies it is particularly hard to predict what the future will bring, and this makes valuation more of an art than a science. These include companies whose existence is based on rights or licences, or institutional conditions, as in the case of pharmaceutical companies or mining companies. It is, after all, impossible to judge on the basis of the prospectus how much gold can be extracted or how hard it will be to drill through the layers of rock. The future value of companies active in the creative sector is also difficult to estimate accurately. How creative will the company be in future, and what will that mean in terms of profitability? Moreover, will the company manage to hang on to its creative minds? Questions of this nature are almost impossible to answer. Generally speaking, all companies that have large amounts of intangible assets on their balance sheet are vulnerable, but they often have potential too. For investors, it remains a difficult judgement to make. The prospectus is also packed full of warnings, which often makes it impossible to see the wood for the trees. In this way, human emotion and imagination once again become a factor in the investment proposition. What, for example, can we say about the value of LinkedIn at the time of its IPO?

On top of this, there is another source of the truth. Companies that start an IPO process hold roadshows at which they can present themselves to the public. While roadshows are primarily intended to win over institutional investors, companies also give presentations to share analysts and the press. Analysts study the proposition and form their own view, which serves as input for retail investors. But are these analysts truly independent? They are often in-house analysts employed by the sponsor banks, and they can hardly be expected to have an opinion of their own. The unwritten rule is that a bank sponsoring an IPO must not frustrate the process by allowing its own analysts to write a negative report. In the past, all too often analysts acted as if they were part of the marketing department. The reports they wrote had little intellectual or analytical value. Retail investors therefore have to depend on independent research houses, but this is the area in which problems are particularly likely to emerge. Securities houses that are not owned by banks in the syndicate generally do not have access to the roadshows, and so they have to obtain information through indirect channels. The second problem is that retail investors do not really want to pay for independent securities research. They would rather be given a lie for free than pay to discover the truth. And then there are the financial journalists. The openness of the prospectus is a powerful tool in the battle against improper dealings. It enables society to comment on the data provided in the prospectus, and some facts may come in for serious criticism. Experts who are not involved in the issue are, after all, free to express their doubts about optimistic expectations. And of course, the important role that the internet plays should not be forgotten. In short, the whole world can have a say in the matter. This aspect touches on the heart of the disclosure regime. The market is to be left to make up its own mind, but companies must be transparent and regulators must focus strongly on the quality of transparency.

The process leading up to the IPO needs to be handled with great care. In the heat of the battle, there is always a risk of deception, no matter how unintended it may be, as was seen in the IPO of Germany's Postbank as reported in the *Financial Times*, 2004.

When Germany's Postbank decided to go public in the summer of 2004, almost everything that could go wrong did. Not only did it emerge that Deutsche Bank – the merchant bank that acted as lead manager – wanted to buy the bank, but, to make matters worse, there was a leak of internal documents which revealed that the federal post office had overestimated the value of its subsidiary Deutsche Post. Then, during the run-up to the IPO, global stock markets fell in reaction to events occurring around the world and developments in the oil market, which made Postbank much less appealing to institutional investors. Next, Deutsche Post CEO Klaus Zumwinkel announced that retail investors had shown overwhelming interest in the offering, which was, with hindsight, a very questionable statement. Although the media and the regulators did not scrutinise this statement, it was impossible to prove. It could not be based on any reliable information, such as a telephone survey or mailing lists, because

Continued

Box *continued*

retail investors were not committed to anything at this stage and could still cancel their orders at any time. However, optimistic statements can easily be misleading. On Sunday 20 June 2004, two weeks making after his positive announcement, Zumwinkel was forced to narrow the bandwidth and cut the number of shares in order to ensure the IPO would not be a disaster. His earlier statement did indeed turn out to be misleading.

All of the marketing material needs to be geared towards the prospectus. Promotional activities aimed at bringing the shares to the attention of investors cannot begin until the prospectus is available. This allows interested investors to consult the prospectus immediately, and put the picture they have formed in its context. At least that is the theory. In addition, any promotional campaigns must end well before subscription starts, so that excited potential investors have sufficient time to cool off. Marketing efforts must be proportionate, because if they are overdone they can be misleading. The following real-life example illustrates this. The notorious IPO of internet provider World Online, which took place in Amsterdam in 2000, was preceded by an advertising campaign that was so intrusive, loud and excessive it created an image of the IPO that was not reflected in the information contained in the prospectus. As a consequence, the prospectus was disregarded as an information carrier. Based on this and other circumstances, regulators now try to prevent institutional funds from being used to hype up a share prior to its IPO. This explains the cooling-off rules. But is hype something we can prevent entirely? Sometimes the whole world is affected by the build-up. We should not be under the illusion that rules can put an end to emotion and greed. In the case of World Online, the hype was not based on the advertising campaign alone; it was based on reality. AOL's takeover of Time Warner in 2000 was front page news around the world. Everyone believed that a new era had dawned in which different rules applied. The World Online IPO was a huge success, but that success literally lasted only a few hours. A number of major shareholders disposed of their stakes on the first day of trading. And even before the IPO lunch had finished, the sell orders had started to come flooding in and the share price tumbled. The banks initially provided support, but after this the free fall became unstoppable, encouraged by rumours that the prospectus was misleading. It literally signified the end of the global dotcom dream, and the start of a worldwide collapse in internet share prices. Investors suffered, but they were also to blame. Prior to the World Online IPO they had acted in the same way as the drivers on the A2 near the Limburg village of Beek. All the investors believed they had won the lottery and only had to wait for the prize money to be paid. It never was. This huge anticlimax was one of the main reasons for the collective anger of investors. They read the prospectus and called their lawyers. To add insult to injury, World Online's campaign had basically been financed with money that had been raised from investors. As the share price fell, investors instinctively realised that they had paid for the marketing costs themselves. When the World Online IPO took place, a small group of demonstrators, a forerunner to the Occupy movement, gathered on the square in front of the Amsterdam stock exchange, bearing large banners and pans. They were selling hot air, because 'the hot air sold outside was a great deal less expensive than the hot air traded inside the exchange'. And this turned out to be true. But could the same thing be said of Google's IPO? Or the IPO of LinkedIn? And what about Facebook's flotation?

The first moment – the birth – is crucial. But sometimes the baby is delivered with the cord tied around its neck and is strangled. This is what happened to Bats (Better alternative trading) Global Markets. The trading platform, launched by David Cummings in 2005, was very successful in attracting trading volume away from major exchanges. Over 11% of share trading volume in the US goes through Bats. The company wanted to be listed on its own platform, which at that point was nothing more than a trading platform. While it had listed some index products successfully, it had not at that point had a 'real' company. It was therefore to be the first listing on its own exchange. All the software had been tested extensively and approved, but none of these tests had discovered the bug in the IPO module. The bug only started to cause problems when trading began for real. Trades were not reported properly to the centralised quote system, as a result of which incorrect prices were published. And this proved to be fatal. In the space of 9.5 seconds, the price of Bats shares collapsed from just over US$15 to zero. In its wake, the platform dragged down other equities with names beginning with letters close to the start of the alphabet, such as Apple shares. The IPO was called off, and the baby was stillborn.

The Facebook IPO that took place at the end of May 2012 incorporated all of the above calamities. The issues surrounding the IPO of Facebook are at the core of this chapter. Was the promise made by the company to the investors an empty promise or not? In the run-up to the IPO, in response to the vast level of public interest, Facebook increased the number of shares on offer and increased the issue price as well. But at the same time, there was news that was similar to a profit warning. It was a first indication that the earnings potential may have been represented too optimistically. Worse still, the earnings model was somewhat in trouble because of the increase in the number of customers accessing Facebook through their mobile phones. This news was not disseminated simultaneously to the entire market. Suddenly there were insiders and outsiders, creating a very awkward situation just before the IPO went live. How did this happen?

Analysts may discuss their views of companies with investors and they can choose which investors they talk to. Few of these investors are private investors. Analysts were aware of the potential earnings problem and they shared their thoughts. From a regulatory perspective, these two aspects are highly relevant. In the US, there is a ban on the release of research prior to an IPO, but that ban applies to written information, whereas in this case the news was conveyed orally. And although selective disclosure of information is no longer permitted, the same does not apply to companies that are not yet listed. So an old practice, which was thought to have been buried, was revived. And private investors were the ones that suffered as a result.

NASDAQ also had egg on its face, and did not make any new friends. Trading was halted at the very moment the IPO took place, and that made the market even more suspicious. It was put down to a computer bug, but in fact it was the result of a processing mistake. NASDAQ run normal auctions by freezing all incoming orders and run an algorithm. However, their IPO model did not include a freeze mechanism, and cancel orders continued to come in while they were running the auction. The only way to overcome this problem was to remove all the orders and freeze the system by hand. Many orders were treated badly. Nothing of the kind had ever happened before in the history of NASDAQ, but there is a first time for everything. Sometimes it takes a whole book to describe everything that can go wrong on the securities market, yet this can all be encapsulated in just one IPO. Facebook should be congratulated for accomplishing this feat. It is only a pity it cost so many investors so much money.

Once the IPO process is over, a new set of worries arise. It is vital that the share price is not manipulated in the aftermarket. For this reason there are strict rules governing the extent to which the underwriting financial institutions are allowed to stabilise and regulate the share price. We previously saw how such provisions can be circumvented by asking third parties to make further purchases if the price falls, in exchange for which they are allocated extra shares in the IPO. One acceptable way of supporting share prices in the aftermarket is through what is known as a greenshoe. The company issues more shares than indicated in the prospectus, the additional shares being referred to as the 'greenshoe'. If the share price in the aftermarket falls below the issue price, the sponsor bank buys back the additional issued shares at a price that is below the issue price. This supports the share price. If, however, the share price does not dip below the issue price, more shares will have been brought into in circulation than in the original issue. In that case the greenshoe option is exercised, as a result of which the issuance of the additional shares is authorised in retrospect.

What determines whether these processes are not only honest at the outset, but continue to be so? The integrity of the actors is vitally important, of course, as is the quality of the rules and laws in the jurisdiction where the shares are listed and in which the company is based for legal purposes. Another vital factor relates to the conditions the issuer has to satisfy on a permanent basis, known as the ongoing obligations. The form of shares to be issued, the rights they represent and the governance structure (as expressed by corporate governance requirements) are important in this respect. Some governance requirements relate to matters such as control, the control structure, and how control over the company, and within it, has been allocated. The structure agreed with the company going public is often crucial to its future success. Many of the seeds of destruction are sown early on, and this can be detected in the structure and documentation that forms the basis of an IPO.

Foreign listings represent a special proposition that is extremely vulnerable from the perspective of integrity. In the battle for supremacy, some Western capital markets are quite aggressive in their hunt for foreign listings. And most of this hunting takes place in Russia and China, both large economies with less well-developed capital markets and, more importantly, issues in the area of integrity.

Companies in countries classified as emerging markets or as frontier markets (one level down from emerging markets) by Morgan Stanley Capital International (MSCI) have an image problem due to the status of their country of incorporation. That means international investors, and certainly investors who invest passively in Western indices, will not be very interested in them. So what can they do about this? Such problems encourage companies to change the location of their headquarters, their legal incorporation and their listing. Some companies based in China (which is classified as an emerging market) transfer their interests to a holding company located in Hong Kong (classified as a developed market by MSCI). This is a pure form of corporate upward mobility. In turn, the exchange officials and competent authorities are happy to accommodate the applicant. It is good for their capital markets and their position in the league tables. But in order to appeal to international investors, especially passive ones, these companies need to obtain a place in the local indices. A good example of this concerns the application for a British exchange listing submitted by Polyus Gold, a Russian mining company that is one of the biggest players on the Russian gold market. Polyus is owned by Mikhail Prokhorov, one of Russia's richest magnates, who has substantial industrial holdings. Prokhorov is extremely flamboyant and a somewhat controversial figure. In early 2007 he gained notoriety when he was arrested in the French Alps for allegedly arranging prostitutes for rich Russian guests. He was eventually released and received an apology from the French authorities. He made the news again in 2010 owing to a scandal in the south of France.

At the end of 2011, Polyus decided to relocate its holding company activities to London and transfer them to a public limited company. Naturally, it also wanted its shares to be listed on the London Stock Exchange. This would give the company much easier access to the wallets of international investors. Until that time, Polyus was a Russian company and investors could only invest in American depositary receipts (ADRs). British listing rules require a minimum free float of 25% for ordinary shares, while a free float of 15% is required in order to be eligible for inclusion in the FTSE 100 index. However, Polyus, with its new holding company, had a free float of just 13%. The British authorities gave no indication that this would be a deal breaker. This attitude in particular unleashed a storm of indignation among institutional investors. Resolve was stiffened as a consequence. The FSA tightened its rules and the FTSE increased its free float requirement to 25%. But that was not the only reason why the listing did not go ahead. The Russian authorities, headed by Vladimir Putin, failed to approve Polyus's relocation request. And that was the end of the story. Nevertheless, this is a good example of how far the Western capital markets are prepared to bow to immigration applications from foreign companies. They do this despite knowing that all these constructions could easily collapse owing to weak foundations.

What are these weaknesses? A recurring vulnerability in the construction concerns the free float, or more specifically the lack of a free float. This is usually due to the presence of one or two major shareholders. In such instances there is usually a controlling shareholder who also has various business relationships with the company, as was the case at Polyus. And when someone has relationships of that kind with the company, they can erode any returns on the company by executing transactions that are not in line with the market. It is tantamount to having the opportunity to commit daylight robbery. International shareholders that sign up to the investment proposition are therefore very vulnerable. The authorities thought that this issue could be resolved by means of relationship agreements. Written promises are made to the effect that all transactions will be done on an objective basis, but in reality this is often all just a sham. How can the protection laid down in the relationship agreement be enforced on behalf of minority shareholders whose rights are affected? The independent directors, who supervise the business on behalf of the minority shareholders, can easily be dismissed if they decide to take action. And this does actually happen. The only thing that could possibly help improve the situation a little would be to add a provision to the articles of association that stipulates controlling shareholders do not have any authority to dismiss independent directors. But just how far should we go in our efforts to put right something that is wrong?

There are many other weak spots in the foundations of such structures involving foreign holding companies and foreign listings. Companies emigrate from a strange, unfamiliar jurisdiction where the rules are not in keeping with Western ways of thinking. This is a recipe for all kinds of problems. One of the questions that arises in this context concerns the choice of accounting principles to be used. Or, as in the case of Polyus, how is it possible to demonstrate with any degree of reliability the company has legal title to the mining reserves and whether those reserves actually exist? One of the main questions relates to whether the company that is incorporated and listed in the UK actually owns the foreign assets. There is very little chance it is the full owner, particularly when it comes to strategic assets. The company is more likely to have contractual relationships with entities in the mother country which own the rights. And how solid are those contracts in the event of conflicts? How easy is it to cancel them or simply fail to comply with them? Polyus is a special case. Prokhorov accumulated his wealth during the wave of uncontrolled privatisations that occurred while Boris Yeltsin was in power. Moreover, he is not a friend of Putin. In December 2011, he announced his intention to participate in the Russian presidential elections, in which he came third with 7% of the vote, behind the communist Gennady Zyuganov. Is it safe for foreign investors to assume resentment in the motherland will not have any impact? There is often a political risk to take into account. Another issue relates to the repatriation of profits. Will the holding company have access to profits generated in the mother country? Some of these companies do not distribute any dividend and instead retain all earnings. That means that shareholders' reserve reported in the balance sheet in euros or sterling are, in reality, stuck in Siberia in the form of roubles. Those holding companies that do pay dividends may well have to borrow them from the bank. The financial relationship between the holding company and the subsidiaries in the motherland therefore becomes very strained. The listing on a Western market is often a facade behind which anything can go wrong and in which Western regulators are unable to intervene. The most the regulators can do is delist the company. The facade therefore serves to give the company undue legitimacy.

It is vital that a substantial portion of the total share capital can be freely traded. As mentioned above, the minimum applying in the UK is 25%. A minimum requirement much lower than this increases the risk of market manipulation. This may be a relevant issue when it comes to controlling shareholders. They often have many other business concerns, and one of those businesses may at some point get into difficulties. It will then be necessary to borrow money from a bank, in return for which collateral will have to be provided. If the free float is small and the shareholder gives the shares as security, he will be sorely tempted to manipulate the share price. In this way, the shareholder remains in control of how much he is able to borrow from willing financial backers.

A controlling shareholder can also create problems at a company that is entirely Western. The founder is often obliged to admit outside capital in order to finance plans for expansion, but at the same time he does not want his influence to be diluted. A structure is created in which a minority of the shares represent the majority, or even all, of the power. The Dutch brewery Heineken is a good example of this, as are many other reputable companies around the world. One company that has been in the spotlight a great deal is News Corporation. In terms of share capital, the Murdoch family does not own the majority of this media conglomerate, yet the family still calls the shots. The position of the independent directors can be very vulnerable, particularly if the majority shareholder also has control at the level of the executive management. Sometimes this control is exercised by a son, sometimes by a daughter-in-law. Minority shareholders are held hostage as a result, and often have no option but to sit back and watch how the game plays out. Independent board members are there purely for show, and are compelled to act as mere advisers.

Following on from the above, the next questions we need to consider are as follows. Should shareholders with identical participating interests be allowed to have an unequal say? What about the principle of one share, one vote? In the context of equality in the financial industry, surely the rule should be one vote per share? Or is there another argument we need to take into consideration? A number of fundamental debates have been held on this subject. The urge to hold on to power is, of course, the main countercurrent, driven by high levels of emotion and the thought that the business belongs to the incumbent regime rather than the shareholders. Companies that have listed all their shares on the public market are particularly easy prey when it comes to takeovers. These include hostile takeovers, with all they imply from a financial and emotional perspective. Should we stop that by denying someone the right to vote? The debate surrounding unequal voting rights has two dimensions. The first relates to whether a shareholder may be denied the right to vote when another shareholder who has contributed just as much capital does have the right to vote. This question should be answered in the affirmative. Shareholders who do not have voting rights are aware of the situation beforehand, and when they decided to invest in the company they consciously chose to waive their voting rights. The second dimension relates to where the voting right ends up. Does it go to the controlling shareholder, or is it managed separately, independently of the existing management? If it ends up with the remaining shareholders, would this not lead to an unhealthy concentration of power? In the most extreme case, all control over the company is concentrated in a single share. With the notable exception of Volkswagen, almost all of these shares, known as golden shares, had disappeared. However, sovereign shareholders in particular are now hanging on to golden shares so that they can protect the interests of society. If a shareholder is denied the right to vote, the control they would have had must be transferred elsewhere. Not having the right to vote is much less of a moral problem than the issue of where those voting rights end up. Why should someone who does not hold any shares have the right to vote? The voting rights could end up in the hands of management or their friends. This corporate governance issue can quickly turn into a major social problem.

However, if the voting rights are held by the shareholders, a different problem can arise. This is because shareholders do not always have any capital at risk. In the recent past, various companies have gone under and have had to be bailed out by creditors, banks or the government. In such cases the shareholders have lost everything and certainly do not have anything more to lose. They no longer have any skin in the game, but they still have the right to vote. As a consequence, besides being full of rancour they also have an incentive to act irrationally. The process of restarting the company is obstructed for no reason other than anger. The lengthy law suits aimed at obtaining compensation for shareholders in the bankruptcy of the Belgian bank Fortis provide a good example of this. When capital is lost in the economic sense, the voting right attached to it should also be relinquished. The rules surrounding living wills (compulsory plans for dealing with specific emergencies) for financial institutions need to give substance to this very challenging idea.

This chapter started off with the birth of a listed company, and we have now reached the end point of the corporate life. As well as being listed on the stock exchange, companies are also delisted. Sometimes this is done as part of a takeover, in other cases the company simply goes bust. But sometimes the company's management violates so many rules that the competent authorities suspend the listing or withdraw the company from listing. This last measure, in effect a form of corporate euthanasia, contains a hidden moral dilemma. Existing shareholders, who were able to invest through the public market, are the victims in this situation. Their property is in fact snatched away from them. The authorities remove companies from listing when they believe it would be irresponsible to allow new, unwary investors to sign up to an investment proposition that has become indefensible. In this way, new investors are protected. The music stops, and the game is over. The existing shareholders are the ones who suffer, but their suffering is necessary for the integrity of the markets to be maintained. Someone always has to pay for empty promises.

Chapter 14

Taming the beast

Little boys like to play football and build sand castles, big boys like buying football clubs and building real castles. What drives those needs? How can excessive behaviour be properly channelled? Real castles made from sand often collapse when the tide comes in. How can the culture of corporate toadying be overcome?

In 1991, the Anglo-Czech media magnate Robert Maxwell fell off the radar, literally and figuratively, somewhere in the vicinity of the Canary Islands. In November that year he was cruising alone on his yacht, the Lady Ghislaine. The yacht was found, but there was no trace of Maxwell. His lifeless body was fished out of the water several days later, following an intensive search. He was thought to have lost his balance and fallen overboard in the middle of the ocean. The official cause of death was drowning, but rumours of suicide soon surfaced. The British tabloids did not rule out murder, as a former Mossad employee contended that Maxwell, who was Jewish, had been a spy and a mainstay of the young state of Israel. In any case, he left the Mirror Group, one of Britain's best known publishing groups, in a state of chaos. There had been suspicions that things were not going well with the group, but following Maxwell's sudden death it emerged that the business was in much worse shape than imagined. The Mirror Group was in serious financial trouble, and bankruptcy was inevitable. As the empire crumbled, more and more sordid details emerged from the rubble, all of them the result of mismanagement. The most fatal decision was related to the Mirror Group's pension fund. In a desperate attempt to avert bankruptcy, Maxwell had pledged the fund's assets to the banks Shearson Lehman and Goldman Sachs. Nothing like that had ever happened before. It was the absolute pinnacle of corporate incompetence. Maxwell was revealed as a ruthless, domineering, headstrong man who did exactly as he pleased and was not prepared to listen to anyone else any more, not least his sons Kevin and Ian. He had lost all touch with reality and no longer had any sense of proportion.

The Italian Carlisto Tanzi, a born entrepreneur, had similar problems. He did not shine academically at university and at the age of 23 he set up a small milk pasteurising factory. He sold his pasteurised milk door-to-door in Parma, a city in the north of Italy from which he took the name of his company, Parmalat (a combination of the words Parma and *latte*, the Italian word for milk). Under Tanzi, Parmalat grew into a major company that handled 50% of all milk processing in Italy. In the late 1990s it began to branch out into other areas. Parmalat became a conglomerate with diversified activities, including a travel agency managed by Tanzi's daughter. But that was not enough for the domineering, self-satisfied Tanzi. In 1990 he bought FC Parma, a small provincial club that played in Italy's Serie B. The club was renamed AC Parma, and things took off from there. Success came quickly, but it proved fleeting, and not only for the football club. In December 2003 Parmalat had to repay a loan of €150 million. Although the conglomerate's books said it had €4.5 billion in liquid assets, the business was in trouble. There were in fact no liquid assets at all, just colossal losses, particularly on the holdings. In addition, there was wide-scale fraud in relation to the financial statements, and documentation on loans had been falsified. Billions had been siphoned off to accounts in the Cayman Islands. A sum of €14 billion mentioned on the balance sheet could not be found. The Parmalat empire subsequently collapsed like a deck of cards, becoming what is still the biggest corporate bankruptcy in European history. In 2008 Tanzi was sentenced to 10 years in prison by a court in Milan. He appealed, of course; how dare they do that to him?

Dirk Scheringa (1950) is the Dutch equivalent of the born entrepreneur; a simple man with a folksy, cheeky-chappy personality who was anything but media-shy. It was difficult not to know him. Scheringa was born in Grijpskerk, in the province of Groningen. After finishing his lower secondary education he began as an apprentice typesetter. He later worked as a sergeant in the police force but quit in 1975 to set up a tax consultancy with his wife, Baukje. They started with filling out tax returns but soon expanded into simple financing activities, initially as a means of helping people meet tax payments, but consumer loans were soon added to their range of products. Scheringa also got into the mortgage and insurances markets. His activities were so successful that he decided it would be a good idea to set up his own bank. He was given a licence, he named the bank after himself, and DSB bank was in business. However, in 2010 things went wrong and Scheringa's empire collapsed. This was not as a result of fraud, but because the bank had been hollowed out by the boss's expensive hobbies and the public had got wise to DSB's dubious earnings model. They saw that the bank was saddling its customers with too much debt and useless insurance policies that came with exorbitant premiums. DSB's business model was unethical, and at a certain point customers cannot be hoodwinked anymore. The company's management failed to change course in time. Moreover, a different business model would have also resulted in a different earnings profile, and that would have meant the end of the king's expensive toys. But when aggrieved customers joined forces and began to file claims, the empire crumbled.

Maxwell, Tanzi and Scheringa all built their companies from scratch and experienced great success before driving them back into the ground again and ending up on the smouldering ruins of their own ambitions. They were each responsible for the bankruptcy of their own life's work. But these three men have something else in common. They were all dictators, modern versions of the traditional patriarch. They knew how to use favours and flattery to bind people to them, and they treated those in their direct business environment as one big family. That was the experience of their courtiers. The price was absolute loyalty; no dissenting opinions were allowed. Those who were loyal benefited from the patriarch's generosity, receiving a dividend of favours and privileges. Those who were disloyal, and dared to challenge the boss, even in the most innocent way, were banned to the back of beyond. They were expelled not only from the business, but also from the family and from the boss's sphere of influence. That is why many chose to make a pact with the devil; they asked no questions and looked the other way. Others left of their own accord. The naysayers gradually disappeared from the family, leaving only the toadies behind. Robert Maxwell had a stranglehold on everyone around him, and his sons Kevin and Ian were pawns in their father's game. There was, however, one exception. While he was a student at Oxford, Kevin Maxwell met the independent and outspoken Pandora Warnock-Davies. They married soon after, against the wishes of his father. Pandora did not hesitate to voice her opinions and she was not afraid to stand up to her father-in-law. The two were frequently at odds. Pandora could not be expelled from the family so Robert Maxwell had to put up with her, but that was the extent of it. It was the only opposition the Maxwell empire would tolerate. Pandora dealt her most famous verbal blow in the early morning of 18 June 1992, when Kevin was arrested on suspicion of involvement in the Maxwell scandal.

Amid all of the media attention surrounding the Maxwell affair, Pandora proved herself a very loyal wife. One night she and her husband were disturbed by shouting at their front door. Leaning out of an upstairs window, she shouted, 'Piss off, or I'll call the police!'

'Madam,' came the reply from the street, 'we are the police.' Her husband was arrested and driven off in a police van. The scene was caught on camera by a news channel which repeatedly broadcast the fragment to the British public. Pandora has never ceased to protest about what she sees as an injustice.

Carlisto Tanzi invested a great deal of time, energy and care in the local community in Parma, and solved many of its problems, both monetary and non-monetary. He had a great deal of influence in the local church, but his power extended beyond the local. In the wider Parma area, people knew it was a sensible idea to stay in Tanzi's good books. The same was true of Scheringa, albeit on a smaller scale. He was synonymous with Spanbroek, and his influence extended into large areas of West Friesland. According to unconfirmed reports, Robert Maxwell's arm was much longer. Some blamed him – and others gave him credit for – helping Mossad to find the nuclear physicist Mordechai Vanunu (who had said that Israel was secretly manufacturing nuclear weapons, see Chapter 15) and deporting him back to Israel.

The one thing that all three men have in common is a football club. Maxwell bought Oxford United, Tanzi AC Parma, and Scheringa AZ Alkmaar. Under Tanzi the once unassuming AC Parma won three national championships and two UEFA cups. Scheringa's AZ was another regional club, which started out at the bottom of the premier league. Scheringa built a big new stadium in Alkmaar, named after himself, of course, and AZ went on to become national champions. Other examples include Silvio Berlusconi and AC Milan, and Roman Abramovich and Chelsea. Men who have influence in society apparently all want to own a football club. Why is this? It is intriguing behaviour, and perhaps somewhat immature. But because it is structural, it reveals something important about the ego and the psyche. Do these men really like football? Or do they like themselves more? Do they want to cheer on their team during important matches, or do they want someone to cheer them on? Do they want the trophy, or do they hold on to it because they want to be admired?

Another similarity, of a somewhat different kind, is shared by Dirk Scheringa and the American, Roland Arnall (and in one sense also by Arnall and Robert Maxwell). Arnall was born on 29 March 1939 in Paris, on the eve of World War II. His parents were Hungarian Jews who fled to France. In the war Arnall was hidden away in the countryside where he was raised as a Catholic; he did not find out that he was Jewish until later. After the war his family moved to Montreal, and then, in the 1950s, to the US. To earn money, Arnall started selling flowers on the street, but soon he became interested in another type of commerce. He discovered that there were people who needed credit but did not qualify for a bank loan. Arnall thought he could provide the solution, and he started a company that focused on providing consumer credit to the poorest in society. It began with loans to buy refrigerators. But if you buy a refrigerator you need a place to put it, preferably a home of your own. So Arnall soon branched out into the mortgage market. He founded Ameriquest, which he built into one of the biggest sub-prime mortgage lenders in the US. In his book *Too Big to Fail*, Andrew Ross Sorkin writes extensively about Ameriquest. He concludes that at that company mortgage data and applications were altered, the conditions of loans were withheld, and exorbitant conditions were imposed on borrowers. It was behaviour that went far beyond the bounds of the ethical. The company was essentially a criminal organisation, stealing from the poor in the US to make Arnall a billionaire. He did have a big heart, and he donated large sums to all kinds of social and political causes. For example, he made substantial contributions to the election campaign of George W Bush. When George W started his first term in office, Arnall naturally got something in return. He was put forward for the position of ambassador to a country which, although an important ally, is not important enough to merit an experienced diplomat – the Netherlands. It also helped that Arnall was really a European, not an American at all. The appointment was not entirely uncontested as the first court case against Ameriquest was already underway. The US Senate expressed concern about the appointment and was reluctant to give approval. However, in January 2006 Ameriquest reached a US$325 million settlement, and that February the Senate approved the appointment. I met Arnall on various occasions in The Hague and found him to be a very pleasant person. In my view, he had a solid world view and a proper understanding of his country's role. After serving one and a half terms in office he suddenly returned to the US. The official version was that his son was seriously ill, but within a few weeks he himself had died of cancer.

What are the similarities between Arnall and Scheringa? Both earned money by providing financial services to the poorest in society. By misrepresenting the situation and focusing on the most basic human needs they persuaded customers to take on too much debt – debt that was also encumbered by unnecessary insurance. Customers were fleeced. And because they were left with no possibility of appealing to any other bank, they were caught in a web of extortionate insurance policies and money lent at extortionate interest rates. Every missed payment was punished by even higher interest rates. Debt collectors went from door to door to collect money from customers. It was an evil system but it flourished and Arnall and Scheringa earned good money from it. The debt arrears mounted up, as did the interest and their income. What did they do with all their money? They gave a significant portion back to society. Tanzi did so via contributions to the church, and Arnall, one of the biggest charity donors in the US, gave a large share of his wealth to the poor. This seems odd. Why should they steal money if they intended to give it back? In fact they actually gave only a small portion of their fortunes away, but the real answer is that what truly matters to such men is something entirely different. It is about power, status, and, above all, vanity. It is also about their own deep-seated anxiety and insecurity. Maxwell was born in Czechoslovakia as Ján Ludvik Hoch to a poverty-stricken Jewish family that was forced, in a divided Europe, to flee from the Nazis. His parents and many other members of his family died in the concentration camp at Auschwitz. Dirk Scheringa came from a poor community in Friesland and began his career as a policeman. Arnall was an impoverished immigrant who sold flowers on the street. An acute awareness of the uncertainty of life must have been stamped on the souls of these men and ingrained in their genes.

The feelings of insecurity, inferiority and vulnerability can easily tip over into narcissistic behaviour.

Someone with a narcissistic personality disorder feels superior to others and has a sense of belonging to an elite. They seem to regard privileges as their due. Blessed with so many unique traits, they have opportunities to be become part of the happy few. Narcissists may display sharp swings in their preferences for and rejection of others. It takes very little for someone they initially idealised to suddenly be discarded. People with narcissistic tendencies are addicted to admiration and attention. Deep inside they are often lonely, but they shut themselves off from the outside world with their inflated self-opinion. They are extremely sensitive to offence and rejection. Criticism is experienced as a ruthless attack on their person. It is a mixture of grandiosity, arrogance and an extreme sense of inferiority. People with a narcissistic personality disorder display persistent patterns of behaviour that serve to maintain or protect self-esteem. Failure can mean others think they are bad or flawed. There may also be a strong sense of envy, and this can lead to feelings of extreme aggression. In their private lives, [narcissists] find it difficult to form attachments as they are unable to let others into their life unconditionally and without criticism.

Source: Muste, E, Cornelissen, K and Harman, S, *Persoonlijkheidsproblemen; beleving en behandeling*, 2008

This internal sense of insecurity can be dealt with by shutting off feelings from the outside world, shouting them down, and protecting them from negative external forces, such as contradiction. Narcissists seek protection in admiration and pursue prosperity to counteract the uncertainty of their existence. They wrap up their feelings in a blanket of money – nice comfortable piles of money. Others can then share in that wealth, because that too offers protection by stifling criticism from others. 'Greatness' can be measured in terms of owning a football club, and also by an even more addictive hobby: collecting art. Many wealthy, successful men start an art collection, which gives them even more status and security. And although they cannot benefit from such security once they are no longer of this earth, they still want their name to be remembered. A fine art collection in their own museum can ensure the rich remain famous forever. Scheringa was a passionate collector. His financial demise was hastened by his exceptional collection of meta-realistic 20th century art, and the construction of a surreally large museum in his home town of Spanbroek, which would never have been home to such a museum if it were not for Scheringa. Tanzi was also linked to a collection of expensive art objects. In December 2009 the Italian authorities announced they had confiscated 19 large paintings from the house of one of his friends. The paintings, which included works by Picasso, Monet and van Gogh, had a combined value of €100 million. Tanzi denied that he owned the paintings, even though his son-in-law was about to sell them.

Why are these stories included in a book about financial ethics? In my view they give us insight into how many leaders within our society think, behave, and, more importantly, how they go off track. They also shed light on whether this is the result of personal failing or the failure of the system. When powerful men lose their way for personal reasons, they often leave a lot of damage in their wake. They become a danger to themselves and to their immediate surroundings, and, if they are truly influential, their behaviour can become a social, and sometimes even a systemic, risk. If it is possible to discover a pattern in their behaviour, then perhaps we can say a bit more about how this behaviour affects companies and how it can be properly channelled or prevented altogether by means of early intervention. This is necessary because every leader discussed in this chapter blazed a trail of destruction through the society in which he lived and worked. They drove people to financial ruin and took away their prospects of future happiness. Thanks to the banks, the Mirror Group's pensioners got back half of their pensions, but the other half is gone for good. Many of DSB Bank's customers have been sentenced to lifelong repayment of extortionate loans, in the form of premium payments for useless insurance policies. We also want to understand the behaviour of these men because it is so contradictory. Those who behave unethically often have a genuine charitable impulse. They steal, but they also give a great deal of money back to society. It is therefore not a question of good *or* evil, but of good *and* evil, which is what makes matters so confusing. Dirk Scheringa is still a hero to some Dutch people, Robert Maxwell was buried on the Mount of Olives in Jerusalem in a ceremony fit for a statesman, and despite the fact that he was essentially the head of a criminal organisation, Roland Arnall was the US ambassador to the Kingdom of the Netherlands, where he was frequently the guest of Queen Beatrix. Good and evil are intertwined, and this presents a new challenge to our capacity to make ethical judgments.

Sometimes big accidents and small accidents are simply permutations of the same phenomenon. A variation on one of the themes already discussed fits seamlessly into this concept. In 2007, two professors, Crocker Liu of Arizona State University and David Yermack of New York University, published a paper with the apt title 'Where are the shareholders' mansions?' Liu and Yermack studied the relationship between the houses purchased by CEOs and the share value of their company. The professors concluded that the more expensive the house was in relation to the houses of other CEOs, the worse the performance of the company's shares. This is a significant finding. A large number of industrial leaders and senior bank executives treat themselves to a beautiful estate at the end of their career. The newspaper magnate William Randolph Hearst commissioned his own Hearst Castle, while the residences of JP Morgan, steel magnate Andrew Carnegie, and the politician Henry Clay have been turned into museums. The exception to the rule is Warren Buffett, who not only wants to pay more taxes but also still lives in a relatively modest house in Omaha. A Dutch example that springs to mind is the flashy estate that Rijkman Groenink built. While ABN Amro ran adrift, his brand new house on the banks of the River Vegt stood sparkling, oblivious to the banking crisis and the fact that it looked out of place in its surroundings. The research conducted by Liu and Yermack also found that the way in which CEOs financed their houses provided information about returns on the shares of the company they control. Other researchers obtained identical results when they looked at the relocation of company headquarters, usually to much better buildings.

It is not my intention in this chapter to depict any particular individual as a narcissist, but it is possible to identify certain narcissistic traits in society as a whole. Emphasising the importance of the individual, refusing to tolerate contradiction, shutting one's self off from suggestions to reconsider past decisions and using power to elicit obedience and admiration are just a few of the countless forms of variant behaviour that can have huge consequences for the management of a company or a social organisation. I would like to look at two of them in greater detail. The first refers to the human biological constitution, and how it is translated into sex, lies and arrogance through the abuse of power, the best examples of which come from the world of politics. The second form of variant behaviour is the lack of self-reflection and the inability to re-evaluate past decisions or actions. There are numerous examples of this in the financial world, but certain cases of judicial error could also be included here.

At the end May 2011, the following question was blazoned on the cover of *Time* magazine: 'What makes powerful men behave like pigs? Sex, lies and arrogance'. The scandal involving the former head of the IMF, Dominique Strauss-Kahn, had prompted an article on the misbehaviour of powerful men, particularly those in the social and political arena. *Time* cited an article published in *Psychological Science* that stated the higher men and women climb in a hierarchy, the greater the likelihood they would be unfaithful. This is because power leads to self-confidence and opportunities for sexual adventures. With self-confidence comes a sense of entitlement. According to evolutionary biologists, fame and power can weaken the mechanism of self-control and erode layers of social behaviour developed in our youth. *Time* magazine also looked at the difference between nature and nurture. It argued that people who are born with a silver spoon in their mouth are more likely to feel a sense of entitlement and may not be able to exercise the same self-control as those who are less fortunate. Discipline and perseverance create great athletes, but once they become famous they tend to feel that the rules they once learned no longer apply to them, according to *Time*.

This was clearly the case with Dominique Strauss-Kahn (DSK), but he is by no means unique. At the time of the DSK scandal, the news also broke that Maria Schriver had left her husband, Arnold Schwarzenegger, after 25 years of marriage. Schwarzenegger had confessed to having fathered an illegitimate child with a former staff member. Eliot Spitzer was another high-profile case. The former New York State Attorney General who famously launched a crusade against Wall Street's misdemeanours turned out to be client number nine in a prostitution ring. Silvio Berlusconi was accused of tax evasion and corruption, and also of having sex with a minor. Sometimes this kind of behaviour is dismissed as being strictly a private matter, which has implications for moral leadership but no further social consequences. That was the case for Newt Gingrich. He was forced to resign as Speaker of the US House of Representatives in connection with tax fraud, but the rest of society was unaffected. There was, however, a great deal of public outrage. People who purport to have high moral standards are more vulnerable in this respect than people who make no such claim. Gingrich had been quick to point the finger at Bill Clinton, but when his own scandal became public he had no choice but to resign. Spitzer found himself in the same position. This was unfortunate for the men in question, but not a problem for society as a whole. However, there are cases in which the self-destructive behaviour of individuals can have disastrous consequences for their surroundings. Their actions become a matter of public concern. Berlusconi's behaviour during his 14 years in office proved a fiasco for the entire country. By being corrupt, he signalled to the public that corruption pays. His tax evasion was a sign that failing to fulfil your obligations towards your country was acceptable behaviour. *The Economist* warned of this several times, most recently in an article published in June 2011 under the headline 'The man who screwed an entire country'. Berlusconi left behind a country with a twisted sense of tax morality and so much debt that it poses a threat to the entire eurozone. Strauss-Kahn's behaviour 'decapitated' the IMF at a time when this major international institution was engaged in a hugely important rescue mission. Behaviour that generates social consequences of this magnitude is criminal behaviour, and it should be treated as such. How was it possible for Strauss-Kahn to carry on with this kind of dangerous behaviour for so long? And why did it take Italy so long to seize back control of its own destiny? Why was the emperor not dethroned? Anne Sinclair, DSK's wife, can provide part of the answer. *Time* magazine reported she told a Paris-based newspaper that she was proud of the fact that her husband was a womaniser because it proved how seductive he was. For a politician the game of seduction is extremely important, and Sinclair was implying that DSK was therefore qualified to hold an important political office.

The second well-known form of variant behaviour that has led to major problems in society, and the business community in particular, is tunnel vision. Tunnel vision makes it difficult to bring decisions to their proper conclusion, especially decisions that have a long incubation period. Before reaching a decision, leaders collect a great deal of information. As they get closer to the actual decision they weed out details and irrelevant information. For the sake of convenience they tend to regard the information they decided to use as immutable. The end goal becomes all-important and factual circumstances are adapted to fit the goal. It is difficult for leaders to the find the inner strength to change their opinion or reverse a decision they have already taken. They see this as a weakness. In addition, because decisions are influenced by so many external factors they have their own momentum, which is sometimes difficult to stop. One of the best-known examples of this is the takeover of ABN Amro by a consortium made up of Royal Bank of Scotland, Banco Santander and Fortis. It was particularly true of the weakest link in the consortium, Fortis. When dark clouds appeared on the horizon, the Belgian-Dutch bank and insurance conglomerate simply went ahead with its part of the acquisition. In fact, there was no going back. If Fortis had backed out, the entire construction would have crumbled. The bank was therefore under enormous pressure because it would have destroyed more than just the plans of the members of the consortium. Almost all of the leading investment banks in the world had elbowed their way to the table and were involved in the deal. The no cure, no pay system was so binding that continuing to work towards a preordained result was the only option. Independent advice was ignored because it was in everyone's interests to achieve the goal. Only one member of the Supervisory Board of Fortis disagreed. He was asked to resign from the board. The entire situation is in many ways similar to the fate of American Airlines flight 1420 on 1 June 1999.

The American Airlines flight was en route from Dallas to Little Rock. It was an ordinary flight at the end of a busy day. The first news of worsening weather conditions in Little Rock came when the plane was already underway. The outlook was not good, and conditions became steadily worse. The crew in the cockpit were well aware of this, but the flight was not going to be diverted. However, a thunderstorm over Little Rock was becoming a serious threat. Would they be able to land before it reached the airport? Probably. The crew consulted air traffic control again, who thought that landing would present an unacceptable risk. They were told that the wind had changed direction and a wind shear alarm had been issued. That meant they would have to land on another runway in any event. Or should the flight be diverted to another airport? The second option was discussed more than once, but was rejected by the crew each time. A diversion would have created major delays and they were not in the mood for that. They wanted to get home on time. They decided to start the landing procedure. Unfortunately, the airplane and the thunderstorm reached the airport at the same time, and visibility was extremely poor because it was raining so hard. When the plane landed it could not get enough traction on the runway, and as the wheels touched down they began to skid. The plane left the runway at high speed and finally stopped on the banks of the Arkansas River. It later emerged that the pilots were so focused on the rapid, difficult landing that they forgot to adjust the spoilers properly. The accident was down to human error, albeit made under extremely difficult circumstances.

But what precisely was the error: forgetting to adjust the spoilers or starting the landing procedure against all advice? The decision had dire consequences. The airplane broke into three pieces and caught fire. The captain and 10 passengers died, and 110 people were wounded, 45 seriously. Nearly a decade later the management of the financial conglomerate Fortis found itself in the same position. The plan called for a landing, and the company's management was in no mood to be diverted. Not long after this, in the autumn of 2008, Fortis skidded off the runway. The bank caught fire and also broke into three pieces.

Although the personal problems of leaders may not always be to blame for errors, it is often true that a problem could have been averted if the leader had acted differently. That is why insiders need to deal with the information gap once and for all. They can do so by making sure they do not get caught in a social and intellectual vacuum. Lehman Brothers could have been rescued if Richard Fuld had realised months before how serious the situation actually was. He had the power, but he was the last to know. The circumstances in which one operates may be the reason why things go wrong. There is no opposition and therefore no self-reflection. In that respect, business leaders and government leaders share a remarkably similar fate. It is a fate that gradually creeps up on them because it is invisible. Early on in their term of office, new leaders usually do a good job, and everything seems very promising. After some initial hesitation they are praised for their good ideas. However, towards the end of their term the once so acclaimed leaders tend to lose their sense of reality and go off course. The lack of a healthy, objective frame of reference can lead to spiritual deformation and a skewed view of their own abilities. That in turn can result in excessive, risky behaviour that often affects their private lives as well. Very few can resist this process. It is perhaps beyond the capacity of our human constitution to meet the challenge. But no matter how self-satisfied a person is, no one, no matter how important they are, including business leaders, can resist the pull of gravity, even though some of them are convinced it must be possible. Take UBS, for example. This bank radiated invincibility and appeared to have a natural right to profit, growth and success. However, in 2003, somewhere at the bank's mid-management level, the suspicion began to grow that something was not quite right. The internal auditors were sent to New York to investigate. Within days the Swiss headquarters of UBS received an urgent e-mail: 'Hello Zurich, this is New York calling – we have a problem'. This euphemistic message was the first indication that, while disaster could be avoided at a 'small' price, the bank was already on a collision course. The head office did not do anything with this information, although within a year the internal auditors who had conducted the investigation were no longer employed by UBS. They had been given the boot. Management stayed put. What could go wrong? The answer came four years later, when the US mortgage crisis forced UBS to write off enormous losses. These were so large that even the Swiss central bank would have had problems coughing up the money. Ignoring the problem had turned it into a life-threatening situation, even for a company as solid as UBS.

Why does the human psyche allow itself to be lulled to sleep like this? To answer that question, let us consider the example of a KLM pilot who flies a 747 back and forth between Amsterdam and New York twice a week. He knows how to land the powerful machine on the runway every time, and this is a wonderful feeling. His young son is waiting for him, sees the plane arriving and witnesses the flawless landing. The little boy glows with pride at what his father can do. The pilot's sense of power is reconfirmed with every successful landing. He feels invincible. He internalises the power of the airplane and attributes this power to himself too. This feeling works its way into his psyche and distorts his self-perception, and hence his personality. The same is true of the managers of large sums of money who are able to move the market with their monetary power, and it most certainly applies to bankers. Feeling competent and powerful corrupts the perception of risk. This false sense of security is a wide-spread phenomenon. Drivers of luxury cars can also be affected. Today's well-equipped vehicles are a bit like a living room on wheels, giving passengers the sensation that they are as safe as they would be if they were sitting at home in a comfortable armchair in front of the fireplace. But if it starts to snow, although he understands it intellectually, the driver is emotionally unaware of the change in the level of risk and that road conditions have become less safe. Things become treacherous when we grow immune to external signals, which must be what happened with the management of UBS. The boardroom of their high-rise office building felt like a living room, and from that height their employees looked tiny and unthreatening. There was not a cloud on the horizon because their view was above the clouds. Management felt protected because the signals warning that the situation was about to turn on UBS filtered through so slowly that they never arrived. They were like the light from faraway planets that will arrive long after they have died. Jamie Dimon CEO from JPMorgan commented on the rumours of large, dangerous positions among his

London-based traders 'as a complete tempest in a teapot' shortly before he had to announce a US$2 billion loss. During the parliamentary hearings, Koos Timmermans, a risk manager at ING, admitted that the management of ING did not see disaster coming until just before it happened. They were busy buying shares and paying out a fat interim dividend. It was snowing outside, but inside everyone felt safe and snug.

There are different ways to mitigate this process. Make sure you organise your own information, both within the company and in relation to customers. The results could dispel some of that comfortable sense of security. But above all, organise your own opposition, not so that they can block the decision-making process, but so that you can get a better sense of what other people think and let them point out the dangers. And then do something with that information. Create a company based on trust instead of fear, and ensure that relevant information reaches management quickly. Management must be imbued with this approach to working and organising matters. Make sure your company has a serious board (and separate Supervisory Board, if appropriate) with critical managers who know how to make a nuisance of themselves, and have the internal auditors and compliance officers report directly to the CEO. It was, after all, a lack of opposition that led to the biggest aviation disaster in history.

Tenerife, 27 March 1977. Captain Jacob Veldhuyzen van Zanten was tired after having been forced to divert his flight and then wait a long time for a new slot. If they did not make a start soon, they might not be able to leave at all. After Veldhuyzen van Zanten had taxied to the runway, he contacted the air traffic control tower. Radio contact was extremely difficult as there were many people talking at the same time and the air traffic controllers spoke poor English. Veldhuyzen van Zanten prepared for takeoff while his co-pilot, Klaas Meurs, was uncertain whether air traffic control had given them permission to do so. Meurs expressed his doubts, but he was overruled by Veldhuyzen van Zanten. Meurs had no choice but to inform the tower they were getting ready to take off. The traffic controllers said 'Yes, yes', but they were talking to someone else. As the KLM aircraft picked up speed, thick fog obscured the sight of a Pan Am airplane taxiing down the runway until the very last minute. The Pan Am plane did everything it could to get out of the way, and Veldhuyzen van Zanten, tried to take off faster, but it was too late. The planes collided and burst into flames. The disaster cost the lives of 583 people. As a consequence of this accident, many aviation procedures were changed for the better. Today, every instruction given by the captain must be confirmed by the co-pilot. The captain has lost his absolute hegemony. It was an important change in the corporate governance structure of the cockpit, and it was a lesson for businesses too.

I would like to add three rules to the arsenal of corporate governance provisions raised by this story. The first is to keep the board that monitors the CEO small. Having more than five non-executive directors on a board dilutes its effectiveness. The members are less involved and are more afraid to ask questions because they think their turn to speak is over. The second rule is that the CEO should not serve more than two four-year terms in office. CEOs who stay on for longer are rarely as effective in their later years and have a tendency to keep kicking past mistakes into the long grass. In the US, the president can only be re-elected once for another four-year term. I am a great admirer of how the democratic system in the US handles the transfer of power. It is amazing that the world's greatest power is able to accomplish this in such a disciplined manner, particularly if you consider what power means to those who exercise it. And that nation turns the transition into a celebration. Even the best president knows that it will all be over in eight years' time. Why does the business community not do the same thing? Instead, we see a lot of Putin-like behaviour by managers who refuse to budge. Josef Ackerman of Deutsche Bank tried to continue as chairman of the board once his period as CEO had ended, when the company had just adopted a two-tier management system. It was a clever attempt to retain power, and it was almost successful. But it would have destroyed any opportunity to rethink the company's position and reassess its ties to society. The third rule is to organise your opposition to the point where it becomes institutionalised. Free up people from different levels and sectors whose job it is to put critical questions to the company's management. Create an internal parliament and give its members a real opportunity to play a part by giving them a certain degree of immunity. This is a process that can rid your company of its toadying yes men.

Beppe Grillo was one of Italy's top accountants before he was discovered as a comedian. In 1979 he did an improvised monologue at an audition for the performing arts, and two weeks later he appeared on television. Grillo began performing on a regular basis and he was celebrated, but also feared, for his sharp tongue. In 1987 he launched an attack on television against Bettino Craxi, then prime minister of Italy, who at the time was visiting the People Republic of China. It changed his career. Grillo quipped, 'If the Chinese are all socialists, who do they steal from?' The joke was a reference to the totalitarianism of the People's Republic, and particularly to its internal corruption. The Italian prime minister's own political party was not amused. Grillo was castigated as a national nuisance. He was boycotted and no longer appeared on television. However, in the 1990s, he decided to fight back with a daily blog that continuously criticised Italy's political leaders. With 350,000 hits a day, it is one of Italy's most popular blogs and an important forum for the free expression of ideas. Prominent thinkers are active on the forum, including Nobel prize winner and economist Joseph Stiglitz. That is how the man who was boycotted by the media became more powerful than the media. The thorn in the side of Italian politics is now even bigger. During a visit to the European Parliament, Grillo told the members that Europe was Italy's biggest problem. Europe gave Italy money without asking what it was doing with it. Grillo claimed the money was being misused. As an Italian, he called on the politicians to stop all subsidies, which he said was like giving money to Jean-Bédel Bokassa, the leader of the Central African Republic who crowned himself emperor.

Long before Parmalat got into trouble, Beppe Grillo's shows were predicting the imminent collapse of the dairy product conglomerate. The court thought that this was reason enough to bring him in for official questioning. How could he know this? Grillo replied that everyone knew but the punishment for speaking out prevented them from saying anything. Many people have an instinctive knowledge of the truth, either because they have knowledge and information due to their position or because the conclusion is an obvious one. However, the influence of those in power often extends far beyond the company itself, and can even affect the minds of individuals. Companies have rules that protect whistleblowers within their own four walls, but these individuals are vulnerable in other ways too. The boss's revenge is not limited to the company, as was seen in Parma, in Spanboek and in the UK.

Power only takes a step back in the face of greater power. And yet that is not always true; it sometimes bows to a small power as well. Beppe Grillo, once referred to as the Clown Prince, has stood up to power and won. The jester's humour can be more dangerous than straightforward criticism. The harlequin's venom, the comedian's criticism, the philosopher-activist: they make people laugh about things not because they are funny, but because they are the sad truth. Comedians are the invulnerable ones. Italian politicians tried to marginalise Grillo, but they ended up with a man who is more effective than the Italian parliament and who has done more to fight the corruption of the people in power than any opposition party. Grillo was the only one who publicly dared to tell Tanzi the truth: Parmalat was built on a big lie. No power is greater than the power of gravity, and no truth is stronger than the truth of the jester.

Chapter 15

The ethical organisation

What criteria does a business need to fulfil in order for it to be considered an ethical organisation? How important is it that it acts ethically? What impact does unethical behaviour have? Sometimes the thieves are the ones who end up duped.

On 28 February 1994, Juntaro Suzuki, the 61-year-old director of Fuji Photo Film Corporation, was stabbed to death on the pavement in front of his house. Suzuki and his wife, Michiko, lived in a modest home in Setagaya Ward, a fashionable area of Tokyo. On that fateful day, Mrs Suzuki was recording a television programme for her son, who lived abroad, when the doorbell rang. Juntaro used the intercom to ask who was at the door. An unknown man said that he had accidentally crashed his car into the wall of the Suzukis' house. Could he please come outside to look at the damage? Juntaro did not hesitate to open the door. It was a fatal decision. The neighbours said they heard a brief scream. Michiko heard it too and ran outside. She found her dying husband lying on the pavement, bleeding profusely. Juntaro was only able to whisper the word 'mamma' before he drew his last breath. The police established that the wounds on his head, legs and arms had been made by a Japanese sword, often used as the weapon of choice by the extreme right. However, further investigation of the brutal murder all pointed in one direction: *sokaiya*, a peculiar form of organised crime. *Sokaiya* originated in the second half of the 19th century, when the concept of limited liability was unknown in the Japanese business community. When scandals or other negative events occurred, the managers of a company were held liable, and their entire personal capital was at stake. The result was that management provided as little insight as possible into the company's affairs. Not knowing meant not being held liable. The practice of keeping shareholders in the dark, and shareholders' meetings as short as possible, also dates to this period. The annual general meeting was purely a formality in which no one was held accountable and all liability risks were avoided. However, this was often not enough. To fend off troublesome shareholders, management often hired gangs to help them keep the meetings under control. Any initiative that might lead to a revolt was immediately quashed. They acted as front men, helping management keep information that might incriminate them under their hat. In the 1960s the gangs shifted their focus from protection to extortion. They were paid for their work, but they blackmailed the management if they uncovered any incriminating information themselves. The information did not even have to be entirely true, as long as it sounded believable. That is how the genie got out of the bottle.

Something needed to be done about the practices of these hired thugs, and both legal and other means were used to combat them. One option was to schedule all shareholders meetings for the same time so that criminal gangs would not be able to hit them all at once. In addition, some managers were courageous enough to refuse to be blackmailed, and, as Juntaro Suzuki's story illustrates, this sometimes cost them their lives. The practice of *sokaiya* is just one example of criminal behaviour in the business world, in this case one that was structurally rooted in one of the world's biggest economies. Business communities everywhere can be affected by criminality, and this is certainly true of the Western world, which I will come back to later. This issue is concerned with the integrity of companies, their managers and – at least equally importantly – their environment. There are many definitions of integrity and how it relates to character traits and virtues. It basically comes down to doing what you say (reliability), and saying what you are doing (the predictability of your behaviour), but there is more to it than that. According to this narrow definition, criminals might also be said to possess integrity, and, with the exception of Robin Hood, that is difficult to imagine. Integrity is also about doing the right thing, which brings us straight to the heart of ethical conduct. Finally, integrity is also related to mutual trust, and the efficiency of the moral process.

What makes an organisation ethical? To begin with, the employees who work for the organisation must act with integrity. But managers, shareholders, suppliers, and, to a certain extent, the broader social context of an organisation must also be above suspicion. A company that is active in a criminal environment will find it difficult to come across as having integrity. Take, for example, the Italian companies that come under the influence of the Cosa Nostra. Is a company simply the sum of its parts, or is it more? An organisation is essentially an independent organism with its own character, which is more than the sum of the personalities of those involved with it. The culture (or personality) of an organisation is capable of change, but for many companies this is a hard-fought battle against bad habits that prove difficult to eradicate. As are the bad habits of people. Corporate cultures are idiosyncratic, are not always linked to individual leaders, and may outlive many generations of managers. The personality of a company has the same virtues and vices as those I discussed in relation to individual people. One of those virtues is integrity; another is the courage to take risks. The list goes on. But vices also flourish. Lack of integrity is one vice. There may be behavioural components present that explain an organisation's loss of integrity. A good example of this is allowing too much scope for conflicts of interest, that is, failing to curb the fundamental drive people have to enrich themselves, which leads to self-enrichment at the expense of the company. A company that allows corruption to continue and also participates in abuses of power has lost its integrity. But less serious infringements can also compromise a company's integrity. A critical lack of expertise and control or a miscalculation of business risks can also lead to a loss of integrity. The same applies to inconsistent behaviour and a tendency to look the other way on the part of management. The mind speaks, and the body should follow.

But let us switch to a more positive approach here. How should an ethical organisation function and what policies should it adopt? To begin with, a company should act in a manner that is befitting of the social and cultural normative framework of the environment in which it operates. Whether or not an action is considered ethical may vary from one country or cultural area to another. There are nevertheless certain general principles, such as justice, honesty, equal opportunities and the equal treatment of internal and external parties. Furthermore, the objectives of a company should make a demonstrable contribution to the general good of the society in which it operates. The general good is the reference point. A company must be accountable with respect to its social responsibility. In addition, individual decisions must contribute to the realisation of the company's objectives, and most definitely not conflict with them, and actions must be taken in accordance with those decisions. Remuneration should be proportionate to performance – another area in which honesty plays a role. Remuneration is not only related to work and individual differences in performance, but also to the difference between labour and capital. Managers have to be accountable across the entire spectrum of integrity. That includes being transparent. In addition, an organisation must enforce normative behaviour. Simply formulating rules of conduct is not sufficient. Every organisation needs a system of rewards, punishment and correction.

As discussed earlier, we have drawn a distinction between the ethics of honour and the ethics of conscience. The ethics of honour were very important in ancient Greece and Rome. It was a time of continuous war and conquest, in which strong warriors who had led their army to victory had high status. Their behaviour was worthy of emulation. The ideal and its realisation – also in the eyes of the bystander – is the guiding principle of the ethics of honour. This is an outwardly directed strain of ethics: what do others think of my behaviour? According to the ethics of honour, courage is good and cowardice bad behaviour. Good entrepreneurs are valued, while the reckless and the accident prone can expect nothing but contempt. The environment disapproves of failure to achieve the stated ideal, and that results in shame, the corrective morality mechanism that encourages people to improve their behaviour. The nature of the ethics of honour is consequentialist. If I act and my standing in the community increases as a result, then my actions are good. But if my honour is damaged, it was not a good action. In the ethics of honour it is the result that counts.

By contrast, the ethics of conscience, derived from the Christian faith, assumes that people have gone through a process of internalising norms and values. If your actions are at odds with these norms and values, this produces a sense of uneasiness (a feeling of guilt). Hence the ethics of conscience are inwardly directed and focus not on the outcome but on the intention behind the action. Guilt, like shame, is a mechanism that leads to self-correction. Both forms of ethical orientation are instrumental in ensuring the integrity of an organisation. They are the two anchors that together prevent good behaviour from going adrift.

The ethics of honour may be as ancient as the Greeks and Romans (or, more accurately, as ancient as humanity) but they are still relevant and they play an important part in the business community. We talk about our reputation instead of our honour, but the principle is the same. We spend billions on our image. We commission the design of flashy logos and slick advertisements, and use all kinds of other clever communication methods to convince the public of the company's high standing. Companies are anxious to avoid negative news because that would be bad for their reputation. It makes financiers suspicious, and clients nervous. Reputation is all-important, especially for entrepreneurs with a big ego. Another interesting factor is the concept of revenge, which is linked to the ethics of honour. An individual who besmirches the honour of someone else may be punished and sometimes even murdered. The business world also recognises this concept. An employee who brings discredit on the company is not likely to have a very long career there, even if he did not violate any internal code.

The ethics of conscience is more principled, and it, too, is highly visible in the behaviour of companies. A company has its own conscience. It is formed by external laws and rules, but also by rules it draws up itself (the company code of conduct) using external norms as its frame of reference, as well as by culture, the unwritten laws. All employees are expected to abide by the code. If they do not, sanctions will be imposed. Here, shame has become guilt. Within a company there is considerable overlap between the ethics of conscience and ethics of honour. The outcome is often, but not always, the same. Therein lies the fatal error. Being right is not the same as receiving acknowledgement that you are right. Take the example of a financial intermediary who is involved in a dispute with a customer about the quality of a product. The intermediary will ask himself a number of questions to determine whether or not his own position is right. What does the prospectus say about the issue the customer is complaining about? What does the marketing material say about it? Were the customer's expectations realistic? What advice did I give and how did I present the situation to the customer? Having asked himself these questions, the intermediary may be convinced the customer has no right to complain or receive compensation. For him, that is the end of the story. But from the perspective of the ethics of honour, there is more to it than that. According to this ethical approach, formal arguments are not important, and the question that needs to be asked is an entirely different one: if the complaint gets into tomorrow's newspapers, can I explain in just three sentences why the customer is wrong? Can I explain it to my mother-in-law and my next door neighbour? Will I get caught up in my own argument? In other words, will the outside world acknowledge that I am right?

As the CEO of the asset manager Robeco, I once faced such a dilemma. Years before any problems arose, we had introduced an investment product that was popular with our customers: a sustainable (green) bond issued in the form of a collateralised debt obligation (CDO). Customers had rushed to subscribe, primarily because of the tax treatment of the product and partly because it was environmentally responsible. The proceeds from the CDO issue were invested in sustainable, green projects, as described in the prospectus, and in accordance with the tax rules. But customers had been promised higher returns. Returns were to be jacked up by concluding credit default swaps (CDSs), which would generate additional income. Customers were led to believe, as they were with all the other products, that the extra credit risk involved would not stand in the way of their earning extra income. Historical analyses of corporate defaults clearly demonstrated that this was the case. Yes, the credit risk in the CDSs was collateralised with the principal of the green CDO, but as this risk constituted a well-diversified, large bundle of credits; they did not present a risk at all. And of course we had included a warning about risk in the prospectus.

One of the credit names was General Motors Acceptance Corporation (GMAC). This was the financing company of General Motors, the manufacturer of the accursed Hummer. However, in the autumn of 2007 it was not just leaves that were falling; the credits fell as well, and far beyond what could be expected given the statistical context. The initial credit losses we experienced at the start of the banking crisis could be offset by the buffers that were built into the product. But as more and more credits went sour these buffers were depleted. The alarm bells went off. Any subsequent disaster would start to eat into the principal. And the leveraged nature of the product meant the capital would melt away as fast as snow in summertime. The moment of implosion was fast approaching. The sobering prognosis was that GMAC could well be the next bankruptcy. Officially, nothing was wrong. Everything had been done by the book, and the risks and the losses had been made transparent. Yet the potential newspaper headlines flashed before our eyes: *'Hummer bankruptcy responsible for green CDO losses'*. Try explaining that. Something like can be fatal for a company that has spent years building its reputation as a purveyor of sustainable investment products. Repairing the damage could take years. Although we were under no contractual obligation to do so, we had no other choice but to take the losses onto our own books. We wanted to avoid the shame, even though, from a legal point of view, we were not guilty.

In its decision-making process the managing board of a company must give careful consideration to both perspectives: the formal viewpoint and perception. In the final analysis, both play an important role. Let us consider another example that may be more striking, and is certainly much more relevant. Neglecting the ethics of honour as an influential factor was one of the leading causes of the 2007 credit crunch. Most large banks had set up special purpose vehicles (SPVs) to keep a supply of structured products on hand. It was a clever way of maintaining a large supply of financial products without tying up too much regulatory capital. Keeping a stock of the products also generated attractive returns. The SPVs financed themselves on the money market by issuing negotiable debt instruments. The regulators approved this construction. After all, they, too, believed that the formal arrangements were watertight. But the markets suddenly lost confidence in the debt instruments, and rolling over the passive financing of SPVs became a big problem. We all know how it ended. Despite the fact that they had not given any guarantees and had carefully segregated liability, the banks were forced, one after the other, to rescue their off-balance-sheet vehicles. Their reputation was more important than the prospective financial losses. Neither the banks nor the regulators had taken honour-related risk assessment into consideration, but in the end it was arguments based on this that forced them to act. In terms of defining good and bad behaviour, the ethics of honour and the ethics of conscience bring us back to a familiar methodological discussion in the study of ethics. Is an action good because the intention is good (that is, because our conscience tells us it is) or is an action good because the outcome of that action is good (that is, honour)? We have to measure every action by both standards.

Which criteria determine whether an organisation is ethical? Here are some practical examples. The first relates to a story picked up by the *International Herald Tribune*, concerning the IMF during Dominique Strauss-Kahn's term at its helm. The *Herald Tribune* reported on the remarkable fact that the IMF had two different versions of ethical rules: one for its employees and another for its 24 directors. According to an independent adviser specialising in business ethics, the directors' code of conduct was extremely lax in comparison with that of the employees. The ethical code for employees was highly detailed and packed with policy and procedure. It included provisions for a hotline where employees could report any behavioural transgressions, and details of complaints were included in the annual report. The adviser who had been hired especially for this purpose had the authority to follow up special cases, and in 2010 this resulted in one dismissal. Not very remarkable for an organisation with 2,400 employees, but at least it was something. On the other hand, the Executive Board lived in a world of its own, which remained closed to the independent adviser. The board had set up its own ethical committee in 1998, but in 13 years the committee did not handle a single case; all it did was discuss its own procedures. That this Executive Board should be covered by a different code is perhaps understandable, since most of the directors are appointed by the countries they represent rather than by the IMF. Their first loyalty is to the organisation that appoints and dismisses them, and not to the institution they work for. While this may be understandable, it is not entirely defensible. It makes the IMF an organisation with a split morality, and that is problematic for an organisation whose key competency is to correct the behaviour of others and lay down the law to them.

Governments in general are important examples of organisations that face serious problems of split morality. They have different standards for themselves and others. As a specialist lecturer in financial ethics, I often use an example I call, for no particular reason, 'The Blue Elephant'. It is an example of an organisation with a significant level of internal inconsistency that makes it less ethical. This big organisation – The Blue Elephant – has not received an unqualified audit report for years. Its auditor gives four reasons for this. The first, and perhaps most important, is that one of the company's biggest operating units is qualified as 'unauditable'. Second, the financial relationships between the different operating units are very unclear. The auditor has also concluded the process of financial consolidation is ineffective. Finally, he has found that certain expenditures he regards as crucial for reporting purposes cannot be accounted for. According to the auditor, the possibility of illegal payments could not be ruled out. After telling this story I always ask my students whether they would be willing invest in this company. Of course, very few of them are. The general consensus is that this is a company to be avoided at all costs. However, until recently this company was given an AAA rating by the leading rating agencies. The Blue Elephant is a metaphor for the US. The 'unauditable' operating unit is the Department of Defence, and the auditor estimates the amount of illegal payments to be somewhere in the region of US$125 billion. In addition, it is primarily the financial relationships with NASA that do not tally with the central accounts. Surprising? Perhaps, but the US are not exceptional. Almost all countries have trouble managing their finances. The European Union, for example, also has integrity issues. At the end of the 20th century Paul van Buitenen, one of the European Union's internal auditors, was involved in a controversy. He and his colleagues in the internal audit department had collected evidence regarding the Leonardo da Vinci programme. The material pointed to direct and indirect conflicts of interests in the allocation of budgets to private companies tasked with implementing parts of the programme. And there were clear irregularities with respect to spending. Van Buitenen publicly denounced what he called the fraudulent behaviour of members of the European Commission and he reported his findings to UCLAF, the anti-fraud branch of the European Commission. The French euro commissioner Édith Cresson was a particular target of the accusations. After a while, Van Buitenen concluded that the relevant European authorities had done far too little with his report. The reaction of the European Union was understandable. They acted as if they had been stung by a wasp and their first response was to try to remove the sting. Van Buitenen was suspended for four months, his salary was halved, and he was subsequently transferred to a less sensitive position. But he persevered. After a lengthy battle, which began to attract more and more publicity, the entire European Commission was forced to resign. The move was unprecedented. Van Buitenen published a book on the subject in 1999 (*Strijd voor Europa*), which met with such a favourable response that he decided to stand for the European parliamentary elections. Although he was elected, he made little impression as a parliamentarian and, disappointed, he has since left the political arena.

It is astonishing that government organisations – the legislators – are especially likely to behave as if they were above the law. Whistleblowers are treated particularly badly by such organisations. Public companies that come under US or British jurisdiction face some of the most stringent anti-corruption laws in the world. Managing boards would not dream of taking conscious risks in this area because the law is merciless. But government organisations appear to be less scrupulous about observing their own laws. What other explanation is there for the US$125 billion worth of questionable payments uncovered by the auditor? This touches on one of the central themes of this book: everyone needs a boss. Because there are no checks on people who do not have a boss, they gradually start to believe they are above the law and that the forces of gravity can no longer hold them back. This means that the integrity of the company is at stake.

Some organisations believe they are above the law, and that they are only accountable to truly higher powers. And God does not concern himself with the small details of earthly matters. Proof of that is provided by the Vatican, where belief and finances have a complicated relationship with one another. In 2009 the Rome police arrested Father Orazio Bonaccorsi because he was laundering money through an account with the Vatican Bank (also known as the IOR or the Institute for Religious Works). The money in question was a subsidy from the European Union for a non-existent agricultural company. The money was transferred as a charitable donation and was withdrawn by Bonaccorsi's uncle, who had mafia connections. It turned out to be a minor event in a much larger scheme. In 2009, Cardinal Ettore Gotti Tedischi, a professor of ethics at Università Cattolica del Sacro Cuore in Milan, was given the task of cleaning up the mess, but in 2012 he suddenly was fired. The bank's board stated nine reasons for dismissal. Tedischi gave no explanation. 'My love for the Pope prevails over any other sentiment, even the defence of my own reputation,' was the professor's response. The dismissal came on the heels of the arrest of the Pope's personal butler for leaking all kind of secret documents, a scandal that was quickly given the name of Vatigate. The most damning leaks related to claims of corruption and financial mismanagement at the heart of the Vatican. It seems as though financial criminality has become structurally embedded in the nerve centre of the Institute for Religious Works and the Vatican. Worse still, it appears that those who want to rectify the situation are being removed. Italy's leading daily suggested that the Pope, just as Jesus, had been betrayed.

There is one special group of companies that I find particularly intriguing from a moral and management perspective. These are companies that produce useless products that have a negative social value, companies that are notoriously unsustainable. This time I am not talking about banks selling useless products. Instead I am referring to businesses such as the logging companies that cut down our primeval forests or companies that force people to perform slave labour in questionable circumstances. In the Netherlands a debate has arisen as to whether or not institutional parties, especially those who manage pension funds, should be allowed to invest in companies that produce cluster bombs. Arms manufacturing can be morally justified by the importance of self-defence, but cluster bombs are designed solely to cause unnecessary civilian casualties. What ethical principles lie behind the actions of a company that regards such behaviour as its purpose in life? Possibly none at all. In that case, we would be justified in labelling that company as unethical, based on the ethical framework we have described. My particular interest is tobacco companies, partly because I once worked for a company in the tobacco industry, albeit on the trading side rather than the production side. But above all because I have an intense dislike of smoking and feel pity for smokers. While tobacco companies were once blue chip shares, they are now the pariahs of the business world. What motivates companies to continue manufacturing products that demonstrably shorten people's lives and condemn many to spend their old age in a worn out, ravaged body? It was with a burdened conscience that I went in search of the annual report of a company: Philip Morris. For a period of 30 years, until the end of the 20th century, Philips Morris secretly purchased the scientific conclusions of Ragnar Rylander, professor of environmental health at the University of Geneva. His research was concerned with the effects of passive smoking. Rylander was prepared – for a fee – to conclude that there were no negative effects, and if there were any they were negligible. It is a disturbing story. Out of curiosity, I searched Philips Morris's website until my eye lighted on a statement on social responsibility. Philips Morris maintains that it is proven that the use of tobacco cannot be stopped. Taking this statement as its starting point, the company's objective is to limit the damage tobacco causes. Furthermore, Philip Morris argues that this approach is not an obstacle to government programmes aimed at preventing and stopping tobacco consumption. In simple terms, the website says that since people are going to smoke anyway, they might as well use Philips Morris's products. And, they add, we will not get in the way of government anti-smoking campaigns. The upshot of this is that the company's moral right to exist is hanging by a thread. Is Philip Morris's intention compatible with cigarette advertising, even if it is only for their own brand? Is it not in effect encouraging people to smoke? Is advertising compatible with its statement, or does the statement itself lack integrity? Was it made for the purpose of misleading people? All evidence points in the direction of the latter. Philip Morris defends its own interests with every means available. This is a problem for the anti-smoking lobby, with its limited budget, and also for nation states. Uruguay has the most stringent anti-smoking policy in South America. That poses a great threat to Philip Morris. After all, what would happen if other countries in South America adopted similar policies? Philip Morris has therefore launched a legal battle against Uruguay, which, to put this in proportion, has a gross national product equal to Philip Morris's revenues. Clearly even countries may not be equal to the power of some companies. And in this case the company has issued a statement saying that it respects countries with policies that discourage smoking. Ironic? There is certain to be a battle with the Australian government concerning its planned legislation to introduce plain packaging, so that in future all cigarette packets will look the same. During that battle, in my opinion it has become clear that Philip Morris is basically determined to obstruct governments that are genuinely trying to reduce smoking.

In 2003 Robeco made a promising acquisition. It bought a small but high-profile Swiss asset manager, Sustainable Asset Management (SAM), from its founder Reto Ringger. In the 1990s Ringger had conceived the idea of setting up activities in the area of sustainable asset management. He also wanted to compile an index made up of sustainable companies. He took his plan to the Swiss Exchange, one of the owners of the DJ Stoxx Index. Ringger was referred to the office of DJ Stoxx in Frankfurt and then to the DJ Index organisation in

New York. So he hopped on a plane, knocked on the door of Dow Jones and presented his plan. He had a strong, simple idea: in the long run sustainable companies will outperform companies that are not sustainable. And if the sustainable companies are brought together in an index, the index will outperform ordinary indices. After some initial hesitation, the people at Dow Jones accepted the proposal and an agreement was concluded. That was the start of the DJ Sustainability Index. The agreement specified a simple division of duties. SAM would do all the research, the outcome of which would determine the composition of the index. The index would be revised once a year on the basis of new insights and circumstances. Dow Jones would handle marketing and service provision in the US, while SAM would do the same in Europe. People who are ahead of their time often have to wait a long time for market recognition, and Ringger was no exception. But the long-awaited reward was that the DJ Sustainability Index gained widespread acceptance. Companies were finding it increasingly important to have external validation of their sustainability policies. And companies were increasingly willing to provide the research department of SAM with the information it needed to sharpen its analyses. Among them were various Dutch companies, including Azko Nobel, Philips, Unilever and Royal Dutch Shell. Akzo was very proud of its leading position in sustainability in its particular category, and boasted about it on its investor relations website. CEO Hans Wijers went even further, including the company's position in the SAM sustainability rankings as one of the key performance indicators (KPIs) that determined management bonuses. Wijers was also on the Supervisory Board of Royal Dutch Shell and the chairman of its remuneration committee. However, the day came when Royal Dutch Shell collided with its shareholders over the remuneration policy for the Board of Directors. An annoying situation, but the solution soon presented itself. The remuneration policy had to change, and Wijers was asked to take the lead. This led to the idea that Shell's position in the sustainability index should also be included as a factor for determining bonuses. At the time, Shell already led the ranking in its category (energy companies), so the idea was approved. The resolution was quickly adopted and announced to the shareholders, who were satisfied. But the next year, Royal Dutch Shell's position in the ranking was adjusted downwards, despite an improved score. This was the result of a discretionary decision on the part of the index compiler. How on earth had this happened? The management of Shell was furious. The angry voices coming from the boardroom all agreed that it was impossible to work with such an unprofessional organisation, whose actions were arbitrary and unpredictable. The DJ Sustainability Index and Shell's position in it could no longer be a determining factor for the bonuses awarded to the management of Shell, so the sustainability criterion disappeared from remuneration policy as quickly as it had been adopted. A letter from Wijers to the shareholders on 2 March 2011 contained the following euphemistic statement.

> The Remuneration Committee has therefore decided to exercise downward discretion and has set the DJSI-linked element of bonus assessment to zero. While the company will continue to participate in the DJSI/SAM assessment, it will focus 10% of the scorecard on three new sustainable development measures.

However, for a long time a situation had been brewing in Ogoniland in the Niger Delta in Nigeria. The local population was diametrically opposed to the start up of Royal Dutch

Shell's activities in the region, but the Nigerian government had ignored their protests. Worse than that, in 1995 the government had tried to break their opposition by murdering nine Ogoni leaders. One of them was Ken Saro-Wiwa, writer and leader of the Ogoni movement. In 2006 a group of independent scientists from Nigeria, the UK and the US described the devastation caused by the activities in Ogoniland as exceptional damage to the global ecosystem due to oil extraction. Shell was called to appear before a federal court in New York and accused of being an accessory to serious human rights violations. In 2010, a report was published by UNEP Ogoniland, the special United Nations department set up to assess the ecological disaster and propose improvements. The report was highly critical of the Nigerian government, and Shell was also given much of the blame, something which might have surprised its management.

In February 2012 Royal Dutch was in the news again, this time owing to its support for a campaign launched by various multinationals against the strict anti-corruption rules of the European Union. Shell wanted to see a substantial dilution of the rules aimed at making payments to governments more transparent. SAM's 2012 Sustainability Yearbook no longer includes Shell (or BP) in its ranking of oil and gas producers, which is now led by Repsol SA. Shell has not been unaffected by these developments. In 2012 Martin Haigh, Senior Energy Adviser to Shell's Scenarios Team, made the following remarkable statement during a speech to an important gathering of environmental scientists in London: 'Royal Dutch could fade away and die if it responds too slowly to global climate pressure.'

However, this makes no difference when it comes to Shell's bonuses; they are no longer linked to the company's position in the DJ Sustainability Index because they are now based on the company's own sustainability criteria. In the spring of 2012, the remuneration report revealed that Peter Voser, the CEO, took home €11.7 million in 2011, more than double his pay the previous year, because a lucrative long-term incentive plan was paid out. Environmental campaigners and shareholders were livid. Just how far can a company go in creating its own reality?

Moving from narratives, back to our discussion of the underlying structure of unethical behaviour, let us revisit the subject of animal spirits, as this is where the causes of unethical behaviour can be found, in the areas of unhealthy interpersonal relationships. This concerns nepotism and corruption. Business is all about the individual, the group, and money. Lots of money. Winning tenders and projects can be of huge value to a business. It is crucial that orders are awarded on the basis of professional considerations and the interests of the organisation. This is where things often go wrong. The world football federation FIFA provides a classic example. Even before the failure of the British bid to organise the 2018 World Cup finals, the British media were breathing down the necks of some of FIFA's officials, whom they regarded as extremely corrupt and easily influenced. When the British bid – technically and commercially, the best bid – was rejected in the first round of voting, the British were outraged and felt they had been humiliated. They demanded a bribery investigation into the World Cup selection process. The investigation was carried out by the FA, the English football association, and in June 2011 *The Wall Street Journal* published the findings under the heading 'FIFA's foul ball'. The FA found that members of FIFA's executive committee had asked for favours in return for votes. One member asked for a school to be built in his homeland and for the television rights to a friendly match between England and Thailand.

However, the investigative team could not prove that the requests had been made with a view to personal enrichment, and for FIFA chairman Sepp Blatter that was the end of the matter. 'There are no elements in this report which would prompt the opening of any ethics proceedings,' he concluded. 'The members of the committee are completely clean.' *The Wall Street Journal's* subtle comment on this was that it said more about the organisation's ethical hygiene than it did about the evidence presented.

The standard pattern of corrupt behaviour in the business world is as follows. An official ensures that the company enters into an agreement with an agent. The agreement stipulates that the agent will provide services, but the exact nature of those services remains vague. The same is true of the performance criteria the agent must meet in order to receive commission. The compensation for these questionable services is often too high. The agent sometimes sews up the whole deal by demanding a confidentiality agreement. If the agent introduces a new customer, the company is not allowed to tell the customer that it pays the agent without the latter's permission, and is certainly not allowed to say what it pays the agent to do. This leaves the field wide open in terms of corruption. An example of this is the insurer Aon, which was reprimanded by the British regulator, the FSA, for questionable commission payments to intermediaries. These were agents who acted on Aon's behalf in difficult countries. This is just one random example taken from thousands of others. Companies that pay agents for vague services deserve the full attention of critical board members. But how many board members actually examine this kind of behaviour with a magnifying glass?

The examples above illustrate just a fraction of the kinds of conduct that can make a company less ethical. Many of the companies, institutions and organisations I have mentioned are prominent and are keen to display their integrity. The lesson we can take home from this is that corruption is everywhere, and in particular it is right under the noses of managers. Managers could do more to prevent it. I have seldom heard a manager ask to see an agent agreement, or enquire about the company's policy towards external intermediaries. Managing boards focus primarily on costs, and only rarely on the details of purchasing agreements, which is precisely where expenditure on corruption is hidden. Unfettered power can create major problems in an organisation unless the person exercising that power has exceptional character traits (or virtues, as Aristotle called them), and, of course, a magnifying glass. But if power is not checked or contradicted, it can go off the rails. During an interview given just before he died, Prince Bernhard of the Netherlands was asked why he had accepted bribes from the American aerospace company Lockheed. The prince gave a simple answer: 'Because no one told me I wasn't allowed to do it.' A lack of checks does not mean that everything is permissible, even though this does sometimes seem to be the case with powerful men.

When safety systems fail, the last resort may be the lone individual who saw everything, someone with a strong conscience that will not be subdued. The whistleblower who has to get something off his chest. Going public with information about abuses is a risky business for the whistleblower himself, as well as for the organisation receiving the information. It is a minefield full of bad intentions, in which it is very easy to take a wrong step. The organisation must correctly assess the whistleblower's motives. Are they genuine, or is the employee disgruntled and out for revenge? Or worse, is the whistleblower an accomplice who hopes that going public will ease his guilty conscience? Is the story true? The whistleblower has to find the right person to give the information to, and ensure that person has no ties to those involved in the abuses. Whistleblowing can have far-reaching consequences and a great many forces may be unleashed in response.

Two of the most effective whistleblowers were Daniel Ellsberg and Mark Felt. In 1971 Ellsberg passed secret documents about the Vietnam War to *The New York Times*. These documents, which came to be known as the Pentagon Papers, revealed that consecutive US governments had systematically lied to the public about the war, their motives and the number of casualties. Their publication marked the beginning of the erosion of public trust. Felt, better known as Deep Throat, provided *Washington Post* journalists with information on a secret operation led by President Nixon, aimed at derailing the Democrat's election campaign. Felt did not reveal his role in the Watergate scandal until the end of his life; it was a role that changed history. Less famous, but no less courageous, was Mordechai Vanunu, who leaked information about Israel's nuclear activities to the British press in 1985.

The organisations that the whistleblowers were addressing felt attacked. The most obvious reaction in such situations is to strike back, and to do so with a vengeance. The office of Ellsberg's psychiatrist was broken into and his report on the whistleblower was stolen. Oddly enough, the break-in would turn out to be the start of the Watergate scandal. Other whistleblowers have not been so lucky. Vanunu spent 11 years in solitary confinement and is still not permitted to leave Israel or speak to foreigners. What criteria can be used as a basis for deciding whether to step out of the hierarchy and report an abuse? The US government has drawn up rules designed to manage the whistleblowing process. They are primarily concerned with the criteria that must be met in order for the whistleblower to enjoy protection. Infringements that meet these criteria include gross mismanagement, excessive wastes of money, and abuses of power. Also included are matters related to 'substantial and specific dangers to public health'. While the whistleblower cannot be expected to bring hard and fast evidence of an abuse to the table, there must be 'reasonable conviction' that it exists.

Why is it important for an organisation to be ethical? Ethical behaviour – integrity – is all about mutual trust. That is an essential aspect of the way in which our society functions. Without integrity society cannot function. If one party is unable to trust the other, the consequence is unproductive forms of behaviour that do not help create prosperity. In the worst case, we are condemned to Thomas Hobbes's natural state. Right now we are confronted with countries in which the tax-paying ethic has been weakened. If some citizens go unpunished for avoiding the obligation to make their national contribution, it becomes difficult to ask others to pay the bill. Mutual trust is a hallmark for how we operate. Without it we all sink into the swamp of suspicion. In the words of the British moral philosopher Philippa Foot, who died in 2010:

> In order to live together successfully and reproduce, people must be able to form attachments based on mutual trust, which means, among other things, holding others to their words and promises. Like other living beings – plants and animals – people have specific conditions for their continued existence. For humans these include observing judicial norms and mutual obligations.

The last example in this chapter is the story of Sino-Forest, a company that operates forestry plantations in China. After many years the trees are harvested and the lumber is sold.

Sino-Forest markets itself as a sustainable operation, and it refers to its forestry methods as ecological. China's long-term plan calls for reforestation in order to counteract CO_2 emissions, and Sino-Forest wants to play a role in this process. The company was set up in the 1980s under the leadership of the energetic entrepreneur Allen Chan. In the 1990s Sino-Forest was listed on the Toronto Stock Exchange by means of a reverse takeover. An empty corporation was given control over assets in China via a contractual arrangement, rather than through a shareholding. Everything went as planned and the share price rose steadily. It was surprising, but understandable, that the company did not pay any dividend because all of the profit was reinvested in the company to finance its growth. Although the company was small it attracted international attention; it was active in an environmentally friendly sector and it was assumed that the Chinese forestry sector was destined for growth. Even major hedge fund managers such as John Paulson had a serious stake in the company. In 2011, however, things went awry, and the share price suffered spectacular losses in the space of a few days. The reason for this was a devastating report on Sino-Forest, published by the small, unknown research boutique Muddy Waters, owned by the American, Carson C Block. The company was said to be one big lie, the mother of all Chinese scams. The report raised two important issues. Sino-Forest's business model was said to be fraudulent, because its proceeds were generated via authorised intermediaries (AIs) who were fully responsible for remitting tax. All of the profits ended up with the AIs, who were in fact affiliated to the company. Moreover, Sino-Forest listed assets on its balance sheet that did not belong to the company, but to local front men.

It was not the first Chinese listing on a foreign exchange to get into trouble. It also happened to Harbin Electric, Orient Paper and Bodsin Biotech. Bodsin did not survive the attack; the company disappeared from the public market for good. Orient Paper withstood the offensive, but share prices never recovered to their former level. The offensive had little effect on Harbin Electric. But what about Sino-Forest? Why had Block published such an extensive analysis and why was he so determined to uncover the truth? Was his concern genuine, or was he simply a sophisticated, professional manipulator?

Carson C Block, a restless young man from New Jersey, first gained experience in equity research when he was a student at the University of South Carolina. In 1998, after he had completed his degree, he moved to Shanghai and set up an equity research company. However, Block had little success in China, and he returned to the US to study law in Chicago. He also worked for his father's business and for a law company, Jones Day. He had a reputation for being arrogant and would later admit to having major disciplinary problems and difficulty accepting authority. In 2006, Block left Jones Day and returned to Shanghai. He worked at various jobs, all of them more or less doomed to failure, and finally returned to his old craft of equity analysis. Block gradually became interested in companies that were active in China and listed on stock exchanges in the West. He was familiar with the Chinese way of doing business and he suspected that some of the stories were too good to be true. He became convinced that the assumptions of Western investors were based on different mores and a different business culture. Block started to dig around for information. His first report was on Orient Paper. He posted it on his website, and then took out a small short position in the share. He was surprised by the consequences of the report: the share price collapsed and he accidentally made his first fortune. It made him hungry for more. Block then turned his attention to other Chinese companies, the last of which was Sino-Forest.

Block collected information about Sino-Forest but he took out a short position before he published his report. This time he was not as cautious as he had been with Orient Paper. He went massively short, while the famous hedge fund manager John Paulson was snoozing on top of his long position. The effect was catastrophic. Investors thought the conclusions of Muddy Waters were plausible and began to sell en masse. Faced with a substantial loss, Paulson lost confidence and decided sell his entire holding. The price of Sino-Forest shares dropped from US$25 to US$1 before closing at US$4. The company put up a good fight but there was a weak spot in its defence. It cited competitive reasons for not wanting to reveal the names of its AIs, and the public smelled a rat. The independent directors and the audit company PricewaterhouseCoopers instigated an investigation, but the results were a long time coming. It proved difficult to uncover the truth in mainland China. Having been heavily criticised, the Canadian regulator decided to suspend trading in the shares until Block's accusations could be verified, which in effect meant until the investigators had published their report. Allen Chan was forced to resign, but he was named founding chairman emeritus in an effort to save face. The independent directors had little alternative because they desperately needed his help.

The story of Sino Forest is fascinating because it features all of the vices that plague the public capital market. Is the company a front for shady practices in a faraway country where it is impossible to verify facts? Was Allen Chen a crook and an impostor? Had the auditors simply failed to do their job, and had they relied too heavily on a local Chinese auditor whose reputation and expertise they had not checked adequately? Perhaps the local auditor was simply lazy and careless; after all, China must have ways of verifying uncertain assets. Or had the auditors perhaps been given fraudulent documents? It may also have been a question of cultural differences and a different way of doing business (the book *Mr. China* (2008) by Tim Clissold provides a good picture of how business is conducted in China and how this differs from the Western world). Or was Block a market manipulator of the worst kind? At the end of the day he had no hard evidence, just strong suspicions and a bit of imagination. He made his case seem plausible, but that is all. After three months of external investigation, the case against Orient Paper proved to be unfounded. Nothing illegal had occurred. Moreover, Block had gone short in order to make money on his report; he was one the parties involved and therefore his interpretation of the truth was compromised. His behaviour was different from that of the hedge fund managers during the 2007–2008 banking crisis (also known as the Big Short). Most of them issued warnings in advance because they were convinced things were about to go pear-shaped. When no one was willing to listen, they decided to take advantage of the situation. Their warnings were not designed to manipulate the market; it was simply that no one heeded their warnings. It was in the interests of Muddy Waters to repeat its accusations of fraud as loudly as possible and for as long as possible. Does that sound suspicious? The investigation instigated by the independent directors revealed that Sino-Forest's cash balances were in order. It was also possible to verify the legal ownership of the majority, but not all, of the assets on the balance sheet. During a trip to China, a very large country, it emerged that in a small number of cases information was not available. It was also impossible to trace the identity of some AIs and backers (individuals with a great deal of social and political influence). Is this fraud or is it the way business is done in China? Are backers an absolute condition for becoming active in China, and are they instrumental to the return that Western investors hope to receive? Or are they parasites feeding on the blood of Western investors? Welcome to China!

The example of Sino-forest brings us full circle: it has much in common with Japanese *sokaiya*. The problem in Japan was that the groups which discovered allegedly dubious facts were criminal organisations and blackmailed the management, threatening to expose the truth. In the last example, Muddy Waters published material which, although unverified, made it seem plausible that something was seriously wrong. Block was not engaged in blackmail, but by going short in Sino-Forest shares he was able to rake in a fortune. It is, in effect, a much more efficient method, but the fact remains that his profits were the proceeds of publishing strong suspicions, and these are not the same as the truth. It is a new form of *sokaiya*.

Making an organisation ethical is profitable. Time and again people manage to make a success of a business that is fundamentally unethical. However, it only takes a small accident to set off a chain of events that can rapidly bring the entire organisation to its knees.

Chapter 16

A bed of nails

Companies prefer to offer their employees above-average remuneration because they like to think their employees have above-average qualities. No company is ever convinced that its employees are generally performing at a below-average level, thus justifying lower than average remuneration. As a result of this approach, the average salary creeps up whenever remuneration is discussed, and this creates a self-perpetuating system of pay rises.

In 2010 I took part in a discussion programme on Dutch television that brought people from different backgrounds together to share their thoughts on restoring trust in the banks. Seated next to me was a woman who had been shifting uneasily on her chair since the programme began. She had had a number of unpleasant experiences with banks and could not wait to tell us all about them. Sitting next to her was a man who ran a flower stall. The conversation quickly turned to variable remuneration. The woman next to me commenced her attack and stridently voiced her views: she thought bonuses were scandalous. She continued to express this opinion at full volume. The presenter allowed her to speak at length. Too long, in my view. The stallholder joined in and started to berate vehemently the system of variable remuneration. I felt quite ill at ease. What was I doing here? Clearly I felt as lost as an actor in the wrong movie. Every now and then I managed to get a word in, but I was basically fighting a losing battle. In this situation, reason was not the best way of building up an argument; emotions were. At least that is what I thought. Later, when I replayed the programme on DVD, I realised I had wasted an excellent opportunity to respond to the stallholder's remarks about variable remuneration. After all, what was his own earnings model? How did he motivate his own employees to brave the cold every Saturday and go to work in the market? Probably not by paying them a fixed salary. That would not sell many flowers. Street markets are a prime example of an environment where variable remuneration keeps people on their toes. And of course the financial markets work in the same way as ordinary markets do: they present hunters with a challenge. Those who fail to bring home the bacon find their position is threatened. The market is a place to practice survival skills and serves as an evolutionary laboratory. It is where our instincts are born. The stallholder fulminating against the banking industry's bonus system made his own living from a system of variable remuneration. I had wasted a great opportunity.

I have already described how safety and security are among the most basic human needs and how they can be traced back to the survival instinct. Financial security is just one aspect of safety and security. On the face of it, this is of course a personal need, focused on individuals, their family and, in a somewhat broader sense, their tribe. Reward systems often trade on these concepts. Companies are organised into smaller units – divisions, departments and groups – and corporate remuneration structures focus increasingly on the performance of these units instead of on the results of the company as a whole. Just for the sake of convenience, let us call this type of unit a tribe. There is an obvious reason why managers make the tribe the specific focus of their organisation's remuneration incentives. It is because this reflects a human scale. The individual has no influence on company results and does not see them as resulting from his or her own achievements. This works in both directions. Employees who do their best in an organisation that is losing a lot of money can easily become seriously demotivated, while an individual who is personally responsible for losses may still be rewarded with a share of the profits earned in another part of the company. In both cases, the link between effort and result is missing. This reduces the incentive to perform and can lead to parasitical behaviour. Employees may start to take things easy, comfortable in the knowledge that they will get their bonus anyway. Decentralised remuneration can prevent this by encouraging and rewarding the team, regardless of what happens elsewhere. The added advantage of this system is that group-based remuneration encourages co-operation and acts as a check on individualism. Without co-operation, no products can be made and no services provided. People need to co-operate in order to achieve results, and that can be accomplished by including group objectives as key performance indicators (KPIs). Another major advantage of variable remuneration is that it only costs money if the company or department is doing well. It transfers operational risk to employees, who need to take this into account in their private lives and adjust their spending to reflect the element of uncertainty. Sometimes, variable remuneration means no reward at all.

Performance-based remuneration is an important means of motivating employees to perform. An anecdote told by Bert Heemskerk, the former Chairman of the Executive Board of Rabobank Nederland, illustrates how effective this can be. Heemskerk was an imposing, charismatic man with a wonderful, self-deprecating sense of humour, who died much too young in the spring of 2010. The anecdote centred on his personal experience of the 2008 credit crunch and society's criticism of the banks' remuneration structures.

> One evening I went bowling with my seven children in our home town of Noordwijk. We had a great time. My sons had brought along a group of friends, one of whom was Jacob, a lanky lad with red hair in his early twenties. As the evening wore on, everyone was in good spirits but I noticed that Jacob had not done very well. He had not scored a single strike and was right at the bottom of the table in our little family competition. I decided to give him some extra encouragement, but it didn't help much. So it was time to change tack. I offered Jacob a deal. I promised to give him €100 for every strike he bowled. It worked like magic. Suddenly he was focused, and from that moment on he bowled one strike after another. The game was starting to get a bit expensive for me and the deal was rather one-sided, so I decided to change the conditions a little. He would still earn €100 for every strike, but now

Continued

there was a malus clause. If he failed to knock over all of the bowling pins he would have to pay me €50. This brought Jacob's winning streak to an abrupt end. The fear of losing money upset him so much he lost his concentration, and he scored poorly after that.

Clearly, variable remuneration has advantages and drawbacks. If the parameters of the remuneration system are set in a way that encourages aggressive behaviour, employees develop a one-sided focus on operational objectives. They are positioned as quasi-entrepreneurs, but a bonus system without a malus clause makes them too eager to take risks. They become more like gamblers than entrepreneurs.

Failure to use the proper dose of variable remuneration creates tensions between competing tribes within the company. Some of these groups have similar responsibilities and they are all competing for the same scarce resources. The tensions create islands within the organisation: self-contained little kingdoms with their own command structure that is no longer linked to the organisation as a whole. There may even be hostility if one kingdom gets in the way of another. This leads to sub-optimal trading results. All of the attention is focused on dividing up the pie, instead of on finding ways to increase the size of the pie. This culminates in the annual circus of infighting between groups and management about the allocation of overheads and capital requirements.

The excessive emphasis placed on sub-goals can result in the payment of huge bonuses by a company that is losing money. In retrospect, negotiations on variable remuneration not only led to sub-optimal results, they spawned structures that were essentially parasitical. Too much advantage was taken of the company, with management entering into agreements that were too one-sided. In this context I am referring in particular to over-reliance on the good name of financial institutions and the banks' risk buffers, exposure to counterparty risk, and capital requirements. The tribe's activities often required more capital than expected and the risk was not adequately compensated. After years of good harvests the caravan moved on, leaving the company behind with all kinds of residual risks, such as aftercare for long-term products and potential claims from customers. As it turns out, quasi-entrepreneurs are not entrepreneurs at all; like Jacob, they cannot cope with a malus clause.

So far I have used the terms 'variable remuneration' and 'bonus' interchangeably. However, the failure to distinguish between the two is perhaps one of the biggest mistakes made in the financial industry. Variable remuneration means agreeing contractually with employees that their income is dependent on performance as measured in terms of volume or immediately identifiable revenues. A bonus is for people who receive a good basic salary and from time to time turn in an exceptional performance that goes beyond their normal contractual duties. This implies that there are 'normal' circumstances in which no bonus is awarded. If this 'normal' situation is unclear, then bonuses are part of a fixed salary, just in a disguised form. Or, as the *Financial Times* put it on 28 January 2012:

> If there are no clear circumstances under which a bonus would not be paid, such an award starts to look like a basic salary that dares not speak its name.

Sometimes variable remuneration is conditional and deferred. It can be paid in cash, shares or share-related pay elements such as options and phantom shares. Because these payments do not have to be made when things are going badly (although they are sometimes paid even then), there is no need to report the costs immediately. Due to their conditional nature, those costs have a deferred effect on results. Tomorrow is left to take care of itself. In the 1990s the subject of reporting rules was hotly debated. Companies in the US had for a long time been successful in keeping management options entirely off their income statements. Options were charged directly to the shareholders, who, even though they had little influence when it came to awards of options, bore the costs because their own rights were diluted.

Since then, remuneration in the form of management options has become slightly less popular, but it is still an interesting phenomenon. Beware, this reward structure is far from moribund and could resurface at any time. How did it begin? The practice of awarding management options started to create major waves in the 1990s. It was first introduced in Silicon Valley in the US as a solution for companies that were unable to absorb direct costs because they lacked income and did not have sufficient cash flow to pay real salaries. The idea was to reward employees with a stake in the future, in the form of options. They were a suitable instrument because management regarded employees as quasi-entrepreneurs. Above all, the value of the company was, crucially, determined by management and employees rather than by outside circumstances. If the value of the company rose, it was the direct result of outstanding performances by management and employees. All of that changed, however, when the practice was adopted by large public-listed companies. If their value rose, it was difficult to determine whether it was due to the efforts of management or to external factors such as market sentiment. The result was that during bull markets managers who did not perform well still received substantial rewards. And during bear markets, managers who thought that they were performing well, and were therefore not responsible for the fall in the share price, tried to renegotiate. It was not uncommon for the strike prices of their options to be lowered so that money could be made even when share prices were heading south. From an ethical point of view, this is a completely unacceptable practice because it involves changing the rules of play halfway through the game. And yet it happened all the time, turning the whole system into a lottery. In their book *Bankroet: hoe Fortis al zijn krediet verspeelde* (2009), Michielsen and Sephiha quote Maurice Lippens, the Chairman of the Board of Directors of Fortis at the time of the takeover of ABN Amro. Lippens wrestled with a similar problem.

> Fortis's annual report stated that Jean-Paul Votron had been awarded a bonus of €2.5 million for 2007 in connection with his part in the takeover of ABN Amro. That brought his total annual salary to €3.9 million. In addition, the annual report informed shareholders and investors that Votron's fixed salary had been increased by 75% to €1.3 million. The response was public outrage. Lippens saw what was coming and anticipated the criticism in his speech to shareholders. 'Jean-Paul Votron's fixed salary is now in line with what senior executives earn at other banks,' he said. 'What Fortis pays is slightly higher than the average.' Lippens pointed out that Fortis had already decided in 2006 to raise the CEO's fixed remuneration, but Votron had refused to accept the increase. According to Lippens, Votron had demonstrated exceptional leadership. He added that

Votron and other senior executives at Fortis had also suffered financially due to the fall in the share price, because 'their options are now worth less'.

The shareholders accepted the dilution of their rights with a degree of resignation. They drew some comfort from the thought that their interests and those of the board were more in synch than ever before. But the real danger lurking in those share options had yet to become clear. The boards of companies that awarded management options were often incapable of delivering the performances needed to lift the share price above the strike price. But there was another way to make money that did not involve lowering the strike price. As the managers approached retirement age, the pot of gold at the end of the rainbow was still empty. They had to think of a ruse if they wanted to secure the main prize. Their clever solution was to position the company as a takeover candidate in the hope that another party would be willing to pay the takeover price plus a premium. They sacrificed the independence of the company in order to increase its value, officially justifying this with the need to create economies of scale. In truth, however, management had a conflict of interests; they were looking for takeover partners that suited them instead of the company. A large number of takeovers can be explained only by the fact that managers, in their race against the clock, gave priority to their own interests.

Share options left one more trail of destruction in their wake. There is only one way to be an entrepreneur, but there are two ways to earn a profit. Good entrepreneurs develop new products and services that customers want, find ways to operate more efficiently and utilise every opportunity. These things are all within the reach of good, talented entrepreneurs, and if they are successful they deserve to be rewarded for it. However, some entrepreneurs who discovered they were unable to achieve success in that way still wanted to increase the yield on their invested capital, so they became financial entrepreneurs, introduced buy-back schemes for shares which they often financed with borrowed capital. This weakened the company's balance sheet but increased earnings per share. That is how they jacked up the share price and consequently, their own remuneration. It did not transpire until much later that these entrepreneurs had saddled their companies with unacceptable additional risk, but it was invisible because it was financial risk. With the encouragement of consultants and shareholders, hollowing out healthy companies became an accepted practice. It also became necessary to defend companies against the 'barbarians at the gate', that is, the threat of hostile takeovers financed mainly with loans that the acquired company would have to pay back (leveraged buy-out). There was virtually no criticism of this approach, which was driven primarily by personal motives. On the contrary, it was seen as bringing grey, old conglomerates back to life. However, the medicine only had the effect of weakening the balance sheet. It is the reason why so many industrial companies entered the 2000 crisis with a weak financial position, and the same thing happened to financial institutions when the 2007–2008 financial crisis erupted.

An interesting point in the controversy surrounding variable remuneration in shares or options was raised during the Republican primaries in the US. Mitt Romney was ahead in the polls, so it was only natural that his opponents would start to comb his past in search of ammunition. As the CEO of Bain Capital, Romney earned his enormous fortune (estimated at US$250 million) in private equity. Private equity managers have 'skin in the game' and share in the profits. A management participation in the company allows them to benefit from the surplus value they themselves help generate. This is referred to as carried interest. In contrast to management options and other types of variable remuneration, the tax authorities treat carried interest as a capital gain, which is taxed at a much more favourable rate. If a capital gain is realised by means of financial leverage, the question is whether that gain is sustainable or has been achieved by creating more volatility, resulting in a temporary upside, a bit of gambler's luck. But surely what we are really talking about here is income that has been derived from employment?

In many cases, a company's management is judged by the profits made as well as by the share price, and this can easily lead to profit manipulation. In their first year, most incoming leaders write off a substantial amount on their predecessor's projects. This affects profitability but the impact is not normally structural. Profits then recover in the course of the new monarch's reign. If the first year is taken as the measure for determining variable remuneration, this strategy can prove very profitable. At least for the manager, that is. In 2008, something occurred at Philips that is symptomatic of this predicament, albeit in reverse. The group sold one of its crown jewels for a price that far exceeded its book value. The sale generated a substantial profit and management stood to benefit in the same year thanks to a proposed extra bonus. However, the shareholders objected to the plan, arguing that the value of the crown jewel was the result of years of hard work, rather than something the current management had achieved in the past year. The shareholders maintained that selling the assets to the highest bidder did not constitute exceptional performance. It was simply part of the job management had been hired to do. Philips's shareholders voted against the remuneration policy. It was a sorely felt defeat for the Supervisory Board, which had defended the proposal at the AGM, and also for management.

In March 2011, when Portugal's António Horta-Osório was hired as the head of Lloyds Banking Group, the shareholders were presented with an even more unusual situation. Horta-Osório had been the CEO of the UK branch of Banco Santander, but in 2010 he moved to Lloyds Banking Group to help solve its problems. Expectations were running high because he was thought to have the necessary skills to get one of the UK's most important financial institutions (and one of the largest in Europe in terms of market capitalisation) back on track. But it soon came out that Horta-Osório stood to earn £13.4 million in salary, bonuses and other extras during his first year on the job. He was to receive a basic salary of over £1 million and a bonus that could be as high as a cool £2.3 million. This was all intended to minimise the cut he was taking in his fixed salary. The rest of the £13.4 million was compensation for the loss of his bonus and pension rights at Banco Santander. This was a very expensive golden hello. The shareholders were astonished. David Harrison of Birmingham told the shareholders' meeting that he had initially assumed it was a typing error. In the words of Martin Simons, 'He gets more than twice the pay of all the senators of the college of justice in Scotland and 56 times what the lord chief justice of England gets. Welcome to a bed of nails.' That comment turned out to be portentous. Horta-Osório worked very hard, but according to his critics he found it hard to delegate and tended to interfere with everything. If that is your nature, there is a good a chance that at some point your body will protest. And that is precisely what happened to Horta-Osório. He had a burnout. According to the newspapers he had gone without sleep for four days. The prediction was correct: he had landed on a bed of nails. After two months of rest, Horta-Osório went back to work in January 2012. What can we learn from this tale? When an institution is being kept alive on state life-support, its CEO cannot expect to receive an exceptional salary if his weak leadership style (or physical weakness) makes him incapable of carrying out his responsibilities. This cannot be allowed to happen. Any manufactured product that cost as much would come with a guarantee. It is impossible to justify to the general public, who, as taxpayers, own a 41% stake in Lloyds Banking Group, why they should help fund a bonus of that size.

In one sense, the same thing happened to Michel Tilmant, the CEO of ING at the time of the credit crunch. In 2005 things were still going very well at ING, but then Tilmant incurred the wrath of the Dutch government. He threatened that if the government pursued its plans for taxing high earners (that is, himself), ING would seriously consider relocating its headquarters to another country. Using the company to promote one's own interests so blatantly is, of course, not very ethical, but what happened later when the crisis broke out was a total reversal of fate and fortune. The tension and the mental pressure proved too much for Tilmant, and he stepped down as CEO. In the end it was the head of ING, not the headquarters, who was forced to relocate abroad, leaving the bank reliant on the state. As for Tilmant, he left and returned to his native Belgium.

This brings us to the moral dilemma of asymmetrical remuneration (heads I win, tails you lose). The problem is ubiquitous and has become even more manifest over the past five years. Corporate managers are rewarded as if they were risk takers, but they are not. If the company does badly, someone else pays the bill. Time and again management's only concern is making sure their booty is safe. How can we avoid this situation? The cases mentioned above suggest a solution: defer share-related remuneration and retain elements of variable remuneration in cash. In other words, shares and options should not vest automatically. Such rewards may well be earmarked and made available conditionally, but they should remain on the table. The amounts can become available after several years, or when the manager's contract ends. Is this the solution for short-termism? Even this will not do away with inequitable behaviour. To start with, deferring payment in shares does not necessarily eliminate the wrong kinds of incentives. This is illustrated by what happened when Lehman Brothers collapsed. The management and employees of that financial institution were paid in shares that could not be sold. It should have been the perfect example of how to apply the latest insights in the area of variable remuneration. However, it did not make management more cautious, nor did it make their policy less reckless. With the collapse of Lehman Brothers, many employees lost their assets – their income from past employment – and they became destitute. Employees need to realise that having so much money tied up in a company creates personal systemic risk. Deferred (that is, unvested) remuneration can therefore create problems for the individual. An inability to cope with a malus clause can lead to inequitable behaviour. I have seen it happen many times. That is why we need to work out what the contractual obligations are when an employee who receives variable, deferred remuneration leaves the company.

Essentially, there are two ways in which employees can leave the company: as good leavers (they retire or die in the saddle) or as bad leavers (they go to work for a competitor and their unvested remuneration reverts to the company). Bad leavers are quite similar to footballers; if they depart before the end of their contract a payment has to be made. If they have to put money on the table to leave their current employer, they need to be promised a golden hello by the new club before they will be prepared to sign on.

Someone who has worked for the same company for a long time may well have built up substantial amounts of deferred compensation and will be keen to hang on to them. Good leavers are often employees who leave by mutual agreement, albeit somewhat reluctantly at times (such as in the case of a negotiated departure a few years before they reach retirement age). They agree to leave only if they can take all of the fruits of their years of labour with them. This places a premium on dismissal. The unvested interest is payable on demand, in its entirety. That can be more financially attractive than muddling along for a few more years. The result is that employees start to display unco-operative and unconstructive behaviour. The company is faced with opposition instead of co-operation, which is the exact reverse of the situation that the remuneration was supposed to create. Another added aspect of this problem is that the amounts involved are often so large that immediate payment results in additional costs which the company cannot justify in a given reporting period. If the business climate is unfavourable the company may try to string the obstructive employee along, but in fact it is the company that is being held hostage.

What about the supervision and control of remuneration? Companies are supervised by a board. The Anglo-Saxon system is based on a one-tier board, while the Rhineland model favours a two-tier system based on a managing board and a supervisory board. In the Anglo-Saxon system, non-executive board members customarily receive variable remuneration, which may include options and shares. The Rhineland model rejects this practice outright. Proponents of this model do not believe that supervision can be independent and neutral if the supervisors' own behaviour is motivated by variable remuneration. Their own financial interests should not play any role, especially when it comes to takeovers and the decision to accept or reject a bid. Their job is to represent the interests of shareholders and other stakeholders, and any suggestion of a conflict of interests is one too many.

But let us return to the issue of excessive executive pay and the notion that the sky is the limit. The decentralisation of remuneration creates little kingdoms within a company, as well as a culture of excess and unlimited willingness to accept risk, which sometimes borders on anarchy. The interests of the groups become so extensive that the control mechanisms of the companies they work for cannot function properly. Control over important aspects of the process becomes hopelessly inadequate. The bigger the organisation, the bigger the problems. And that becomes visible to the naked eye. Citicorp was once the champion when it came to instigating compliance problems, but has since been surpassed by UBS. Their corporate services departments seem doomed to clean up one mess after another. There is no end to the misery. Now even JPMorgan is sharing in the uncontrolled misery. Excessive remuneration puts ethical behaviour under pressure. The employees of Citicorp and UBS (and of all other conglomerates) had so much at stake that they overstepped the boundaries of legality. Employees who are under this kind of pressure create the wrong products and sell them to the wrong consumers.

The grey, passive organisations of the mid 20th century have changed forever as a result of takeovers and dramatically different remuneration structures. They have become far too big, their management structures are too decentralised and their reward parameterisation is too aggressive. Too many interests have piled up, one on top of the other, and they are conflicting. Conflicting interests have become a business model of their own. Employees no longer have a clear view of the company's broader organisational and social objectives, and they have become slaves to their own quest for higher pay. All of these factors help to make organisations a breeding ground for vice, while taking away any control management had. The process is no longer manageable. It is out of control.

Horta-Osório decided not to accept his bonus for 2011 (which was said by insiders to be worth up to £2,390,000). It was not a bad haul for someone who fell ill from overwork halfway through his term as CEO. In Germany, Commerzbank saw its share price collapse after the fatal acquisition of Dresdner Bank in 2007, from which it never recovered. German taxpayers still hold a stake of 25%. And yet after some years of restraint, the remuneration cap of €500,000 for members of the board was lifted. 'How come your salary has been raised by 160% while the shareholders have not received a dividend?' asked Markus Dufner, an investor in the bank, of Martin Blessing, Chief Executive Officer, whose basic salary will now be more than €1.3 million. Stephen Hester, CEO of The Royal Bank of Scotland, found himself in a different situation. The British government owned 83% of this group, having paid around 50 pence per share at the end of 2008 and the beginning of 2009. After remaining at that level for a long time, in 2011 the share price fell by 40%. The board of The Royal Bank of Scotland had already halved Hester's performance bonus to £1 million, but even this met with strong political and social disapproval. Although Hester thought he was entitled to receive a bonus, in the end the pressure became too much and he decided to make the best of a bad situation. But there was more to come. A computer failure at RBS in 2012 left millions of customers without access to their bank accounts. The word 'sorry' was not good enough anymore. This time, Hester realised his only option was to announce he would not take any of the bonus he would be entitled to for 2012, and would instead hand it back to shareholders.

On 29 December 2011, an editorial in the *Financial Times*, with the heading 'Restoring faith in the banking system', reported:

> But the real problem banks face is not that people regard their services as being unnecessary or without merit. It is rather that they question the culture within banking institutions. The asymmetry of risks and rewards has led to some very poor outcomes for society.

We have now come more or less full circle and arrived back at the story of Richard Grasso and his 9/11 bonus. If a bank gets into trouble, there is essentially a state of war. All leave is cancelled and everyone is called on to do their patriotic duty. The war has to be won. A bank that is being kept afloat by the British or German government cannot pay its generals a bonus even if their efforts justify it. Can executives still demand pay that is in line with the market if the bank itself cannot survive in that market alone, without the support of taxpayers? Are arguments based on market forces legitimate or even morally just? And what about the precious alignment between the CEO's remuneration and the shareholders' interests? Where has that concept gone astray?

When there is a war on, bread is rationed. Soldiers do not fight for a good salary or a bonus. They fight for a just cause, and they do it for a soldier's wage. They may, however, be decorated for an outstanding performance. Richard Grasso should have been given a medal or a ribbon instead of a bonus. Stephen Hester falls into the same category, and so does Martin Blessing. That may sound a bit Spartan, or Calvinistic if you will, but it is how John Reed responded when Citicorp needed him, and also what Mario Monti, a Catholic, did when Italy asked him to govern the country. It is the sacrifice that gave these leaders the freedom, and above all the moral authority, to push through the necessary changes because their rectitude stopped all counterattacks in their tracks. Hester and Blessing may have had slightly different personal positions, but they could have lived quite comfortably on their basic salary even when capped. The rest is a matter of personal morality, something that was clearly missing.

Throughout this chapter I have attempted to get to the core of the system's inability to tame the bonus culture and find out why bonuses that lead to public indignation are still being awarded, even though they make a travesty of promises of restraint. But before I do that I would like to say something about the American philosopher, Robert Nozick (1938–2002) and his thoughts on justice and the equitable distribution of income. Nozick had very clear views on the latter. His approach is somewhat formal and legalistic. According to him a distribution is equitable if it is arrived at in a correct, legal manner, but his main concern is the beginning of the process of distribution rather than the end result. Simply put, if a labourer works twice as long as his colleague, it is right for him to earn twice as much. The government should not redistribute money merely because someone has an income that is twice as high as that of others. It is not the amount of income that is relevant, but how it is earned that determines whether it is equitable. Nozick used the example of the famous American basketball player, Wilt 'The Stilt' Chamberlain. He analysed the equitability of the exceptional basketball player's income of a quarter of a million dollars, which was considered excessive at the time. Chamberlain played for the Philadelphia Warriors, leading his team to victory over the New York Knicks on 2 March 1962. I will not go into Nozick's story, partly because the amounts involved do not seem very spectacular by today's standards. Instead I shall retain the essence of the story while considering a modern-day hero. When FC Barcelona plays, everyone hopes to see Lionel Messi, also known as La Pulga (the Flea), in action. Over 10 million people watch these matches on television. What would happen if Messi refused to play unless he was paid extra? Each of those viewers would prefer to watch a match involving Messi and would be happy to pay an additional 10 cents to see him play. Based on these factors, the amount that the market would be prepared to pay to watch Messi play is €1 million. What if, armed with this knowledge, the star player went to his employers to discuss the matter and demanded a sum in the region of that amount? Would there be anything morally wrong with this behaviour, given that all the viewers would be prepared to pay more to see Messi play? This is a difficult dilemma, and one that is at the heart of the issue of excessive bonuses. Ethically speaking, there are two relevant criteria for determining whether or not income distribution is equitable. According to Nozick, equitable distribution is determined by effort (that is, labour), not by the results of that effort. It is driven by input, not output. John Rawls, who turns up in Chapter 19, is a proponent of the output-driven vision. Nozick, by contrast, belongs to the school of thought which maintains that equitable distribution is determined by how that distribution comes about; if the origins are equitable, then so is the outcome. If you see an opportunity, seize it and become successful, that success is yours. But Nozick ignores some important facts: work is often not done in isolation but as part of a joint effort involving several individuals working together within a given structure. That is where distribution often goes wrong. However, the theory of contractual rights also falls apart in another way. Even if I am entitled to a bonus based on a profit-sharing plan, a vital issue concerns how the profit was made. Was it earned honestly? In the case of the Libor rigging scandal, one can easily argue that the profits made by banks involved in the scandal were income from fraud. The moral entitlement of thousands of bank employees to contractual bonuses is in such cases corrupted as well, even if in Nozick's narrow analysis their entitlement may still be legitimate. One last question remains unanswered. The policy of monetary easing pursued by central bankers influences the profits made by banks, since the policy bolsters the margin that banks earn on interest. How legitimate can the bonus of any individual banker be if the profit on which his or her bonus is based was supported institutionally?

It is important to distinguish between the individual, the institution and the structure. This brings us back to the Boeing 747 KLM pilot in Chapter 14. Every performance is a combination of either labour and capital or the labour of several individuals (in the case of a group). A pilot makes an exceptional effort. However, without his machine he is just a human being, and some people are nothing without their machines. What is Francesco Schettino, the captain of the Costa Concordia, without his ship? Or guitarist Keith Richards without his amplifier? We live in a society that has enormous operational leverage. People in Hong Kong may find a British comedian such as Mr Bean highly entertaining, an American songwriter can make a couple in Germany so happy they decide to play one of his songs at their wedding, and if Tiger Woods plays a game a few strokes under par the whole world cheers. Which part of the globalised value of our work is down to the individual, and which part is down to the world? No matter how big and powerful the world is, individuals seem to have the upper hand. They decide whether they will write a song, or perhaps call off a game because they have a cold. Individuals are apparently in a very strong negotiating position compared to the structure they use. Why is that? Maybe it is because the world, when viewed as an organisation, incurs costs beforehand, just as the airline does for the pilot, the banking institution for the banker, and Barcelona for Messi. The management of these organisations calculate the cost on a marginal basis. If Messi plays, the club earns more than it would otherwise and the extra earnings (minus the marginal cost) are down to him. The fact that Messi benefits from the club, or from football in general, does not form part of the calculation. The structure's contribution to the results is consistently undervalued. That is the fault of companies that allow themselves to be put on the defensive by greedy individuals who make excessive demands as they scrap for individual talent. The result is rich footballers and poor clubs, rich bankers and poor banks, and rich pilots and poor airlines. The CEO of a company is like the pilot of the Boeing: he thinks the performance is down to him, but it is actually down to the company and represents a collective achievement. Succumbing to the temptation therefore creates rich CEOs and poor shareholders.

Bankers are not footballers and it is much harder to determine whether members of the public would be willing to pay an extra 10 cents each for any of them. Their bonuses are determined by remuneration committees. The economist John Kenneth Galbraith described executive remuneration as a warm personal gesture by an individual to himself. Robert Nozick would argue that such awards are not arrived at in an equitable manner.

Chapter 17

Mutuality

Solidarity and individualism are not contradictory concepts. Parasitism, by contrast, erodes solidarity and also has an impact on individual interests. This chapter deals with how social concepts such as co-operation and individual effort have an equivalent in the financial world, and how derived financial concepts have come to dominate the imagination of the real world.

Which aspect of human interaction should a healthy and successful society emphasise: solidarity or individualism? This question is prompted by the many different visions that exist of the ideal social structure. These visions are formed by environmental factors, culture, history and similar circumstances, and, of course, by social interests. The US, for example, has an open, liberal immigration policy, based on solidarity at the gate. Others are welcome to come in search of their dreams, but once inside the country it is up to them to make those dreams come true. Individualism dominates. Americans show solidarity when it comes to letting people into the country, but they are much less willing to pamper newcomers to the promised land. They have to make their own way, social Darwinism. In the eyes of Europeans, it is incomprehensible that so many Americans are uninsured, as they have no social safety net to catch them when they fall. In Europe, and particularly in the Netherlands, the social welfare system ensures that no one has to go hungry, do without insurance or live on the streets. Americans view this as a socialist paradise that can only serve to make its citizens weak and vulnerable. Europeans tend to show less solidarity at the border, but once the immigrant has been given entry they find themselves in much more comfortable surroundings. Immigrants share the same privileges as other citizens, but sharing has a price. Admitting more people to a country who contribute less, and make more use of social welfare, tends to erode the sense of solidarity. That is why Europeans are more reluctant to increase the size of the group; they instinctively realise that solidarity depends on keeping the system affordable. The concept of dilution is a familiar one in the financial world.

Human beings are a part of nature, and their behaviour has strong similarities to that of other species. Individuality and solidarity are both important survival strategies. There are many good examples of individualism. Animal predators are not prepared to share their hunting grounds or their catch. The tawny owl aggressively defends its hunting grounds and will scare off or even kill its own offspring once they become adults. This is the tawny owl's method of survival. Penguins can only survive the harsh Antarctic winter if they huddle together. Those on the outside of the group are most exposed to the wind, and their body temperatures fall the fastest. After a while these penguins are brought back into the middle of the group so they can warm up, and others take their place in the outer circle. Many animals live in groups and schools. Solidarity and individualism are two basic survival strategies. So what are these examples from the animal kingdom doing in a book about ethics in the financial world?

In effect, the same two structures exist in the financial world. Communality and individualisation provide the two basic patterns for financial concepts and products and structures based on these concepts. Sometimes we are tawny owls, sometimes penguins. This is reflected in financial jargon. The mutual fund is an example of co-operation, unification and joint liability while other structures represent individualisation. Collective pensions contrast with individualised pensions based on defined benefits. It is up to us to choose: do we want to arrange matters collectively or individually? What is best for me, and what is best for the group? To survive as human beings we have to choose the basic financial strategy that will maximise our chances of survival. Our choices may be influenced by pragmatism, and sometimes also by our own philosophy of life.

The communal approach to future financial security is sometimes a choice but it can also be a necessity. We cannot take out insurance without anyone else being involved at all because this would be the same as being uninsured, and even borrowers need someone to borrow from. But within the confines of that reality, collective arrangements can be made with others or on an individual basis. Arranging matters mutually may be the cheaper option, for example in the case of insuring risks that are easier for the group to bear than for the individual. The same is true of old age pensions. For example, all harbour pilots in the Netherlands have arranged all of their insurance as well as their pension funds collectively through one professional organisation. Their collective arrangements means that, like penguins, they can huddle together to survive the winter. Doctors, dentists, bakers and people in the hospitality sector have also set up similar pension funds. They feel connected to one another and this has led to the realisation that it is sometimes better to join forces, even though at other times they may operate as tawny owls. They go out hunting on their own, competing with one another to the bitter end. And yet there are things that unite communities. In addition to insurance, there are co-operative forms of banking. Banks and insurance companies are often the product of local solidarity. The local population may agree to share responsibility for certain risks, such as bad debts, fire damage, sickness or death. These are financial arrangements, but they reflect a social desire to demonstrate solidarity in certain circumstances.

Economic co-operation is usually supported by legal structures, such as co-operative societies. These are 'self-help 'organisations set up by producers and consumers of goods with a view to increasing their economic clout. They are also designed to create economies of scale by organising the joint purchase, distribution or financing of harvests or supplies of particular goods. These co-operative efforts are more likely to exist in communities where people feel connected to one another and solidarity prevails over animosity. It is above all prompted by the realisation that their connectedness and communality make them stronger.

Originally there were no limitations placed on these communal benefits. This grew out of a feeling of social obligation to care for the less fortunate. However, it was sometimes a very costly obligation. If the situation required more money than was available, the members of the community were required to deposit additional sums. Sometimes the relevant risks were so one-sided that the obligations became too large for the community to bear. The limitations of communal structures such as this are immediately apparent. In addition, risks were often correlated. In such environments, correlated risks can have a major impact. If the village burns down, the capacity to pay out is going to be severely affected. The European 'village' is facing a similar problem with its EFSF emergency fund. If too many European houses catch fire, it will no longer have the capacity to insure the damage, which is why we want the IMF to participate.

As spreading risk became more important than local solidarity, other solutions were found that involved the entire market instead of a single community. These commercial solutions came from financial services providers who were out to earn a profit and who could be more effective than co-operatives because they were able to operate on a much larger scale. It was a case of the market versus the community. Nevertheless, community-based structures were often cheaper and more efficient. Co-operative organisations know their customers, and they are also more familiar with the risks. They tend to have a more conservative risk profile, a common sense approach, and greater integrity when it comes to expense accounts. They are aware that they are dealing with community assets, and know that their neighbour is watching them. It is a well-known fact that the amounts paid in sickness benefits are lower in agricultural communities than in urban areas where people are more anonymous. On the other hand, the market has a much greater capacity to absorb risks due to its scale and diversity. Co-operative and commercial solutions are two effective means of providing financial services, and they will continue to compete for the customer's business. They reflect two different visions of society: united we stand, or every man for himself.

Sharing risk is not just a problem for the members of a fund, but also a generational issue. That is why I began with the example of a pension fund, which is one area in which the question of solidarity plays an extremely important role. The matter is becoming increasingly urgent. Intergenerational solidarity is an emotional issue with a strong moral dimension. We care for our children, and they care for us. Many people's old age provisions have traditionally consisted of producing enough children, but today this concept is showing signs of wear and tear. As women have assumed their rightful place in the labour market, their part in producing and caring for children has changed. It is also the result of greater mobility in the labour market. Parents may live in the country while their children migrate to cities to secure their own livelihood. Or in more extreme cases, parents may be left behind in North Africa by children who have migrated to the US because they cannot find work in their own country. Labour market mobility has made it increasingly difficult for parents to rely on their children in their old age; care in kind has been replaced by government care. Countries such as China are still in the early stages of this process, and their development will stagnate if the community, the state and the market do not take over significant aspects of care from children. This frees up young people to put their talents to productive use in the cities.

In many countries that has led to the development of basic provisions which may or may not be offered on a commercial basis. It may be a financial product or an employment benefit. Pension schemes are an example of arrangements funded by society on a pay-as-you-go basis. Rather than paying exclusively for their own family, young people now pay for the elderly in a generic sense. This expands the circle of solidarity to national borders and reduces the economic pressure to start families. The pay-as-you-go pension system works as long as the population continues to grow. However, in many countries the demographic balance has changed and populations are shrinking. Fewer children are being asked to care for more older people, and those older people are living longer. What was once a system based on solidarity between the generations is becoming an increasingly heavy burden resting on fewer shoulders. Those taking from the system enjoy a pension funded by the next working generation. Members of that working generation are uncertain whether they will find others are willing to foot their bill when are retired, and are quite justified in questioning this. Pay-as-you-go pension systems are in effect Ponzi pension schemes, and they are not sustainable in the long run, particularly in view of the declining population, since these schemes always collapse if there are more people taking money out than bringing money in. In the future, Western countries with pension schemes based on the pay-as-you-go method are therefore likely to experience serious social disruption as a result of the cost of maintaining them. The concept will start to creak at the seams, placing considerable pressure on intergenerational solidarity.

Another form of pension provision that has evolved over the years is one in which the next generation does not pay for the older generation, but each generation takes care of itself. People save for their own pension so that future generations do not have to pay. A pension is a deferred salary. But there are problems associated with this system as well. In countries such as the US, Great Britain and the Netherlands, pension systems have traditionally created entitlements that are earnings-related. Some are based on the member's final salary, others on average salary. The size of the payment guaranteed under these defined benefit schemes is fixed. The idea is that since people will need an income once they retire, they set aside a fixed amount (usually around 22%) of their income during their working life so that it can be paid out later as deferred salary. These pension commitments are often nominal rights which are indexed to pay rises, and that gives rise to major problems. In effect the former employer will continue to bear financial responsibility in future for the cost of its retired employees. And when a funding deficit arises, the finger of blame inevitably points to the employer. It is guilty because it was the one that made pension commitments to employees which it now cannot honour. Who should foot the bill? There are many reasons why deficits arise in pension funds, including the greater life expectancy of pensioners and the disappointing investment returns on the pension fund's investments. Deficits may also be caused by a decline in the reinvestment rate compared to the discount rate used to calculate the obligations. The same thing happens when purchasing power declines as a result of inflation and investment results are unable to compensate for this. Who takes up the slack in this situation? Every country has its own rules that create or eliminate the possibility of passing the buck in one direction or the other. The UK has laws prohibiting cuts in existing pension commitments. In the Netherlands, cuts are definitely a negotiable option; in fact it is the most obvious solution and one that is likely to be widely used in the future. Who else can be expected to foot the bill? The company that sponsors the pension fund? We have all heard the horror stories about the US automotive industry, where the cost of a car today is partially determined by pension obligations originating in the past. Should we dip into the pension pot and allow the funding ratio to fall even further so that future generations are stuck with a system that only partially covers its obligations? The debate about who should pay the bill is about intergenerational solidarity, and for that reason it is a moral debate that goes straight to the heart of how our economy and businesses function. And because of the nature of the response to this issue, it is also a question that belongs in the realm of financial ethics. It is very easy to say that the company that sponsors the pension fund has the obligation to pay more money into the fund. However, the pension fund is often so big that financing a further contribution from the company's current operating results is not a realistic option, because that would seriously threaten the company's continued existence. The companies facing this problem are those that are much smaller now than they were in the past. The American automotive industry, British Telecom and the Dutch postal services are prime examples of this dilemma. Many banks are also troubled by their own version of demographic decline. Even if these companies have legal obligations originating in the past, when economic reality catches up these obligations will be difficult to enforce.

To determine whether or not the sponsor has the moral obligation to continue to provide additional financing for pensions, we should ask ourselves the following question. In the past, did the company act reasonably and in good faith, setting aside funds in accordance with accepted standards? If so, is it reasonable to expect the company to make additional contributions? The costs are a ghost from the past, but they are charged to current operating expenses. It seems unnatural to force a company to make supplementary payments, and in some cases to accuse the managers responsible for pensions in the past of mismanagement. The extra contribution poses a threat to existing jobs and reduces the company's ability to compete. The postal services are a good example of this. There is now so much competition in the postal delivery market that past costs destroy any chance the company has of becoming competitive. The current crisis means that all obligations need to be fully funded, with no residual risk. Facing this kind of pressure, defined benefit schemes will migrate to collective defined contribution schemes, and end up as individual defined contribution schemes. We are moving from the collective to the individual, from solidarity to individual responsibility. The risk of future fluctuations in investment returns (and therefore uncertain benefits) will shift to the members. The unions are the biggest opponents of this trend, but their opposition is primarily driven by the emotions of their aging membership. They should know better, because forcing the sponsor to make substantial extra contributions threatens the opportunities of future generations. Union leaders rail against what they call casino pensions as the members have to absorb all of the market risks. Is that pure demagoguery? Yes, because the investments do not have to be risky; risk-free investments can be chosen instead. But that brings us to the crux of this moral problem: the market has robbed us of every form of risk-free return. If German government bonds are the proxy for risk-free investment, the risk-free return is no higher than 2%, and that is not enough in itself to cover pension commitments. In fact, the situation is worse since if annual inflation is also 2%, as the investors' risk-free return is only just enough to compensate for inflation. The time value of money has disappeared, and we have come full circle to the real problem, one that we have already discussed. Driven by the animal spirit, we have entered a phase in which every form of risk-taking is punished, and risk-free investment is overvalued (and therefore offers a very low effective yield). However, that is not all down to the animal spirit. Interventions by monetary authorities, such as quantitative easing, are a major contributing factor to low interest rates, especially long-term rates. These are all consequences of the current crisis, and the reckless borrowing that landed market players in so much trouble they had to be bailed out. Keeping interest rates artificially low is, however, not the only way out of this mess. The alternative is inflation. This authorities are keeping this possibility on the cards by using inflationary financing and increasing the supply of money. And so the buck is passed yet again. The debtors who borrowed too much money will not foot the whole of the bill for this stealthy form of debt restructuring. Creditors will also bear some of the cost; in other words savers have to contribute. The older generation should not pass its debts on to the next generation, nor should the younger generation dig itself out of a hole by depriving the previous generation of any form of risk-free return.

Let us now move on and consider what Lorenzo Bini Smaghi said in an interview with the *Financial Times* following his resignation from the board of the European Central Bank. Bini Smaghi left the bank ahead of schedule at the end 2011. He was forced to cede his seat to a Frenchman after his fellow countryman Mario Draghi took over the chairmanship of the ECB from the Frenchman, Jean-Claude Trichet. It is well known that the French president, Nicolas Sarkozy had supported Draghi's appointment on the condition that Bini Smaghi would give up his position to a Frenchman. In his final interview the frustrated Italian hinted that the subject of quantitative easing had been discussed at length by the ECB's board, but that he had lost the debate to policy-makers who opposed this strategy. 'I do not understand the quasi-religious discussions about quantitative easing,' he said. Later in the article Bini Smaghi also noted that the most important lesson he had learned was that 'ultimately central banks, as policy-makers, cannot opt out of their own responsibility for taking decisions'. But who is Bini Smaghi talking about here? The ECB and government leaders? Surely the problem is Italy, where the behaviour of the country's top leaders continued to encourage tax evasion until shortly before the resignation of Bini Smaghi? Where the wealthy did not contribute their fair share to their country? Former prime minister Berlusconi laughed off every problem with a platitude about there being nothing wrong with Italy, since the restaurants were full every night. They probably were, but that was not the point. The point is that when they leave the restaurant, the guests pay for their meal with a credit card. Italy is living on top of a rubbish heap of debt. But apparently that was not what Bini Smaghi was referring to when he vented his frustrations to the *Financial Times*. He was undoubtedly referring to his colleagues at the ECB and to European government leaders. Bini Smaghi is a proponent of quantitative easing, in other words of printing money. Paul de Grauw, a lecturer at the Catholic High School of Leuven, agrees with him. He concluded that although the ECB helped the banks out with long-term, low-interest loans, in the end no one pays the bill, because there is no bill to be paid. But is he right?

Money is like a share in a company. Or to put it even more succinctly, money is a share in the European economy. We could give our economy a name, perhaps Global Euro GmbH. As with any company, the current shareholders will not be happy if Global Euro GmbH suddenly decides to issue new shares and give them away for free. On 15 January 2012, the *Financial Times* reported the following.

> Ms Le Pen said she would solve France's debt problem by quitting the euro, printing money, slashing immigration and setting up protectionist barriers... In an attempt to

attract a broader range of voters, Ms Le Pen plans to raise the wages for poorer workers by €200 a month...paying for it by putting a 3% tax on imports. She would return the country to the French franc, authorise the Bank of France to print the equivalent of €100 billion a year and borrow €45 billion a year from the bank in interest-free loans.

Quantitative easing is the equivalent of issuing new shares that entitle their holders to the same amount of real economy assets as old shares. As the new participants in the circle of solidarity do not provide anything in return for these shares, the rights of existing share-holders are severely diluted. This is parasitic behaviour. The consequence of dilution is a process of creeping inflation. The issue of dilution was discussed in the previous chapter, in the context of management options, proponents of which also argued that the options were not issued at anyone else's expense. Companies issued options to employees. Because dividends did not increase, the interests of existing shareholders were diluted. Supporters of the system viewed this as a way of making free money. Companies made more profit, but because there were more shares, profit per share remained the same and shareholders did not benefit from the increase in the value of the company. They were the ones who paid the bill, which brings us back to one of the maxims of this book: is a little bit of stealing acceptable? Tax evasion and insider trading are not really the same as stealing, and no one pays for quantitative easing. With so much money already in circulation, surely a little more could not do any harm? This is the reasoning behind this policy, to which supporters add the comforting thought that the inflationary effects are likely to be limited. Moreover, they claim that the inflationary impact of the increased amount of money in circulation will be mitigated by the slower rate of circulation. This last argument may hold true, but only if the monetary authorities can take money out of the system again if the rate of circula-tion picks up and inflation rises again. That, however, is a major challenge, and not many policy-makers are likely to have the backbone to implement the necessary changes in these circumstances. This is a reflection of the asymmetry of political and monetary motivations. It requires more courage than the captain of the Costa Concordia had, which is why quan-titative easing has become a permanent fixture that is being sold as a temporary measure. One of my former colleagues compared quantitative easing to holding a barbecue party in a haystack; things may go well for a while but the risk of the haystack catching fire is huge. And once it starts to burn, it cannot be extinguished. People who get into debt should not count on dilution and expect others to pay back a portion of their debt, even if De Grauw regards this as free money, because it constitutes an attack on the two main principles set out in this chapter: collectivity and solidarity.

In every society there are a variety of factors that necessitate the transfer of wealth. These include covering the cost of governing the country, and paying for collective benefits and infrastructure, public safety, and the preservation of the nation's cultural heritage. But the transfer of wealth may also be a necessary form of social solidarity. Healthy, talented people with a good job and a decent salary need to contribute to the cost of supporting people who are not well or are unable to contribute for some other reason. Babies are a cost to society, and so are the elderly. This transfer of wealth takes place via a legitimate, democratic process: taxes. In many countries, including some in the eurozone, that process simply does not function, owing to poor budgetary discipline, the lack of a tax paying ethic and faulty tax collection systems. This is one of the primary reasons why many countries are unable to solve their financial problems. They prefer to take the easy way out, using the improper and undemocratic solution of inflation by artificially expanding the amount of money in circulation and keeping interest rates low. This is in effect a tax on savers, but it is a tax that has not been through the democratic process. Is a tax union the answer to the eurozone's problems? I do not believe it is. The real solution is a uniform tax-paying ethic. A tax union of countries with different tax-paying ethics will simply result in countries with a strong ethic paying more than those with a weak ethic. Countries with a strong ethic will end up feeling cheated and in the end will refuse to accept the situation. The countries that would benefit from this arrangement would feel no pressure to change their attitude. There are already examples of this. In economic terms, Germany still consists of a Western and an Eastern half, and there is still a substantial transfer of wealth to the East. However, this does not lead to excessive tensions because the difference in the work ethic and the tax ethic between the two halves of the country is not significant enough to erode the sense of solidarity. We might say the same thing about England and Scotland, even though the Scots are pushing for independence. It is less true of a country such as Belgium. It is a tax union, but the steady transfer of wealth from the Flemish part of the country to the Walloons has created tensions and is also the cause of the paralysis that grips the political decision-making process. People on both sides of the language border perceive differences in the morality of the other side, and whether their perceptions are accurate does not really matter anymore. Both sides are intransigent. That is why the tax and budgetary unification of Europe would not guarantee an end to the tensions. On the contrary, it would simply fan the flames of the sense of injustice and powerlessness, which will lead to political unrest. At some point, something will have to give. A tax union is not a solution as long as there is no uniform morality. Europe will have to work very hard to create a uniform morality that can serve as a basis for mutual help in difficult times. And that means that for the time being the Italians should pay their own bills.

> One of the most interesting infringements of that tiny bit of solidarity that Europe still feels when it comes to a common, healthy budgetary policy took place when the Spanish Minister of Sports, Miguel Cardenal, told the sports newspaper *Marca* that the government was looking into how it could cancel the debts that the football clubs Real Madrid and Barcelona owed to the public. Together the clubs owed more than €750 million in taxes and €600 million in social insurance charges. The German newspaper *Bild* was quick to respond. Was it up to German taxpayers to pay the salaries of Messi and Ronaldo? Messi is paid €2.5 million a month, Ronaldo more than a million. To make matters worse, Bayern Munchen had lost to these top clubs.

A question that is often asked is whether Southern European countries should become more German. In my view, that is the wrong question. Some issues are culturally determined, others are not. Not taking on more debt that your own community can afford to pay back is not a Western or Northern European concept; it is a natural law. A squirrel that gets through its store of acorns before the winter is over reduces its chance of survival. Natural laws also come into play if the squirrel borrows some acorns from its neighbour and refuses to pay it back. The cultural difference is not reflected in the law of nature, only in the degree of discipline exercised in complying with that law.

Picking up the thread of solidarity and group solidarity, let us look at some specific groups, such as Dutch civil-law notaries, American taxi drivers, market makers on the New York Stock Exchange, and of course the unions in most Western countries. We show solidarity with one another not only because of our feelings of social empathy, but also because of naked self interest. These groups have stopped being solidarity groups and are becoming interest groups. There is nothing wrong with that, but the next phase is that in the group's drive to protect its own interests, the interests of other groups are harmed. Solidarity groups are inclined to show very little solidarity with other groups. Existing positions are defended tooth and nail, even when this goes against every sense of social justice. This brings us to the principle of economic rent. Economic rent refers to having an institutionalised position in society, protected by rights and privileges or by customs that have a great capacity to withstand pressure and survive. Newcomers are hampered by those who enjoy protection. The rights, obligations and privileges that form the hard structure of a society – the structure we need in order to function properly – become dysfunctional. Rent seekers in the form of lobbyists try wherever possible to protect political and social positions. Economists regard rent seeking as a waste of economic potential and one of the leading causes of social stagnation. Studies have shown that the US loses 3% to 12% of its gross national product to rent seeking. In Europe rent seeking, that is, maintaining vested interests, is partly responsible for the economic crisis we now face. That is why in addition to spending cuts there is so much insistence on the need for reform as well. However, unions are not in favour of this, and nor are associations of commercial airline pilots, employers' associations or political parties. And those that do express support for reform all have different opinions. The solidarity groups have become parasitical.

Earlier in this chapter, I talked about pension funds and health insurance, fire insurance and other forms of mutually shared risks and security. Should we be obliged to take out insurance, or should that be our own choice? Solidarity originates with the desire to help others, and from our dislike of seeing others suffer; there is therefore an egotistical element in feelings of solidarity. Companies have pension schemes, and in many countries these schemes are obligatory. Businesses see it as their responsibility to provide a good pension scheme, but it is also in their own interests to do so. The scheme may be made mandatory by law or under the terms of an employment contract. We previously looked at autonomy, and this is an issue that infringes on the employee's autonomy. The same is true of health insurance and many other types of social benefits. In the Netherlands, where people are obliged to build up a pension, the choice of a pension fund is often laid down in their employment contract. This is an example of enforced solidarity and a closed shop system. If we see a pension scheme as a financial product instead of as part of an employment package, this obligation comes dangerously close to being a form of unfair competition that prevents market forces from doing their work. This kind of enforced solidarity with one's self, the obligation to take out insurance, which is common in Europe, is the crux of the opposition to Obamacare, the new healthcare legislation designed to provide all Americans with health insurance. How far can we encroach on individual freedoms in order to promote a social objective?

The pension issue, which we have considered in detail in this chapter, is in my view one of the purest examples of overlapping social and financial orders. The financial world, with its knowledge and experience of creating crises, should be able to offer some assistance. From an evolutionary point of view, it is natural that parents should care for their children and for their own parents too. Both of these burdens are being shouldered by the working generation. Governments have made pension commitments that are unfunded and so vast they defy all comprehension. They are not included in the national debt, but are in addition to it. But are these really financial obligations? There are new icebergs on the horizon. Can we turn the ship around in time? Can we continue to believe in the fairytale of our own rights and privileges, or should we accept future impoverishment as part of our duty towards intergenerational solidarity? One thing is certain: the solidarity group of pensioners will defend its economic rent tooth and nail.

The following chapter considers our planet as an entity for solidarity. But are we ready to think of it in those terms?

Chapter 18

Scarcity in abundance

The concept of scarcity is at the core of economics. Society as a whole is not willing to take radical decisions in order to solve problems when it comes to our consumption of scarce resources. We find it difficult when such solutions require us to make a sacrifice today in order to achieve benefits in the future. However, it is no different from a standard investment proposal.

On the last day of October 2011, the United Nations Population Fund announced that the world population had reached seven billion. Today, half of humanity lives in cities, which represents a demographic change of historic proportions. The global population is growing faster than ever before, and there still is no end in sight to this rapid increase. It is expected that in 35 years' time two-thirds of the global population, which by then could be as high as 10 billion, will live in urban agglomerations. This means that there will be nearly seven billion people living in cities. How many of these people will be able to live above the poverty line? Will it be possible for them to enjoy a dignified existence, or will human dignity finally collapse under the weight of the masses? With such huge problems facing the world, this book focuses instead on matters of ethics and, for instance, on whether the outcome of an action should be judged from a deontological or consequentialist perspective. Is this merely a micro debate conducted as we head straight towards a macro problem? And is the problem now unavoidable and inescapable?

The unstoppable growth in the world's population, most of which is found at the bottom rung of society, is fundamentally unbalanced. People who own barely anything dream of the lives they see portrayed in advertisements and films, of the lives lived by their sports heroes and pop idols, of a life that everyone longs for but which will remain unattainable for most people. What strain will that place on our political and social systems and our ecosystems? And by extension, what will it mean for our financial systems? These issues are interrelated and together they are by far the greatest moral dilemma we currently face. They are also directly related to the biggest moral issues in the financial industry. What can the financial sector and the financial markets do about them? These ethical dilemmas therefore deserve a place in this book. Although there is not enough room to discuss them in detail, not mentioning them at all would constitute a serious shortcoming.

In 2008, during my term of office as Robeco's CEO, I asked IRIS (a research agency created by a joint venture between Rabobank and Robeco) to study global demographic developments in order to determine their economic impact and possible consequences for the world of investing. The study led to the publication of a report entitled 'Scarcity in abundance', which took a strategic look at tomorrow's world. I had been prompted to order this study by the warnings made by Al Gore in his documentary, *An Inconvenient Truth*. That said, Robeco had had a more general need for a better understanding of the world of the future for some time. IRIS was to consider how demographic, climatological and physical trends would affect the financial industry, and attempt to identify the approach the financial industry needed to take in a rapidly changing world. This is something that needs to be done with a strong conscience, paying attention to how future generations will be affected. The report was also aimed at identifying the financial and monetary consequences of such developments. Although it was something of a stab in the dark, we assumed that anything that could help us find our way was a bonus, and that above all we needed to give these issues some serious thought.

When giving presentations on 'Scarcity in abundance', I used a standard example based on the consumption of clean water. I postulated that many people in the Western world spent far too long in the shower every morning. If every global citizen were to adopt this behaviour, there would soon be no clean water left. The issue is our footprint, whether it is seen in terms of our carbon footprint or the amount of clean water and other natural resources we use. It relates to the use of scarce resources, of commodities that either are incapable of being reused or require unsustainable production processes, such as water desalination. If we multiply our individual Western footprint by seven billion, the problem becomes clear. The rapid rate of population growth, and migration to cities in particular, will lead to an exponential increase in demand for basic goods such as food, clean water and energy. People who live in the countryside are able to lead a simpler life because they are closer to nature. If they are lucky, they can eat locally grown food and can find water close by. By contrast, food and water need to be transported in to cities, and waste and sewage need to be transported out. This creates major dislocations in small societies that are the excrescences produced by global consumption patterns. Is this development sustainable?

It is not the first time that this serious issue has been raised. In 1798, the British economist and demographer Thomas Robert Malthus (1766–1834) published *An Essay on the Principle of Population*, a treatise in which he argued that population growth would inevitably outpace economic growth. Malthus predicted widespread starvation on the basis of calculations made using a simple model. However, that was over 200 years ago. There has been explosive population growth, but it has not outstripped economic growth. The predictions made by Malthus were incorrect, because he had underestimated human ingenuity. Even the conclusions drawn by the Club of Rome in the 1960s seem, at least for now, to have been far too pessimistic. But is human ingenuity still able to save us? Or will humanity's ability to stay one step ahead of its own growth come to an end one day? And if so, what kind of future will we face? Will we perhaps have to deal with a Malthusian catastrophe? As well as a scarcity of physical goods, the reverberations of the financial and monetary changes this would entail would be felt throughout the financial world.

We presented the 'Scarcity in abundance' report in 2009. It received a great deal of attention in the Dutch press and also in Anglo-Saxon media, thanks in part to the fact it was published at the same time as oil prices broke through the US$100 per barrel mark.

This was a significant moment, and the report provided a good basis for considering the issue of high oil prices in a more structured way.

The problem can be put simply. Demand for goods – initially food and water, and then energy and specific minerals required for our mass market – will continue to grow. If the current pace is maintained, the planet's resources will become exhausted. While opinions may differ as to when this will happen, what is certain is that nothing in life lasts forever. The closer we come to the moment the planet becomes exhausted, the higher the costs of extracting natural resources will be. If we do not want matters to reach this point, or if we want to delay this until such time as other solutions have been discovered, we will have to curb consumption of these resources by introducing measures aimed at population control, reducing individual consumption and increasing efficiency substantially. This is the only way in which we will be able to contain the depletion of our planet's resources to any extent.

Besides exhausting the earth's resources, we are also polluting our home planet. What we are doing on a global scale can be seen on a much smaller scale in the Italian city of Naples: we are surrounded by waste matter, but we have become blind to it. We do not even notice the stench it produces anymore because it is the only odour we know. It does not bother us, and so we have stopped clearing up. The use of energy generated from fossil fuels produces waste matter such as carbon emissions. The use of fossil fuels is not the only way in which we pollute our planet, and we do not know how much it would cost to clean up such pollution, or, perhaps more accurately, we do not want to know. Nor have we taken any measures to deal with the situation. The same can be said with regard to the waste matter produced by nuclear energy. We have in effect mortgaged the future. This attitude borders on parasitical behaviour, with one generation living off the host and future generations. We saddle our descendants with the problem without leaving them with a solution. We carry on squabbling about which solution has the most potential. Alongside drastic cuts in fossil fuel consumption, the best option when it comes to our future energy supply would appear to be solar energy. There is plenty of sunshine and models for this kind of energy are replicable, particularly in countries with the highest levels of population growth. However, we do not yet have the technology needed to develop solar energy on a large scale at acceptable costs. Moreover, solar energy itself indirectly utilises scarce resources. There is not enough of a sense of urgency to deal with the underlying limitations associated with this alternative form of energy. Developing solutions for the issues of pollution, shortages, debts and population growth will require a great deal of time, and it may be time we no longer have.

Climate change will have major consequences for food production. Failed harvests and the need to shift areas of production are just two examples. Coastal areas will be flooded as sea levels rise. And on top of this there is the issue of urbanisation and population growth. What will the economic, social and political impact be, especially if the problems cannot be solved on time, if at all? Scarcity will lead to price increases for many goods, and this will mean that many inhabitants of our planet will see a decline in prosperity. Sometimes the problem will go beyond mere scarcity, with raw materials simply not being available anymore. They will vanish from the face of the earth, as the dinosaurs did. The social and political consequences of this will be enormous. The recent unrest seen in the Middle East provides just a taste of what is in store. Rising food prices fuelled smouldering discontent in North Africa. It is striking that no matter what the social order may be, food shortages lead to uprisings in every social structure and society.

When supply fails to keep up with rising demand, the standard response given by economists is that a new balance will be found in which there is a different relationship between supply and demand, even if there is a scarcity. But what if there is no price elasticity on the supply side? What if scarcity leads to a de facto cessation of supply, with supply no longer responding to price increases? After all, how much would I have to pay in a pet store in order to buy a living Mauritian dodo? Increasing the price does not make any difference, because dodos, too, have been wiped out. The new balance perspective is only applicable if a new balance is found between supply and demand, and provided that new solutions, that is, supply, can be brought to market quickly enough. Carbon dioxide pollution may have already gone so far that the processes are irreversible. A scenario emerges in which humanity is increasingly taken over by events and supply can no longer keep up with demand. In that scenario, it is impossible to strike a new balance. In this scenario, human ingenuity has been beaten and Thomas Malthus has finally been proved right, albeit perhaps a little late in the day in his view.

What effect will all these developments have on the world of finance? What role could the financial sector play right now, and what could it perhaps do in future? Let us start by considering the effect that is the least relevant in the bigger scheme of things. Countless accusations will be made against the financial sector, some of them justified. People will be angry, particularly at players in the financial markets. Price rises may be only the messenger, but they are likely to be seen as the source of the evil. Speculators are already being blamed for price rises because they profit from scarcity. Justified or not, the anger is inevitable. It is therefore important that we formulate our answer now. And if this answer requires us to change our behaviour, let us go ahead and change it now. There are plenty of areas in which we need to take more responsibility and change our policy. In combination, they can offer some protection against future criticism. Given this, let us identify these responsibilities.

The financial world knows all about how markets operate and how they can be organised and maintained. The financial sector will need to use its knowledge of markets to allocate and price resources that become scarce, or create institutional scarcity in order to change the consumptive behaviour of market participants. For example, the broken system for trading carbon emission rights will need to be repaired. Financial players have experience in the area of markets and this could prove of enormous benefit when it comes to solving the problems and creating a market that provides regulation in the areas of pollution and scarcity, just as the financial market provides an opposing view to budget anarchy. Take on this responsibility, even if you only play a small role. It is bound to be an important one.

One of the few positive upshots of the climate change conference held in Copenhagen in 2009 was the agreement that money would be released to help poor countries tackle the effects of climate change. It is immensely important that the capital markets are open to projects that help solve the problems. These markets have the very important task of supporting and accommodating the process of innovation, especially when it comes to initiatives developed from the bottom up. Innovations that come from the market should be symbolic of human ingenuity. Financial resources are vital for the development of new initiatives; money and a willingness to take risk need to play a part in speeding up the search for solutions.

But the financial world can do more than finance innovations. Besides providing money, translating genuine social concern into influence is vitally important. Such influence can turn out to be of overriding importance. The initial widespread serious concern about demographic trends and the climatological consequences for human life on our plant has given way to a certain level of scepticism or even resignation; after all, people prefer warmer summers and winters. This is fuelled primarily by short-term thinkers: people whose horizon does not extend beyond the next Christmas party, the disbelievers and those who have a major interest in maintaining the status quo, as well as government leaders and politicians who ultimately pursue other interests. Often these interests appear close to home. Some politicians publicly express doubts that climate change is due to human activity, despite the overwhelming amount of scientific evidence. Rather than providing evidence to the contrary, they try to bring insight obtained through scientific research into discredit. The ridiculing of the problem for political ends represents a moral challenge in itself, but it is not a specific concern of the financial sector. This is in contrast to the responsibilities of shareholders.

Big businesses make use of substantial resources, which are the property of shareholders, in order to wage a political war on measures designed to help us act in a sustainable way and keep the planet fit for human habitation for future generations. They do this based on the conviction that the status quo is best for them and should therefore be defended using every possible means. Is that morally acceptable, or is it an unacceptable use of funds belonging to members of the public? Well known cases involve mining companies and companies that produce fossil fuels. Recouping economic rent plays a key role in this context. All changes are welcome, as long as they do not affect our own privileges. In this context, an important role is reserved for the voice of international capital, of shareholders united in pension funds or represented by asset managers that act on behalf of collectives consisting of private or institutional investors. Shareholders need to speak up; it is after all their money, and it is not their opinion that is being reflected with that money. Unfortunately, investors and shareholders do little to oppose the use of more or less public funds to influence political processes. However, this challenge needs to be taken on as soon as possible.

This is not the end of the story. Shareholders need to do more. They need to reward good behaviour as well, because some companies stand out from the crowd and the actions of some CEOs are more than courageous. Unilever, for example, wants to shift the focus of its business back to the long term again and away from short-termism. For that reason it wants to move away from publishing quarterly accounts. Its attitude is that it is in it for the long term, and that is what shareholders should reward management for. Shareholders who believe in such values ought to support CEOs that swim against the tide.

The World Business Council for Sustainable Development (WBCSD) is sponsored by more than 200 leading international companies that want to bring about a change in the behaviour of institutions when it comes to the environment, and believe that change should come from the business community in particular. The chairman of the WBCSD is Peter Bakker, the energetic former CEO of the Dutch-based TNT. The council's premise is that the world has only a limited number of years in which to effect change before we will be locked into a state of global warming that cannot be reversed. The pressure on the earth can be grouped into five categories: water usage, waste production, carbon emissions, air pollution and land usage. The scenario presented by the WBCSD is a simple one. In order to reduce our footprint, business has to reduce its impact on the environment in all these areas. But reduction cannot be achieved unless there is a way of measuring the impact, and that requires a methodology based on global standards. The idea is that once such a methodology has been agreed, each footprint will have to be monetised. This simple solution provides a representation of a real cost that nobody has been charged for so far. In other words, we need to act as our own agent and calculate our own bill for renting the earth. And eventually the monetary value will need to be charged to the profit and loss account. If we do not attach costs to pollution, poor behaviour will be subsidised and good behaviour will go unrewarded. This will ultimately kill off all the good intentions of responsible CEOs, such as Paul Polman of Unilever. One of the companies leading the way in costing the use of resources is Adidas, the German sports clothing manufacturer. Adidas publishes a detailed report on its environmental impact every year and sets targets to reduce its impact.

Investments in assets that score negatively may become a burden for the company in future, once that effect is monetised. Banks have a responsibility, and they should fulfil it now by adopting a lending policy in which they incorporate the cost of footprint aspects of such assets in their decision-making process. This means that their lending policies will become selective and encourage investments with a more sustainable profile. Is this ideology in its purest form? No, it is a necessary move. If the cost to the environment is to be monetised at some point in the future, many assets with a high pollution output will become inefficient and be discarded. Banks do not want to find themselves back in a position where they become the ultimate owner of dysfunctional assets that are a burden on their own balance sheets and threaten to render them insolvent again, just as real estate assets did. Adopting such policies is therefore common sense.

Our report, 'Scarcity in abundance', also described the potential monetary consequences of the disastrous developments described above. To put matters in more radical terms than used in the report, can our monetary instruments still be used in a scenario of permanent imbalance? If prices rise, demands will be made by participants in the economic process, particularly in the Western world. They will want to be compensated for the fact that life has become more expensive. But besides creating problems in terms of reallocation (which inflationary pay demands attempt to rectify), rising prices also create, more importantly, problems in the form of generic pauperisation. Pauperisation is due in part to the reallocation of wealth (owners of raw materials will receive more for the same performance), but it will primarily be down to a global organic decline. This is because the raw materials we need will be scarcer and greater efforts will need to be made in order to extract them, which means paying more for them. The exchange ratio between our labour and commodities that were once thought to be free will change drastically. If suddenly every litre of air we inhale had to be produced in an oxygen plant, our level of prosperity would plummet. A similar trend may be seen in food production. We will soon need to start using more expensive production methods so that growing demand can continue to be met in the changing arena. If these trends continue, their impact will be seen in the financial markets in the form of inflation, most probably hyperinflation. Fortunately, we will still have our monetary authorities. Or do they merely lure us into a false sense of security?

In our society, and in particularly in the financial industry, we have the firmly encoded belief that inflation has to be fought. Central bankers have a whole range of means at their disposal for this, including the interest rate mechanism and control of the money supply. But will they be successful in the scenario described above? Inflation has traditionally been tackled by restricting the money supply or increasing interest rates. However, in a world of rising prices we need a larger money supply to serve as a lubricant so that we can pay the higher prices. If the money supply is restricted, the inflationary process is suppressed by monetary measures. But can this process of rising prices due to physical scarcity be dealt with by making money more scarce? I do not believe it can. The problem of higher commodity prices is structural and so difficult that monetary measures will no longer be able to provide a solution. Monetary intervention can push up interest rates substantially, but no consumer wants to be faced with higher financing charges as well as higher commodity prices. In such a situation the political pressure will be great, and the outcome is impossible to predict. The willingness of the ECB's current management to bow to political reality and move away from monetary discipline is clear for all to see. What will happen when tensions really are running high? Monetary instruments will become blunt and lose their effectiveness. Even central bankers who do have a backbone will not be able to do much more than Gadaffi, who continued to order attacks while he was up against the wall and stood no chance. When the tsunami of price increases comes, the dykes constructed by the monetary authorities will deteriorate into sandbanks in an ever-rising sea.

I have painted a very grim picture, but it would have been wrong to have omitted the greatest moral issues of our time in an account of morality and ethics in the financial industry. When responding to these issues, the financial industry needs to live up to its responsibilities. It cannot look the other way or trivialise the problem. Nor can it pass the problem on to future generations, as this would be the ultimate moral failure. Evidently there is little willingness within society to solve future problems if this means difficulties today. The same attitude can be seen in respect of Europe's debt crisis; there is very little willingness to take radical decisions out of choice. We find it very difficult when solutions require us to make a sacrifice today in order to achieve a result in the future. However, it is no different from a standard investment proposal. We only take action when we are surrounded on all sides by a huge abyss. Too often, obstructing the course of action and stopping any resolution of a future problem pays off.

A good example of this concerns the way in which carbon emissions are defrayed, or the carbon tax. In this area, two courageous women have played a role with great passion. Connie Hedegaard, the European Commissioner for Climate Action stuck to her guns when it came to the carbon tax applying to all planes flying through Europe's airspace. The carbon tax is a pollution levy for all aircraft landing anywhere in Europe. China, India and the US were, for once, in agreement; unfortunately these countries had chosen the wrong subject on which to agree. They headed an alliance of countries that threatened a trade war, and when China threatened to withdraw Airbus orders the European lobby swung into action too. This embodied the principle of economic rent in classic form. However, the Danish politician kept her cool, retorting, 'Instead of trying to derail the only attempt to curb aviation emissions now operating, the countries meeting should make concrete suggestions for a better, global solution.'

Another political drama in this area took place in Australia. The country is one of the biggest greenhouse gas polluters in the world on a per capita basis, and it also has a large mining sector with vested interests. This is one sector in which doing nothing definitely pays off. Thanks to constant increases in commodity prices, things just keep getting better for mining companies. Five years ago, the introduction of a tax on carbon emissions was fiercely debated in the Parliament of Australia. The careers of many political leaders were cut short as a result, but in 2011 the Prime Minister, Julia Gillard managed to get legislation approved. In November 2011, the bill, which was largely shaped by the Australian Greens, was approved by the Senate, with the Labour Party and the Greens forming an alliance. The country's top 500 polluters are going to have to pay for their emissions. Although the introduction of the tax is a significant political victory, few people are happy with it. Tony Abbott, the leader of the opposition and a climate change sceptic, went so far as to announce that he intends to overturn the legislation if his party comes to power following the 2013 elections. Nevertheless, the current decisions on carbon tax represent a victory, especially for Greg Combet, the Australian Minister for Climate Change and Energy Efficiency, and his chief of staff, Allan Behm.

Before discussing Behm, let us take the opportunity to consider once again the issues raised in this chapter. The grim picture they paint, with elements of conceit at times, is akin to a true Malthusian drama. Would I, the author of a book on financial ethics, be going too far if I were to offer my suggestions on how the energy problem should be solved and what I believe to be the best clean alternative? I am, after all, an economist, not an energy expert. I know a great deal about monetary intervention and inflation, of course, but have I been too fatalistic? Should we not just allow the market to do its work without any interference on our part? Perhaps, but we can certainly help the market a little by encouraging the market mechanism. We can make carbon emissions much more expensive by means of taxation, and charge the polluter for the actual costs of its own pollution. That will translate indirectly into a sharp increase in fossil fuel consumption costs and allow the market mechanism to do its work. It will do what it would have done anyway, namely respond to scarcity, only more rapidly. If the market mechanism is encouraged at an early stage, this will give us more time to adjust supply and demand, enabling the process of change to go more smoothly. The sooner price trends render new forms of energy economically viable, the more time we will have to develop them to their full technological potential. Only then will there be a level playing field for alternative forms of low-carbon energy of any kind. Let us consider the following example.

SimGas is a small company, based in The Hague, that is specialised in the development and installation of biogas systems for use by households and small businesses. The systems produce gas from human and animal waste, such as food scraps. SimGas wants to install its biogas systems on a wide scale in developing countries. This is a natural energy solution for rural areas. In addition, SimGas has developed technologies for use in urban areas. Biogas is replacing forms of energy that generate much more pollution. The amount of biogas a household can generate from food waste using one of the systems is sufficient for cooking, lighting and other small-scale applications. The system eliminates the need to transport bottled

Continued

gas or burn wood, and as a cooking fuel it does not have the detrimental health effects that charcoal does. Moreover, biogas systems solve a generic household waste problem. Installing and using biogas systems is a superior solution in terms of sustainability, but this is not always the case from an economic perspective. Biogas systems will not be able to compete fairly as long as there is no cost attached to pollution. The defraying of carbon dioxide emissions and the resulting carbon emission rights form an important tool that offers a solution. By putting a price on existing pollution, it creates fair competition. And by placing a tiny microchip on every flue, the savings compared to previous levels of emissions achieved by a household that uses biogas can be measured very precisely. When it comes to such solutions, the financial industry has a responsibility in terms of defraying the purchasing cost of the system. Organising fair markets for carbon emission rights is another of its duties.

At this moment in time we are facing a number of problems of some social relevance. The first is the population explosion and the related exponential increase in our footprint, including our carbon footprint, and the development of more sustainable energy solutions to reducing carbon emissions. The second concerns the issue of government debt. How should this be reduced so that future generations do not have to deal with our mountain of debt as well as the mountain of waste? We can tax pollution so that money is made available to defray the cleanup costs. We can levy a carbon tax, which can be used to cover carbon emission rights to reward carbon savers. However, if we can make the levy punitive enough, the additional income could be used to help solve our debt problem. Rather than a Tobin tax for banks, it would be a Tobin tax for our environment. Let us suggest this to our government leaders. If they are keen, I will become a little more optimistic.

To wrap up, let us return to Allan Behm. He took his daughter along to attend the vote on the introduction of the carbon tax in November 2011. It was to be a very special moment in Australia's parliamentary history. Clad in her blue-green school uniform, the girl viewed the spectacle from the public gallery and listened intently to the debate. Above all, she was extremely proud of her father. The next generation is keeping an eye on us. But more than that, they are holding us responsible.

Chapter 19

Epilogue: a walk in the Polis

Thus, fairness in financial markets includes some considerations of social impact of activity and responsibility of financial decision makers to balance the competing interests of various groups.

John R Boatright, Ethics in Finance, *2007*

The formation of integrated social communities in Ancient Greece, around 700 BC, marked the beginning of Western philosophy. The inhabitants of the nascent cities were forced to work together as a community and this naturally led to work being differentiated. Reaching agreement on how to interact with one another and how to manage the process of communication was an inevitable part of co-operation. The philosophy of the Ancient Greeks focused on the search for wisdom in practical areas such as economics, government and the law. The literal definition of philosophy is the love of wisdom. The Ancient Greeks used the classical system to define areas of philosophy: natural science (physics), knowledge of language and thought (logic), and knowledge of morality (ethics). When acquiring knowledge about nature they tended to concentrate on the observation of mostly fixed natural processes, and on deducing natural laws from these processes. Once these had been identified, they could be used as a basis for predictions. One of the first natural philosophers in Ancient Greece was Thales of Milete (circa 625–545 BC). He was the first philosopher in the world to try to explain the world from something other than a religious perspective. For him, a solar eclipse was not a mythological phenomenon, but a natural occurrence caused by the moon obscuring the sun. According to Thales, observations and calculations could be used to determine when this would happen again. There was no angry sun god involved, and once the relevant natural law had been discovered, the phenomenon would become entirely predictable. This process of determination is called empiricism. We formulate unifying principles on the basis of observation. The material is the determining factor. Logic completely reverses the relationship between idea and material. It is not the world but the idea that is fixed. The world is constantly changing, and we have to use a fixed concept, the idea, to change it in a positive way. This school of thought is known as rationalism.

The traditional distinction between empiricism and rationalism is just as recognisable in the modern world as it was in classical antiquity. It is as relevant now as it was to the Ancient Greeks. Let us take as our starting point the assertion that the financial world is actually a modern form of the Greek city state, the Polis. The parties have to work with one another, and this almost automatically leads to specialisation and differentiation. Agreements about how we behave and about how the entire system of the financial Polis should be governed are necessary aspects of this process. The difference between the empirical approach and the rationalistic approach is relevant in this context. The empiricists among us are searching for unifying principles and natural laws. The result is the formulation of a theory that gives us insight into those (fixed) natural laws, which can be used by every participant in the financial industry to gather outcomes with a predictive value. Theories based on models, the economist's mechanical formulas and the toolbox of models we use to determine the value of financial instruments and portfolios are all part of the empirical approach. These are tools given to us by scientists such as Louis Bachelier, Paul Samuelson, Milton Friedman, Fischer Black, Myron Scholes, John Cox and Stephen Ross. As noted above, the rationalists among us are more inclined to believe in the fixed nature of the idea, and in a changing world. Honesty and justice are two such concepts; others include equality and transparency. The subtitle of this book, *Today's perception is tomorrow's norm,* encompasses the unchanging nature of the idea as well as the changeability of the world. If we decide today that we need new definitions of the concepts of honesty and justice, the world of tomorrow will have to be organised differently, on the basis of the new norms. Insider trading and transparency are just two examples of fixed concepts that have required the world to change over the years.

What is the scientific status of economics? Does it deal with unchangeable natural laws or is it based on fixed concepts and a desire to change the world? Is economics concerned with the method rather than with passing judgment on the objective? Or does it concern itself with the objective and worry less about the way in which the objective is attained? Is it a science that judges whether attaining that objective is worthwhile, or is that a question best avoided? In other words, what is the economist interested in? Imagine him standing on a tower with a brick in his hand, which he intends to drop. Does he want to observe how fast the brick falls and whether that rate is in accordance with the laws of gravity, or is he also interested in the likelihood of the brick hitting a passerby (mechanics)? Or maybe he sees a wider economic benefit in letting the stone drop. Does he also think about whether this action is the right one (morality)? In this book I have tried to demonstrate that economic thinking has been far too mechanical, as has the thinking of the managers who have received economic training for the financial industry. They were good at calculating risk on the basis of models, but they paid too little attention to questions that touched on norms. In a sense, this made them value-free. They calculated the likelihood of the brick hitting a passerby, but ignored the question of whether their actions were principled. Economics cannot, however, remain value-free. It must concern itself with the outcome of actions, and whether or not actions are principled. It should also be concerned with questions regarding the sustainability of actions, and with determining which system results in the lowest risk of economic derailment and infringement of fundamental values. I hope that after reading this book you will in any event be a little more convinced of the need to pursue concepts such as honesty, equality and transparency in the financial markets. Such thinking ensures our actions are no longer value-free.

What do the concepts of honesty, equality and justice actually entail? In the financial world the focus is on concluding transactions to increase the prosperity of the participants, and perhaps also on increasing the general prosperity of a larger group of people who are directly or indirectly involved in these transactions. We have already established that the parties reaching agreement are different from one another and are therefore unequal. How, then, can honest agreements come into being? In this context, we can turn to contract ethics and to insights developed within the framework of game theory, both of which provide useful tools. The American philosopher, John Rawls (1921–2002) developed a vision of honesty and justice as part of his theory of distributive justice. Rawls based his vision on what he called the original position. Someone who is just starting to participate in society and in the agreements reached by society does not know which party he is: the stronger or the weaker, the richer or the poorer, the smarter or the less smart. In other words, he is still hidden behind a veil of ignorance. When basic agreements are reached on the structure of society and the rules that apply, the original position of every participant is that they may be the weaker party. The focus of their concern will be on not wanting their weakness to place them at a greater disadvantage. This led Rawls to develop two principles. The first is the principle of equal liberty, which maintains that all freedoms should be equally distributed, without discrimination. This applies to freedom of religion, and also to the freedom to acquire knowledge and pursue an education. In the financial world it also applies to the freedom to receive good advice and information, but above all to the freedom of equal access to markets and services. Because of their uncertainty about the relative weakness or strength of their position, every participant will be satisfied with negotiation outcomes that maximise the minimal gain (including for the weaker party). This is the outcome most likely to be considered reasonable by both parties. It is referred to as the maximin rule. An outcome arrived at in this fashion is fair. If parties freely reach a decision, and if compliance with that decision does not have to be enforced, this produces the greatest likelihood of a fair outcome that both parties will accept. When applied to the distribution of wealth, this conclusion may sound somewhat socialistic, but the maximin rule is actually an important principle of day to day operations in the securities markets. We need to ensure that the weakest party does not feel disadvantaged by giving that party the benefit of the doubt when a question arises. This brings us back to the dilemma of conflicting interests and how the interests of a professional can be fairly weighed against those of the customer. It also touches on the dilemma in Chapter 12, namely the conflicting interests of private and institutional investors. Who is the weakest party here? If in doubt, the weaker party should be given the benefit of the doubt.

Ethics is the study of norms and values, and of the virtue of traditions and customs. Socrates is seen as the first ethicist in Ancient Greece. He paid little attention to physics, focusing instead on human behaviour and what humans hoped that behaviour would achieve. Ethics is the knowledge of morality, the study of virtues and the justification of customs. In the words of Socrates, moralism is the end of that search for knowledge and the imposition of ready-made rules to live by. All of the rules that have been introduced in the financial world – which fill many volumes – are, in a sense, moralistic. They prescribe correct behaviour and leave the thinking to someone else. At times, this book may have been guilty of moralism too. Moralism is dogmatic and, in the end, fundamentalist. By contrast, ethics is about exploring the boundaries for one's self. The logic of Socrates was based on inductive reasoning. He unpacked the problem by asking fundamental questions and tested ideas to determine actual meaning. What exactly is honesty, and what are equality and transparency? This method of validating an argument and deferring judgment until all questions have been addressed is referred to as Socratic dialogue. Inductive reasoning based on concrete examples can produce insights into more general laws of nature. For Socrates, virtuous behaviour was based on insight. I have tried to use the Socratic method in this book to form judgements about what constitutes good and bad behaviour in the financial industry.

There are a number of significant differences between the financial world and the real world, and that means we must be very careful about applying real world wisdom to our own financial city state. It is useful to remind ourselves of those differences. The financial world is abstract, while the real world is tangible. And although financial products have real names, they are not concrete objects. We can comprehend them with our minds but we cannot touch them with our hands. They are, in effect, concepts or ideas. There are many more differences from the real world that make it difficult for us to form proper judgements. In many cases the victims of financial crimes are anonymous, and they will remain so. Other people do not even realise they are victims. How can we possibly tell whether we have been disadvantaged by someone else's use of insider knowledge? Do we feel the pain when a broker lets a privileged party see our order for a tenth of a second? No, not unless the abuse is made public, in which case we all experience it as a great injustice. Leverage – the fact that small differences can generate big returns – makes matters worse. Consider, for example, the case of a group of bank employees with criminal intentions who rigged the payment system so that one cent out of every payment was diverted to a separate account. It took a long time for the scam to be uncovered because the amounts involved were so small. Who notices one cent more or less? However, the amounts that the bank employees were able to earn with this scam were substantial. There was also great public outrage, even though no one had noticed anything at all.

The financial world is characterised by a strong compulsion to regulate. We are moralistic, according an article published in the *Financial Times* on 8 December 2011 under the headline 'Financial groups hit by flood of new rules'.

> Regulators around the world announced 14,215 changes in the 12 months to November, up from 12,179 for the same period a year earlier, according to a study by the Thomson Reuters governance, risk and compliance unit.

We have a great many rules, and they have become virtually sacrosanct. They obscure our view of the underlying principles and values, programming us to become unthinking robots. If we do start thinking, there is a reasonable chance that we will get into trouble.

One final thing that needs to be mentioned is that people in the financial world work in groups, and these groups develop their own informal rules. These rules sometimes differ from what is customary in society. They become distanced from the normative thinking of wider society. In fact, a strong sense of group discipline deprives individuals of their ability to distinguish between group norms and norms that serve the general good. This applies not only to groups which we perceive as outsiders, such as the Hells Angels, but also to some groups which, although seemingly normal, occupy dominant positions in large financial institutions. Perhaps the products Warren Buffett calls the 'real weapons of mass destruction' are a sort of bankers' Hells Angels tearing through the financial city state on big motorcycles, sowing fear and panic.

Now that we have seen how much damage the participants in the financial game can wreak on the rest of society, it is worth taking another look at the inverse relationship between the financial world and the social world. Society categorises a large number of issues as financial problems, when in fact they are not. The financial industry acts as a kind of safety valve for real-world tensions. If society is unable to solve its problems, the temperature rises as reflected by the change in monetary aggregates. The most important measures of this include inflation and interest rates. Inflation is a monetary phenomenon, but by no means all inflationary tendencies are driven by monetary issues, and many can be traced back to a failing process of redistribution. This may involve the redistribution of wealth, but as often as not it also entails the redistribution of economic decline or poverty. It is the struggle between capital and labour. Pay rises that outstrip improvements in efficiency can lead to price increases. In the struggle for a bigger slice of the national or international pie, one party demands more while the other refuses to moderate its demands of its own accord, and the government is unwilling or unable to compel it to do so. The market will accomplish this instead, through inflation or unemployment, and as a result the participants will lose some of their entitlement to the pie. The consolation prize offered by inflation is that our nominal position remains the same; consequently the actual pain hurts a little less. The debt crisis is a classic example of problems arising in the real world that have such enormous financial consequences we refer to them as a financial crisis. But it is not a financial crisis at all.

Narratio, the Latin word for narrative, is one of the ways in which people have learned to think and a source of human development and tradition. Stories from all corners of the globe reveal that some basic values and norms have much in common, in spite of all the cultural differences. I encountered one example of this in my capacity as an independent non-executive director of NASDAQ Dubai. At a conference in Dubai I ran into Homa Siddiqui, whom I had already met when I was CEO of Robeco and she worked for Credit Suisse. She asked about my current work, and the conversation quickly turned to the subject of financial ethics, for which I launched an impassioned plea. I expressed my concerns at the enormous greed of people working in the financial industry and their tendency to take much more than they give. Homa Siddiqui was born in Kuwait but her family originally comes from Hyderabad. As a child Homa lived at first in the Middle East, and then in Italy. On her 16th birthday she moved with her parents to the US, where she completed her high school education and attended university. She ended up working for Credit Suisse in New York. Homa told me the following parable she had first heard from her mother when she was very young. The story has survived for many generations and its message is as valid today as it has ever been.

> A man living in a city in the Middle East was invited to a wedding in another city. To get there he had to travel for a day through the desert, and as he did not want to do that alone he asked a guide to accompany him. The two men left on horseback that same evening. After riding across the desert for hours, they came to an oasis and an inn where they could spend the night. They would continue on their journey the next day. However, when the traveller awoke the next morning, the guide and both horses had disappeared. He was alone, without

Continued

Box *continued*

> a horse. Having considered the best course of action, he decided to return to the city on foot. There was nothing else he could do. When he finally reached the city after a long, gruelling walk, it was bustling and a market was being held. Tired, he trudged past the people and the stalls on his way home. He was in for a big surprise: his very own horse was standing there. He was astonished to see his own loyal companion for sale in the market. He confronted the merchant who had the horse and asked him how he had come by it. 'It's my horse,' the traveller said. 'It was stolen from me.' The merchant told him he had purchased the horse that morning from a trader and had paid a hundred dinars for it. 'You know,' the traveller said, 'that is how much I would have paid the guide to take me safely to the other city.'

The moral of this story is that the guide would have made 10 dirhams in any event, but it was up to him to decide whether to go about this ethically or not. This is the kind of judgement we all have to make every day.

In this book I have examined a whole range of human behaviours in the financial sector. I hope that it will give the reader a better understanding of how one should act in complex, and sometimes unstructured, situations, in which standard answers and behaviour do not suffice. How should we judge behaviour, and how should we act? Should we be guided by our emotions, our intelligence and logic, or our senses, or perhaps by some combination? To obtain an answer we must return to Jan Verplaetse's insights into our moral instincts. He identified five forms of moral systems. Four of them are hard-wired in us as a result of the process of human evolution. They are automatically driven by our instincts and emotions. Intelligence plays no role at all in this process. In fact, it just gets in the way, as does reason. In Chapter 3, I cited Robert Trivers and his views on economics as science. A biologist who has done extensive research into social theories based on natural selection, Trivers is a fervent Darwinian. His book, *Deceit and Self-deception* (2011), includes an interesting comparison of human and animal behaviour. In addition to co-operation, deception has always been an important means of evolutionary survival. Deceiving one's enemy is a highly effective method of self-preservation. Butterflies do this by taking on the colour of flowers, snakes do it by resembling the branches they hide in. Genetic improvements are constantly perfecting the system of deception. Self-deception is one aspect of this process. Trivers describes how people are also prone to self-deception:

> Self-deception occurs when the conscious mind is left in the dark. Correct and incorrect information may be stored at the same time, but the truth will be stored in the subconscious mind and the lie in the conscious mind.

I discussed the possible consequences of deceit and self-deception in Chapter 14, using the example of the harm that powerful men can cause to customers and employees. Disguised as philanthropists, they were able to carry on their dubious practices much longer than they should have been. Maybe it is next to impossible to stop such behaviour. It is important for us to realise that, so that we can at least have a better understanding of our behaviour. Once we have given all of our internally programmed instincts and emotions free rein, and we are ready to enhance the mixture with a dose of reason, we come to the fifth moral system, which Jan Verplaetse calls the morality of principles. This is the part of our behaviour that is not hard-wired, the part we can shape and guide with our intelligence. Our emotions are still involved, but so too are our powers of reasoning. And this is where ethics comes in.

Jan Verplaetse argues that in bygone days only the morality of principles, that is, the rational moral system, was visible to people. The four other moral systems he described (which for the sake of convenience I refer to as the biological moral systems) were not yet on the radar. Thinking in terms of biological moral systems is something that has enriched our thinking only in the last 20 years. It raises an interesting comparison with the animal spirits which form the basis of teaching in behavioural finance. The biological moral systems have much in common with insights into animal spirits, while the concept of the morality of principles – the rational part of Verplaetse's construction – fits perfectly into the thinking that produced the concept of *homo economicus*, the rational man. And yes, it is true that not only the moral philosophers but, for decades, economists, too, focused solely on the rational side of human beings.

Which basic areas of the financial industry offer participants scope for improving their behaviour, so that a more balanced judgment can be made of the kind of behaviour that can help create a better world? The fundamental question each of us needs to ask is where we belong in this Polis. Everyone who works in the financial industry should ask themselves whether they are acting in the role of an agent or as a principal. When acting as an agent, the customer's interests need to be borne in mind at all times, and these interests need to be properly segregated from the own interests the agent undoubtedly has. It is vital to check whether there are interests in the background that might also come into play. If so, they need to be excluded, and if that is not possible the agent needs to recuse himself from the decision-making process.

The agent and the principal must be fully aware of their relative positions of power. Unwary participants in the financial process are sometimes intimidated by those who make financial services their profession. Cautious advice is often taken to be the absolute truth, and the combination of knowledge and experience can carry disproportionate weight with the recipient. This applies to individuals who borrow money, invest, take out insurance or accept tax advice. It is the imbalance that allows for the mis-selling of products which have no real social utility and which no one wants. Beware of playing on people's emotions in order to make a sale. Is it right that 25-year-old students with a bright future but virtually no current income should be urged to take out funeral insurance so that their surviving relatives do not have pay the costs? Funeral insurance policies play on emotions, and young people are an easy target. Statistically speaking, a young man will live for a long time, and that means he will pay premiums for years to come. This kind of thing happens every day. The financial world is full of information asymmetry. Even more important than the knowledge discrepancy is the difference in emotional experience. If one party is more emotionally invested in a product, the other party can take advantage of this. Examples of products in which parties become emotionally invested include houses, bathrooms and travel; financiers see customers of such products as easy prey. The party who has too little knowledge and too much emotional involvement should recognise this and if necessary ask for help. And the party with the surplus of knowledge needs to exercise self-control. A respite period is a good technique to use in such cases, because it gives customers time to reflect on the decisions they are being urged to take.

Ethical behaviour is based on allocating attention properly to competing interests. It is about a proper allocation between the interests of the agent and those of the customer and between the interests of two customers, especially if one is more important than the other. The balance between short-term and long-term interests is another important factor. If these interests call for opposing actions, the long-term interest should prevail. Short-term interests should be sacrificed in order to achieve long-term objectives. This is not an easy task, and that is why it is advice worth repeating.

This book has also touched on various basic values in financial services, which I will briefly summarise below. Equality is a very important principle. Naturally, we are not all the same, but that is no excuse for discrimination. Inequality cannot be allowed to stand in the way of equal opportunity. Everyone has the right to fair financial treatment that is balanced and appropriate. The foundation of fair treatment is information equality, and its guiding principle is transparency. The information that leads to decisions being taken, or to earlier decisions being changed, has to be made available simultaneously so that all participants have equal opportunities. A second important principle is meritocracy. The best price should have priority; if the price of an order improves the market, that order should be given priority. The corollary of this is that the customer who wants to execute a transaction or buy a product should always get the best price or the best product. An intermediary should not sell the customer a product that is inferior to another product that costs the same. Another significant value centres on the question of appropriateness. Selling funeral insurance to 25-year-old students is an example of inappropriate tactics. There are many other examples of equally worthless products cluttering up the landscape. Some mortgages are linked to useless, extortionate insurance policies that pay too little when disaster strikes. Emotion does not have a price. The long-term consequences of purchasing such products are certainly not favourable. The practice of favouring long-term interests over short-term gains is one possible solution. A determination to question constantly the morality of selling such products is another.

We have also discussed the issue of customer autonomy. Should customers be allowed to decide everything for themselves, or should the authorities help them by taking away certain choices or banning certain practices? Although this goes against the grain of our stubborn belief in freedom and the right to make our own choices, the world – deprived of some its illusions – does appear to be moving in the direction of greater government intervention in the affairs of its citizens.

The next value I would like to mention in connection with financial services is solidarity. When we insure ourselves against the risk that our partner or ourselves will die, we are in fact buying solidarity from the market. After all, everyone who buys that insurance product pays a premium which forms the basis of any amount the insurance eventually pays out. We have encountered solidarity in all financial constructions that are based on mutual or market concepts, such as pension funds, investment products and insurance policies. Even more important is the fact that part of our banking systems is based on collectivity and solidarity. It has become apparent that this is also the more successful part of our banking system. The final, all-encompassing value I would like to mention is sustainability. Services must be sustainable. Customers should be satisfied not only at the time of purchase, but also throughout the entire lifetime of the product. The solution the customer hopes to achieve with a particular product should be able to withstand the test of time.

Just exactly how bad are things in the financial world? Have we completely detached ourselves from the real world and are we behaving like heathens in a church (even though you do not have to be a heathen to misbehave in church)? Fortunately, the reality is not quite so grim. The financial world is not fundamentally worse than other parts of society, such as the worlds of sport, business and politics. Stringent regulations manage to keep participants under control reasonably well. Some practices can even serve as an example to other sectors of society. However, there are no grounds for complacency. The financial sector has immense leverage because of its important role and its level of penetration in the real world. The multiplier effect means that a small deviation can have catastrophic social consequences. We can compare it to a ship setting sail from Liverpool; if it goes less than one degree off course it runs the risk of hitting an iceberg and never reaching a safe harbour.

This brings us back to one of our maxims. People are the root of the evil, and because people act collectively, the root cause of systemic risk is collective failure. Time and again, we prove ourselves incapable of rational thought. And even when we do manage to think rationally, we fail to act rationally. In fact, by acting irrationally together, we reinforce each other's irrationality instead of correcting it, and the social norm itself goes adrift. Italy is essentially a very rich country, yet collective tax evasion in Italy poses a threat to the stability of the entire eurozone. If one person or country gets into debt, others are likely to follow. Improper behaviour becomes the norm. This also applies to Japan and the US, as well as to financial players and many other institutions that bring benefits to society. Spain used to have a very active building sector and excellent football teams. Real Madrid may well be the most successful football club in the world, but it was built on enormous debts. Only Chelsea has more, and FC Barcelona's financial predicament is almost as bad as that of Real Madrid. The clubs are playing on credit, and who knows how sustainable that is. Are we in danger of being blinded by the game? The amounts paid to footballers, merchant bankers, property developers and CEOs are out of all proportion. The norm has drifted away from reality like an ice floe.

Over the past 20 years, low interest rates have encouraged people to take on too much debt, and consumption has become the new standard. Irrationality is the norm. Gravity is suspended, until we all come crashing down, landing us in a situation that is a real threat to the social and monetary system. Systemic risks have one very dangerous feature: they are stealthy. When the consequences are finally revealed, it is too late to avoid disaster. The incubation period is long, as is the recovery period. The long incubation time provides us with a false sense of security, while in fact the irreversible drift has started.

On 1 April 2012, the Russian press agency TASS announced that a total of 675 Russian fishermen were trapped in the frozen Sea of Okhotsk, to the west of the Kamchatka Peninsula on Russia's eastern seaboard. Although it was spring, the fishermen were still ice fishing, as was their custom, but warmer weather had caused an ice floe to break off, which was now drifting out to sea with almost 700 fishermen on it. Boats and helicopters had been sent to rescue the men, and the mission had been underway for over six hours. This illustrates how a crisis is set in motion long before the consequences became evident. When the ice floe broke away, it was already too late. When the consequences of the crisis become clear, the fishermen's only course of action was a collective cry for help. When the group is lost, only an appeal to our fellow human beings' sense of solidarity can save the day. Indebtedness follows a similar pattern. When interest is low we manage to pay it, but because of the size of our debts we get into difficulties as soon as the wind changes direction. How else can we explain why countries with a 3% interest rate can control their debt, but go under when it rises to 6%. Historically, an interest rate of 6% is not that high. Interest rates rise like the temperature in Russia's far east, and we have already ventured too far out onto the ice floe of debt to turn back. The rescuers are the real victims. In 2008 governments were forced to bail out banks, but now it is the European economy that has to be rescued via the rough remedy of printing more money. We will need to create more money to pay off our debts. We are being held hostage and there is no other choice because the survival of our system is at stake. In 2007 we realised that we were being presented with a bill that the innocent were going to have to pay; in 2012 massive quantitative easing programmes are still underway, and printing money seems to have become normal monetary policy.

This book describes different manifestations of the animal spirit and how it affects all areas of society. The animal spirit is inescapable, especially in the financial world, and this means that we can no longer make assumptions based on a rational financial industry with rational markets. Every theory has let us down. The animal spirit takes us back to our primal instincts, which are geared chiefly towards survival and the preservation of only those closest to us. People, and not just Libyans, Aboriginals or Maoris, are still oriented towards their own tribe. Today's society is reverting to tribal culture, albeit a more modern version. We even have network tribes, such as on Facebook, Hyves, Twitter and LinkedIn.

We show solidarity with our friends from the rugby team or cycling club, our neighbours in our village, and our colleagues in the structured products team, but not with the company or bank we work for, or with the country we live in. The company or bank has become so big we no longer have any real connection to it. And the government is there for others, not for us. That is why we are not there for the government either. We have formed groups that make the world smaller, using our own resources to reduce matters to a human scale. Once again we have become individuals trying to optimise our own outcome. We operate in a network with others in order to increase our own opportunities. The goal is self-enrichment, driven by the fear that we will otherwise not survive. In that scenario we have detached ourselves from the greater good, which no longer interests us much. We avoid paying taxes, even if we know that tax evasion is happening on such a scale that it ultimately threatens to destroy the country. Does that make it our problem? The risks we build up in our financial institutions also pose a threat, and they are no longer proportionate to the returns they yield. But we will be long gone when the bomb goes off, so why should we care? The caravan moves on and the tribe will survive. One person's truth is the collective lie. This mentality is the greatest threat to the stability of the financial world. There is much room for improvement in this area. We need technical improvements (such as the creation of structures that solve the problem of companies and countries that are too big to fail), improvements in regulations, and above all improvements in behaviour. Sustainability should be the guiding principle, and long-term considerations should always prevail over short-term gains, particularly if the outcomes conflict. However, sustainability means more than this. The key to acting sustainably is to add value to one's environment, with the aim of leaving an organisation in better shape than when one joined it. The same is true of participation in any social organisation. Sustainability within the context of the preservation of our planet means living in a resource-positive manner. We should be giving back more than we take from the earth. We can do this by giving future generations the technologies they need to replace the resources we have utilised.

I began this book with the crisis, and I will end there as well. The American economist, Hyman Minsky has written extensively about financial markets and crises and can be regarded as a post-Keynesian. The theories Minsky developed link the vulnerability of the financial markets in normal economic cycles to speculative investment bubbles, which in his view are an endogenous feature of the financial markets. The moment when stability tips over into fragility is known as the Minsky moment. According to Minsky, the cash flow of companies and governments in times of economic prosperity should be used to pay off debt. In reality, the opposite occurs. A speculative euphoria takes over and debt levels quickly go beyond the point at which they can be paid back from generated income. Minsky differentiates three kinds of borrowers. The first is the hedge borrower: people who borrow and are able to pay back their debts because the investments they finance with the money they borrowed generate enough income. The second type, the speculative borrower, has sufficient cash flow to pay the interest on the loan, but probably not enough to repay the principal. This borrower has to keep rolling over his financing. Finally, there is the Ponzi borrower, who cannot repay either the interest or the principal from the income generated from his investment but is confident that the value of the assets purchased with the loan will increase, enabling him to repay the debt and the interest when he sells the assets. A large number of Western governments – foremost among them the Europeans – are now in this third stage of debt formation. The only way for them to extricate themselves is by increasing the value of their assets. That can be accomplished via the process of monetary devaluation, in other words inflation. Minsky died before anything was known about the sub-prime lending crisis, and long before European countries got into financial difficulties, but he is cited more and more frequently these days. We have forgotten Minsky's lessons, and we have certainly not acted in accordance with them.

Finally, I would like to conclude the account of my stay in Dubai, which I started at the end of Chapter 5. As I viewed a vast building site with thousands of cranes and saw the contours of what would become the tallest building in the world, I wondered how this was possible. The answer is Minskyian: cheap money was made readily available because people assumed they could sell all the apartments to pay off the loans. It was a speculative property investment, with apartments being purchased by people who would never want to live in them but believe they will be able to flip them like a coin. If a star footballer such as David Beckham wants to live in Dubai, surely everybody would be interested in buying a property there, or so the reasoning goes. Credit is an important instrument, and it can be used to prevent bad behaviour. It determines the scope people have to act irrationally, and the shorter the reins, the easier it is to prevent new bubbles from developing. Too much cheap credit allows us to behave irrationally. Credit is addictive, and once you are addicted, it becomes toxic.

One of the aims of this book is to strengthen and recalibrate our moral compass. It advocates a break with our addiction to rules, and a revaluation of the kind of behaviour that could lead to better outcomes in the financial world – outcomes that could help humans avoid becoming the root cause of the next financial crisis, especially one that threatens the livelihood of billions of households. This book argues that we form a collective market which, despite having major shortcomings, is still a key auxiliary mechanism for influencing behaviour and governing people. It is, however, important to reflect more on what our individual behaviour in that market should be, so that it can be held up as an example for collective behaviour. Understanding our world may help us to improve it, so that we can stroll through our financial Polis day and night without causing incidents.

Chapter 20

Why newborn babies cry

Suddenly we can no longer deny that we have been checkmated, and we are now caught in a trap of our own making. Government finances have gone off the rails owing to the fact that, for years, society spent more than it received in tax revenues. Countries also got into difficulties because the underlying economic processes turned out to be so poorly balanced they collapsed the moment the wind changed direction. Sovereign economies took on the shape of property hedge funds, and when that gamble failed to pay off the debts were offloaded upwards, on to the government. They became the rescuer's problem. In this way, apparently healthy economies with sound government finances were unexpectedly forced to raise a red flag.

But before things went wrong, there were good times. We were happy, euphoric even, and full of confidence. We felt we were truly rich, and we had every reason to, thanks to rising house prices and inflated financial asset prices. We were privileged. We tapped into the increase in the value of our assets and used it as collateral for loans obtained from willing banks. Even though we had not even asked for it, the money was ready for the taking, just asking to be spent. And we spent it as if there was no tomorrow, on items such as sailing boats, trips to far-flung places, skiing holidays, school fees, early retirement, yet more travel, and perhaps a second home abroad. We also accepted that many of our social processes were corrupt, including tax evasion, favours for friends and acquaintances, and benefits for ourselves. Drunk on low interest rates, we continued to build and manufacture in order to meet the incessant demand. Prosperity was in the air.

And then the moment arrived, unmistakably, if imperceptibly, when our luck ran out. It is at such times that the mechanics of the economy come into play, when the boat finally capsizes, so to speak. The immediate cause is an insignificant incident, a sound, a scream, or a badly timed warning from a regulator. As a result, the imbalance takes on the most frightening form. Its power is devastating. House prices tumble – something we have never experienced. And on its downward journey, the value of the house meets the level of our debt. There is a nod of recognition, and the decline continues. We now enter the territory of negative equity. It is at this point that we suddenly realise that everything we previously consumed was bought with someone else's money, not our own, and we have debts that are no longer covered and are far too high. Deflated, we realise the time has come to pay back the debt, but we have no idea how to do this.

A company that runs aground because it invests too much in the wrong areas needs to face the facts. It actually has no choice, since it will be forced to do so by the market. They have to cut their coats according to their cloth, write off assets and absorb losses ('impairment charges' in accounting parlance). Companies that find themselves in this situation define survival strategies, downsize, cut wages as part of deals to ensure future job security, and sell many of their assets that are not essential for their new future. They continue to shrink until they manage to find a point at which they can start to work on a new, credible future. They have to go back to the essentials. Agreements are reached with shareholders and creditors. In return for downsizing, the nominal value of shares is cut and a portion of the debt is cancelled. These measures enable companies to start believing in themselves, their own strength and their future once more. They communicate this belief to the market, and their drive to succeed returns.

Countries are no different from companies, even though they do not act as though they are. Countries are much more unassailable and arrogant. No one provides an answer to the question of who will end up paying off the debts. Repeating the question only elicits a noncommittal response: the future. Nevertheless, countries that get into difficulties as a result of wastefulness, corruption and debt also need to go back to the essentials. They need to downsize, reorganise, cut their coats according to their cloth, and get back to a point where spending is in line with their earning capacity and with social circumstances that are both defensible and sustainable in the long term. We need to get back to basics when it comes to moral values, which among other things means we need to live within our means as a society. This applies to governments and citizens alike. Does this mean that the economy will shrink by several percentage points? If it does, we will be as affluent as we were in 1990. How terrible. Yet a fall of just 1% in the rate of growth puts us in much more of a panic than a 1% increase in government debt. Unemployment today is more important than future debt. The old Keynesian argument is revived: the way to get through the bad times is not by making cuts but by stimulating the economy, using public spending to make up for the shortfall in demand. Governments can kick-start the economy by investing. But would that economy, doped up on money, generate enough income to recoup the additional spending? This is a fundamental question.

Given the current rate of GDP growth in Europe, even a government deficit of just 3% is unsustainable. National debt will continue to increase faster than GDP, based on today's low growth rates and government deficits of 3%. We are overestimating our wealth yet again. As a result, absolute interest charges are rising, as is national debt as a percentage of GDP. Who is going to finance the shortfall, and at what price? The economy cannot be stimulated without incurring more government debt since we do not have any money of our own left to spend. The downside now becomes clear. Someone has to finance the additional deficit. We could try approaching the market. It would ask, in a very clinical way, whether it would get its money back. A very rational premise underlies that question. Can the additional deficit provide enough of a stimulus to reassure the market that not only will the government be able to pay back the loan with interest, but that thanks to the stimulus the rest of the economy will also be better off once the costs have been deducted? In other words, will the investment generate a return? International lenders will demand higher rates of interest, and this creates a real danger that such investments may have more of a negative impact than a positive one. If that is the case, and the stimulus fails to provide the expected boost to the economy, or, worse, the net effect turns out to be negative, we will be left with yet another failed investment. We will then all sink even deeper into the morass.

We will have reached our Minsky moment. During the good times we failed to set aside enough money to allow us, when times got tough, to stimulate the economy using our own money rather than someone else's. We are like an army that is finally able to wage a war but has already used up all its munitions on exercises.

So far, our debate has failed to touch on a very different point. Rather than growing, we need to reorganise. We got into difficulties because our business model is outdated and we have relied on old assumptions for too long. There have been many new developments but we have not dealt with the old structures. We have become stuck in our old patterns of behaviour. We therefore need to make changes to our national economies and in doing so change our social order. Economies need to tackle their problems in the same way as companies. They need to rediscover themselves and find a new basis on which they can build a sustainable future. In other words, they need a new business model. Privileges need to be taken away from those who have an economic interest in disrupting and frustrating the functioning of the market and who deny opportunities to newcomers. Obstacles that form an impediment to market forces and do not contribute sufficiently to the good of society need to be cleared away. Endeavours that do not have a positive focus, corrupt practices and people who fail to contribute their fair share to the nation's finances need to be stopped. We have to put an end to nepotism within powerful families, politicians who give their incompetent friends jobs for life, and governments that are too large to be sustained by the underlying economy. In short, there needs to be a cultural and economic revolution. Countries are like companies with too many overheads that do not lead to productive efforts. Prosperity will be seriously strained, and that strain will need to be reduced.

By spending less we could create a vicious circle, ending up in a downward spiral. While that may well be the case, why should that spiral be any different from the upward spiral we experienced during the period of euphoria? During the upward spiral, it seemed as though the party would never end, yet at some point it did, and similarly our pessimism will also bottom out somewhere along the line. The downward spiral will therefore lose its energy in due course and reach an end point. The sooner we are willing to face reality, restructure debts, reform the economy and take very firm action to tackle ethical issues that contribute to the problem, such as tax evasion, nepotism and corruption, the sooner we will reach the bottom of the downward spiral. However, more than anything else we all need to be willing to make improvements together. Credibility needs to be restored, and, more importantly, so does our fighting spirit.

Sovereignty is a key concept in Europe and the principal remains intact when European countries help each other out. Given this, calls for the introduction of eurobonds are illogical. Such a move would mean giving up sovereignty when it comes to debt, and mutualising liabilities but not rights. This conceals an inconsistency that will not be able to withstand political pressure. Keynes had a clear vision of who ought to solve the problem, and believed that both debtors and creditors had a responsibility to help pull economies out of the morass. In 1923, he wrote that 'The absolutists of contracts are the real parents of revolution'. In the eyes of Keynes, a bystander has a certain moral responsibility to a drowning man because he is partly responsible for the situation that has arisen. However, some bystanders cannot, with the best will in the world, be ascribed any responsibility at all. Nevertheless, they may well still be asked to help, based on a sense of charity and an appeal to their own self-interest.

215

European countries may decide to help each other on the grounds that this could limit the damage to their own national economies, and therefore be motivated purely by the self-interests of the rescuer. The rescuer will then consider how likely it is that it will also be pulled under if it goes to the aid of countries drowning in debt. A similar fate was suffered by some of Europe's national governments that allowed their economies to go off the rails in 2007, as if they were hedge funds. In the end it was the rescuers that paid the price. This explains a great deal of the reticence that can currently be seen in Europe.

If no international investors are willing to provide finance, the ECB will have to intervene by inflating their balance sheet and printing extra money. Is that the right course of action? Is the ECB the institution where the buck stops? Might it not go bankrupt itself? The erosion of debt by means of inflation is the ultimate solution. It essentially amounts to debt restructuring through the market. The bill for the party that no one was willing to pay for is left on the doorstep of the first house we pass. It is not the home of the drowning man but of someone who had nothing at all to do with the situation. It could be the home of a working couple who live frugally to avoid taking on too much debt, have built up a little in the way of life savings and just about manage to keep their heads above water. Or it could be the home of a pensioner who has seen his hard-earned savings evaporate due to inflation or has been forced to accept a cut in his pension because inflation exceeds long-term interest rates. This is the failure of the democratic decision-making process, which has proved itself incapable of either distributing the costs of the downturn properly or carrying out reorganisations. Politicians would rather tell fairytales and sidestep the difficult issues. They do this because voters want to believe them and they are rewarded for doing so. As a consequence, the national decision-making process has also become irrational.

The house where the bill is left could also be the place where a new life has just come into the world. Before its umbilical cord is even cut, the baby is presented with its first savings book by the country in which it is so lucky to have been born. Unfortunately, the balance of these savings is negative; in the Netherlands the deficit amounts to more than US$34,000 for each man, woman and child. The figure for the UK is US$28,990, excluding unfunded state pension obligations, while for the US it is US$42,267. I now understand a little better why newborn babies cry.

Chapter 21

A final wink

Rino Verpalen, lawyer and vice-president of the District Court in Haarlem, is a lover of poetry. On the evening of 18 March 2011, during the trial of a massive Dutch property fraud case that finally went to court after years of preparation, he thought it would be a good idea to recite the first eight lines of 'The Plumtree', a poem by Hiëronymus van Alphen (1746–1803). He used a metaphor in order to help the defendant relax a little following a long, tough interrogation:

> Johnny saw some fine plums hanging,
> Oh! like eggs, so very large;
> Johnny seemed about to pluck them,
> Though against his father's charge.
> Here is not, said he, my father,
> Nor the gard'ner near the tree,
> From those boughs so richly laden,
> Five or six plums – who can see?

This was not such a good idea on Verpalen's part. By announcing that the case he was trying reminded him of these eight lines, the judge ran the risk of being perceived as prejudiced by the defendants. At any rate, it created the appearance that he was prejudiced. This was in spite of the fact that the first eight lines do not reveal the moral of the story. The rest of Van Alphen's poem is as follows.

> But I wish to be obedient,
> I'll not pluck them; off I go.
> Should I for a trifling handful
> Disobedient be? Oh no.
> Off went Johnny, but his father,
> Who had overheard his talk,
> Just then forward stepped to meet him,
> In the garden middle-walk.
> Come my Johnny, said his father,
> Come, my little darling boy,
> Now for you some plums I'll gather,

> Now you are your father's joy.
> Then Pa gave the tree a shaking,
> Johnny stooped with laughing face,
> Johnny filled his hat quite brimful,
> Off then galloped in a race.

Hiëronymus van Alphen, Poetry for Children, *translated by FJ Millard, 1856, p. 20*

Unsurprisingly, Verpalen's position of chairman of the court was challenged by two defendants in the property fraud case. The challenge was declared admissible, and Verpalen was taken off the case.

At the heart of this poem, which was written for children more than 200 years ago, lies the same principle that guides the vast world of finance – the ability of people to exercise self-control. I started this book with the tale of greedy drivers on a motorway, who had their eyes on money rather than fruit. Nevertheless, 'The Plumtree' can be viewed as an excellent metaphor for the financial sector and its bonus culture. The first eight lines sow seeds of doubt about little Johnny's intentions. What is he going to do? Is he just like the man in the story told by Homa Siddiqui's mother, who made the wrong choice and obtained the fee for his work by stealing, rather than by delivering his side of the deal? On reading the whole poem, we can see that little Johnny is not like that. He is a virtuous boy, in contrast to the many people in the financial sector we have looked at in this book. These people believed that they could get away with stealing all the fruit from a tree because no one would notice. Little Johnny, however, has more character. He can control himself and keep his greed in check. He obeyed his father and he was rewarded for this.

This seems a fitting conclusion to our look at ethics and self-control in the financial world.

Maxims

1 Today's perception is tomorrow's norm.
2 By becoming a value-free science (a kind of mechanics), economics has become estranged from the root causes that determine the outcomes of academic endeavours within that field. No wonder economists are so often wrong.
3 Customers would rather be given a lie for free than pay to discover the truth.
4 In remuneration policy, the concepts of effort (variable pay), exceptional performance (bonuses) and going above and beyond the call of duty (honours and distinctions) are constantly confused.
5 Organisations are like cars: they have an accelerator and a brake pedal, and the two need to be used in alternation. The outcome of any process in which just one of these pedals is used will be futile. Alternatively, if both pedals are stepped on at the same time, which can happen in organisations full of internal conflicts, a great deal of energy will be lost. There will be a lot of noise, but the organisation will not move forward.
6 'Uncork the champagne, we've got it made!' The ECB's liquidity support for weak banks in countries with large deficits had the effect of encouraging those banks to buy even more bonds issued by their governments. As a consequence, market discipline was removed and the governments could continue to accumulate debts.
7 Many governments fund pensions on a pay-as-you-go basis. The French and British governments have hundreds of billions outstanding in firm commitments for the future pensions of state employees. Under this pay-as-you-go system, the entitlements of leavers are funded by contributions made by new entrants. It is a Ponzi scheme in its purest form and the biggest in the capitalist Western world. And if the population shrinks it will break down, just like every other Ponzi scheme.
8 The older generation cannot pass the bill for their pensions on to the next generation. For their part, the younger generation cannot solve their problems by depriving the older generation of risk-free returns. It is a matter of intergenerational solidarity.
9 If a time comes when a policy of monetary tightening needs to be pursued, whereby money, having been brought into circulation through monetary easing, is then taken out of circulation, we must hope that the central bankers and the monetary authorities are more courageous than the captain of the Costa Concordia.
10 Is a little bit of stealing acceptable?
11 The root cause of systemic risk is people.
12 Market makers are like foxes. They feed on securities orders from the public. If the foxes are hungry they become bolder and approach the customers' homes. They raid the chicken coop and the dustbins.

13 Chinese Walls have been put in place at financial institutions, with complicated security codes being used to keep doors locked, but these can be peered over, metaphorically speaking, by using Skype or Facebook. What is the point of Chinese Walls if they can be circumvented with text messages?

14 Credit cards are popular in some countries, whereas debit cards are used more frequently in others. The difference may seem to be mere semantics, but in the world of finance and consumer spending this reflects two fundamentally different mentalities.

15 Diseconomy of scale: the term exists, but is it a fallacy?

16 If, as Adam Smith argues, the government needs to leave the market alone, the market should also leave the government alone. But can the government live without a market? Who will discipline governments in that case?

17 The shareholders of insolvent companies lose everything. All they are left with are their voting rights and a healthy dose of rancour. Who would have us believe that investors always act rationally?

18 If my judgement tells me to turn left and the herd turns right, what then?

19 Italy is not in crisis, because all the restaurants are full. However, the bill for the meal is always paid with a credit card.

20 Dutch students automatically receive student loans. They have to go to great efforts to prevent this. It is as if the government were handing out free heroin to people who have not yet developed an addiction.

21 Despite what many people think, the fact that fraud always involves money does not in itself make it a financial crime.

22 Everybody needs a boss, and no one more so than the boss himself.

23 It is easier to look in the rear view mirror than it is to peer into a crystal ball.

24 Huge numbers of mortgages taken out in low-interest-rate foreign currencies are turning countries such as Hungary, Iceland and Poland into one huge hedge fund. The same can be said of Ireland and Spain: they became property hedge funds. Matters may turn out well, but history has shown that many hedge funds end up self-destructing.

25 They used to want a football for their birthday. Now they want a football club.

26 They used to build sandcastles, but now they build castles on shifting sand.

27 Every court needs a jester.

28 The rescuer usually ends up as the victim. It is the lifeguard who drowns.

29 When it comes to eurobonds, we are willing to surrender sovereignty, but only as far as our debts are concerned.

Bibliography

Chapter 2
Baxter, C, Brennan, M, Coldicott, Y and Möller, M, *The Practical Guide to Medical Ethics & Law*, 2002, PasTest.

Chapter 3
Bernstein, P, *Against the Gods: the remarkable story of risk*, 1996, John Wiley & Sons.
Dunbar, N, *Inventing Money: the story of Long-Term Capital Management and the legends behind it*, 2000, John Wiley & Sons.
Greenspan, A, *The Age of Turbulence*, 2007, Penguin Press.
Gude, R, *Geschiedenis van de Filosofi*, 2010, Luister Wijs.
O'Rourke, P, *On The Wealth of Nations*, 2007, Atlantic Books.
Reinhart, C and Rogoff, K, *This time is different*, 2009, Princeton University Press.
Taleb, N, *Fooled by Randomness*, 2004, Thomson Texere.
Taleb, N, *Black Swans*, 2008, Penguin.
Trivers, R, *Deceit and Self-deception*, 2011, Allen Lane.
Van Liederkerke, L, van Gerwen, J and Cassimon, D, (eds), *Explorations in Financial Ethics*, 2000, Peeters Publishers.

Chapter 4
Gasparino, C, *King of the Club*, 2007, HarperBusiness.
McLean, B and Nocera, J, *All the Devils are Here*, 2010, Penguin.
Strober, D and Strober, G, *Catastrophe: the story of Bernard Madoff*, 2009, Phoenix Books.
Verplaetse, J, *Het morele instinct*, 2008, Nieuwezijds.

Chapter 5
Akerlof, G and Shiller, R, *Animal Spirits: how human psychology drives the economy, and why it matters for global capitalism*, 2009, Princeton University Press.
Gert, B, *Hobbes (Prince of Peace)*, 2010, Classic Thinkers, Politybooks.
Johnston Bagby, L, *Hobbes's Leviathan: a readers guide*, 2007, Continuum.
O'Rourke, P, *On The Wealth of Nations*, 2007, Atlantic Books.
Paulson, H, *On the Brink*, 2011, Headline Business Plus.
Phillipson, N, *Adam Smith: an enlightened life*, 2011, Penguin Books.
Skidelsky, R, Keynes, the Return of the Master, 2010, Penguin Books.
Van Liedekerke, L, Van Gerwen, J and Cassimon, D (eds), *Explorations in Financial Ethics*, 2000, Peeters Publishers.

Chapter 6
Driver, J, *Ethics: the fundamentals*, 2007, Blackwell.
Gensler, H (ed), *Ethics Contemporary Readings*, 2004, Routledge.
Kinneging, A, *Geografie van Goed en Kwaad*, 2010, Spectrum.

Chapter 8
Boatright, J (ed), *Ethics in Finance*, 1999, Blackwell.
Schwed Jr, F, *Where Are the Customers' Yachts? or A good hard look at Wall Street*, 2006, Wiley.
Sorkin, A, *Too Big to Fail*, 2010, Penguin Books.
Tett, G, *Fool's Gold*, 2009, Little Brown.

Chapter 10
Bogle, J, *Enough: true measures of money, business and life*, 2009, John Wiley & Sons.
Lewis, M, *The Big Short: inside the doomsday machine*, 2011, Penguin.
Posner, R, *A Failure of Capitalism*, 2009, Harvard University Press.

Chapter 11
Levitt, A, *Take on the Street*, 2002, Pantheon.

Chapter 12
Bolkenstein, F, *Grensverkenningen (Dagboek van een Eurocommissaris)*, 2005, Uitgeverij Bakker.
Kynaston, D, *Liffe a Market and its Makers*, 1997, Granta.
Mifid Directives and SEC releases.
Shorto, R, *The Island at the Centre of the World*, 2004, Random House.

Chapter 14
Burrough, B and Helyar, J, *Barbarians at the Gate*, 2004, Arrow.
Cohan, W, *House of Cards*, 2009, Doubleday.
Gibbs, N, 'Sex. Lies. Arrogance. What makes powerful man act like pigs', *Time*, 30 May 2011.
Liu, C and Yermack, D, 'Where are the shareholders' mansions?' *Journal of Finance 63*, 2007, pp. 1575–1608.
Muste, E, Cornelissen, K and Harman, S, *Persoonlijkheidsproblemen; beleving en behandeling*, 2008, Boom.
Sorkin, A, *Too Big to Fail*, 2010, Penguin Books.

Chapter 15
Clissold, T, *Mr. China*, 2008, HarperCollins.
Szymkowiak, K, *Sokaiya*, 2002, Armonk.
Van Buitenen, P, *Strijd voor Europa*, 1999, Ten Have.

Chapter 16
Bebchuk, L and Fried, J, *Pay without Performance*, 2004, Harvard University Press.

Byron, C, *Testosterone Inc*, 2004, John Wiley & Sons.
Depuydt, P, *De Kloof*, 2010, Prometheus NRC boeken.
Michielsen, S and Sephiha, M, *Bankroet: hoe Fortis al zijn krediet verspeelde*, 2009, TerraLannoo.

Chapter 17
'The man who screwed an entire country', *The Economist*, 11 June 2011.

Chapter 18
Malthus, T, *An Essay on the Principle of Population*.

Chapter 19
Boatright, J, *Ethics in Finance*, 2007, Wiley.
Trivers, R, *Deceit and Self-deception*, 2011, Allen Lane.

Chapter 20
Boatright, J (ed), *Finance Ethics*, 2010, Klob Series in Finance, Wiley.
Boatright, J, *Ethics in Finance*, 1999, Blackwell.
Mandelbrot, B and Hudson, R, *The Misbehaviour of Markets*, 2004, Profile Books.
Voorhoeve, A, *Conversations on Ethics*, 2009, Oxford University Press.

Chapter 21
van Alphen, H, *Poetry for Children*, Millard, F (trans), 1856, Partridge & Co, p. 20.